MOVIES ON CHATHAM PRESENTS

MOVIES ON CHATHAM PRESENTS

Group Conversations About
Diversity, Equity, and Identity
in Film

Pam Hassebroek, Ph.D.

with Lucy Cota and Mary Reed

Triple Synergy Press
Atlanta, Georgia

Copyright © 2021 by Pam Hassebroek

Cover Design: April Leidig, *Copperline Book Services Inc*

Cover and Chapter Art:
Maria Skrigan, *Skeptical Cactus*
GraphicsFuel

Cover and Interior Typefaces:
Arial Black, Arial Nova, Sabon Next LT by *Microsoft*
Bebas Neue by Ryoichi Tsunekawa
Windsore by *AF Studio*

ISBN: 978-0-578-96543-7

For our movie group

Everything I learned, I learned from the movies!

—AUDREY HEPBURN

CONTENTS

PREFACE

OUR SEARCH FOR MEANING IN MOVIES

For the movie-struck, the essentially naive—those who would rather see a movie, any movie (a bad one, a stupid one, or an evanescent, sweet-but-dry little wafer of a movie, like this one), than do anything else.
—PAULINE KAEL, *Day for Night* movie review[1]

And like any family's stories, like most families' stories, they have been used in the service of one of humankind's great and perennial tasks: to figure out and explain what on earth it all means.
—ANDIE TUCHER, Columbia University[2]

THIS BOOK MAY PROVE INDISPENSABLE if you love movies and enjoy discussing them with others. Our group has spent years together watching and discussing films, which is a pretty fantastic way to employ social science. We have learned a lot from this experience, and you will benefit from reading about it. What we present illustrates how film portrayals have reinforced discrimination—which is among the world's most pressing matters—in keeping with the prevailing ideologies.

Suppose you have wondered how individuals born with certain

---

[1] Kael's review of *Day for Night* was first published in *The New Yorker* on Oct 15, 1973, and found more recently at *Scraps from the Loft* (2019).

[2] *See* Tucher, A. (2007).

characteristics get ranked higher or lower down on a society's list of people. Of course, I am talking about all who take that same breath of air as they emerge into life on Earth. Yet, some have social privileges without doing anything to earn them, and some carry social burdens others never encounter.

In movie settings from the early 20th century forward, we observed inequalities of social position. We found that what created the disparate situations was neither direct influence entirely nor a complete conspiracy of ulterior motives. Not surprisingly, our investigation shows that both then and now, ignorance and unjustifiable bias has a hand in maintaining that list.

We can see how this happens and how things change through film depictions and historical, social backdrops. A revolutionary change does happen now and then, but more typically, change in our social environments comes about slowly. By watching these movies, we can notice the positive trend toward a more equitable social order. We attribute the movement to the complex ebb and flow of societal issues, changes in belief systems, persuasive communication, and the vagaries of human nature.

Unexpected Consequences from Watching Movies

When we started this gathering to watch movies, we expected to learn more about the amazing filmmaker complex, including writers, directors, performers, and countless others. And we have. However, we didn't imagine or expect a most treasured consequence. As a result of the experiences, we have developed a new awareness of who we are—our history and our human culture—through the expressions of films and film technologies. And, new understanding often arises through group members' words in discussions about what they noticed in a movie.

The group has pondered why we remember certain movies, lines, and soundtracks while forgetting a hundred more. And we think about why certain types of films may have come into being at some times but not at others. What is it about that film that had such an impact? This idea relates to our emotional responses to films and our own historical and cultural contexts as spectators. If you are curious about how this happens, this work can be enlightening.

Fundamental to the group undertaking has been a mission to explore what and how movies communicate to give them power. Like other media sources with their sometimes-controlling messages, movies have quietly, unobtrusively persuaded us toward particular values, perspectives, and emotional responses.

TV and radio ads ("commercials") continuously and sometimes effectively tell us what to buy and how to cast our votes. Unfortunately, their influential practices have also intruded into our networked electronic devices. Besides coping with annoying ads, we must now be alert for biased news. Recent studies alarmingly report that the more sinister fake news and deepfakes—distorted videos, images, and recordings that appear authentic—can even bring about false memories (Briscoe, 2021; Murphy, Loftus, Grady, Levine, and Greene, 2019).

Fortunately, several groups are preparing resources to help people better distinguish truthful information from the devious.[3] Still, considering today's menacing media environment, should we feel anxious about movies' communication too? Well, that depends.

Movies' impact depends on interpretation, and people interpret

---

[3] Examples are the Associated Press Institute (API) ("News literacy," 2021), The Center for News Literacy (2016), School Journalism ("Fake news," 2016), and the News Literacy Project ("About," 2020).

films differently. We discovered that our local audience members often notice different things when looking at the same scene. They combine what they see and hear with the ways of thinking they've already established to create different meanings when watching the same movie. (Think about the Rorschach inkblot test.[4]) We have investigated why this happens and how different meanings come to mind.

In exploring meaning and influence, we use film criticism to consider the meaning of individuality, equality, and diversity. Over a series of films from *Summer and Smoke* (Glenville, 1961) and *Peyton Place* (Robson, 1957) to *The Bird Cage* (Nichols, 1996), this study observes the movie industry's changing expressions of femaleness, sexual orientation, and gender identity. The chapter critiques show how gender roles reflect social conditions and how movies, like other communication media, can inspire and influence social change.

Meanings Reflect Contexts and Circumstances

Some film analysts may consider meaning solely in terms of the beliefs and intentions of filmmakers. Our view of meanings considers their story contexts and the situations of individual spectators.[5] Spectators' situations include personal experiences, group sanctioned and inflexible attitudes, and regulative norms— beliefs that express themselves differently at different times among different people and groups. Moral values and etiquette are examples of regulative social norms, as are public policies.

---

[4] When people are asked to interpret a vague and indistinct image like an inkblot, their minds will try to create something to bring meaning to the image. What people tend to see is something from their own experiences.

[5] Carey's milestone book, *Communication as Culture* (1989), promotes this idea.

Throughout the movie industry's 150-year history, research has continuously probed the complicated subject of movies' influence. Over the decades of your life, you may have been drawn to, yet had reservations about, movies' violence, sexuality, morality, diversity, and gender politics. And, perhaps like most of us, you watched and wondered in silence but pursued no fundamental understanding yourselves. So we decided to spend some time doing that and recording our progress.

Our movie gathering is akin to a book club or civic organization. We gather monthly to socialize, advance our common interests, discuss, and learn from each other. Thus, we created this book with a similar idea in mind. *Movies on Chatham Presents* will easily fit into most film groups' programs. Students, as well as those who facilitate learning, will find it equally valuable. Whatever your calling, you will learn from reading it, possibly something you didn't even know you wanted to know.

Book Appeals to a General Audience

We wrote the essays and articles for a general audience; hence, there is truly something of interest here for everyone. Further, our writing appears in many forms—informal, formal, familiar, and argumentative compositions. With sometimes debatable views, the essays can serve as catalysts for discussions that employ critical thinking and analytical skills.

Our book's target audience includes but is not restricted to:

THOSE WHO

★ Appreciate movies as part of our art and culture and the entertainment and enlightenment they bring to us

★ Enjoy experiencing a different world as a getaway moment

★ Discuss movies to consider others' perspectives

★ Love observing and analyzing human behavior from within good stories
★ Are open-minded and curious about human diversity
★ Are sociable and like to participate in groups
★ Study movies
★ Teach to expand students' experience with critical thinking

Like other artistic methods of communication, movies connect to the heart of human culture. We believe you will profit from a closer focus on this, particularly as a group endeavor. Among other rewards to be gained, you may expand your concept of and appreciation for our diversity. You may discover a community of interest you didn't realize you were missing. Or you may even meet your best friend or soul mate in a film group. Imagine that.

Today's technologies and movie enterprises offer everyone something that was available only to professional film critics a generation ago. Now that something has exploded to represent a movie enthusiast's wildest dream. It's the opportunity to watch almost any movie you wish to see within your fingertip-reach (or voice range or brain wave). All you need is access to an Internet connection and a streaming device to get started.[6]

Over the years of watching together, this group has taken full advantage of all movie content sources available—purchased VHS tapes, Netflix DVD rentals, and subscriptions from several streaming providers. Then as our 10th year arrived during the COVID19 pandemic, we stopped all input to prepare this report.

---

[6] Your local public library likely provides this. Further, with your library card, you can get free services such as Kanopy, Hoopla, and Access Video on Demand, and sometimes a meeting space as well.

Recognizing Human Differences

The book's focus on diversity led us to spotlight two groups specifically:

1) Women, regardless of sexual orientation or gender identity, and

2) Individuals who identify as LGBTQ (lesbian, gay, bisexual, transgender, queer).

This work is broadly attentive to individual uniqueness and narrowly attentive to group identities. It is otherwise similar to other research exploring gender, sexual orientation, and gender identity across historical periods. In a parallel fashion, we strive to shed light on attitudes about the heterosexual male dominance that has limited lifestyles and livelihoods for all others.[7]

Please note that some terms in this book represent concepts colloquially used in different ways. For example, notice the word "gender" in the above paragraph. The Movies on Chatham group understands that gender is complex, a varying concept that extends beyond the two traditionally broad male-female categories.

In the past, people regarded sex and gender as the same. Yet, sex is a biological term, and gender is a social construct. Therefore, we think about gender expansively and non-traditionally as encompassing all gender-related characteristics, not only physical appearance. The meaning of gender—the physical, psychological, and behavioral attributes often associated with gender—fluctuates depending on context. In a 2017 *Time Magazine* article, Steinmetz reports, "*Facebook*, with its more than 1 billion users, now has about 60

---

[7] Others include those whose status is socially inferior as reflected in civil and human rights when compared to that of a straight, non-transgender male.

options for users' gender."

Investigating Sex, Gender, and Sexuality

We see today's meaning of sex, gender, and sexuality as a dramatic change from the rigid concepts in 20th-century texts and contexts in films, medicine, and academia. Women's Studies as an academic field began in the 1970s and '80s as an outgrowth of the feminist movement. In 1990, Emory University became the first to establish a PhD program in Women's Studies.

LGBTQ Studies began in the spring of 1970, when The University of California, Berkeley offered a course. Still, research had begun long before that—in Europe in the 19th century and the U.S. in the 1930s. Interdisciplinary research centers in both study areas have developed worldwide since then.

Now expanded as Gender Studies, the field takes in all genders, sexual orientations, and gender identities. Thus, Emory University's program is now called Women's, Gender, and Sexuality Studies (WGSS). Pertinent to this book is the Geena Davis Institute on Gender in Media at Mount Saint Mary's University in Los Angeles ("The Geena Davis Institute," 2020).

Like a college class's scheduled study, we focused on each equity and diversity subtopic for four or five months, as is our group's practice. We investigated meanings by collectively perceiving, interpreting, and discussing film narratives and their contexts.

Beyond the group's social camaraderie, a significant added benefit for this study is its range of views and observations. And mine don't always align with those of other group members. Affirming Staiger's (2000) ideas of how we make meaning as movie watchers, I believe that we are all "perverse spectators." In assessing our movie-watching experiences, our personal, contextual factors account for spectators' varied observations and feelings after watching the same movie.

Movie-Watching in Small-Town America

For example, growing up in a rural environment, my background is similar to only one of our members. However, unlike everyone else in the group, I grew up on a dairy farm in Grayson County, Texas, outside Sherman's city limits. My sister Carla and I thought living out "in the country" was a little bit of heaven, free to roam the land, fish in the ponds, and ride horses to bring in the cattle for milking. On some Saturdays, we rode in the truck with our dad to deliver milk cans to the Meadowlake pasteurizing plant in town and to visit our grandmother. She lived by herself in the house at 524 S. Walnut Street where our dad grew up; our grandfather, who started the dairy enterprise, died before my fourth birthday.

Ours sounds like the life in the *Little House on the Prairie* series (Wilder & Williams, 1932–1943). Because of similar difficulties, our grandmother didn't share our love for the setting. On the farm, we had no neighbors or city services, no sidewalks, or paved roads. Winters were bitter cold, and scorching summers brought the daily horror of rattlesnakes, scorpions, and tarantulas. Compared to other kids in school, our family was always the last to acquire modern technologies. But, we did have a party-line telephone, thanks to Ma Bell.

And we had movies! Our mother often dropped us off at the movies in summer and on school-year weekends. We had four theaters in town: one that showed the first-run features; a second, the Plaza Theater, was for the Black community; and the other two had the second run or lesser star-value films. The smaller theaters were side by side on Travis Street, the main street in town, and on either side of them were dime stores, Kress's and Woolworth's. Before watching movies in those theaters, we would first go to a dime store to get candy (sold by weight) and then take the candy into the theater with us. At the Texas Theater, the larger movie house, we bought snacks at the concession stand.

Looking back now, I am sure that movies served a practical function for our mother—almost free babysitting. While we were safely occupied, she could run errands and shop for groceries without pesky kids. Of course, it is possible that during our growing-up years, we saw every movie that was showing at the Texas, the State, or the Ritz.[8] But we didn't know about movie studios or censorship or propaganda. To us, what we saw at the movies was simply the world as it was.

Since leaving the farm, I have never stopped going to the movies as a preferred entertainment. However, until the last decade, I hadn't understood much about filmmakers, musicians, artists, playwrights, actors, and writers other than their star power and their works' creative and entertainment value. So, after spending most of my career in the STEM (science, technology, engineering, and math) realm, I decided to press forward into social science, the humanities, and the arts, toward an emergent STEAM (STEM plus Arts) education. There I encountered the fields of communication, media studies, and public policy.

---

[8] I was inside the Plaza Theater only once, to see *Porgy and Bess,* a movie based on George Gershwin's opera. Somehow as younger children, we assumed we were not allowed to go there, even though it was prominently located on the courthouse square. Regarding *Porgy and Bess*—after an initial unpopular public reception in 1935, the Houston Grand Opera's production in 1976 brought new recognition. It is now one of the best known and frequently performed of all operas.

I now recognize that all creative arts are valuable in documenting humanity at specific moments in time. (Well, some of the documentation does reflect bias and filtering by institutions and institutionalized thinking.[9])

However, this is not only *my* experience that forms our viewing context. It is a group project. Each person in the Movies on Chatham group offers input from a unique frame of reference. And what each one brings adds meaning to our conversations.

Three Takes on Our Collaboration

I now switch scenes to offer background—brief takes on the Movies on Chatham group's collaborative foundations. I discuss this under three headline topics: 1) media influence, 2) critical thinking, and 3) group discussion.

Ideas on the Meaning and Influence of Media

During his trial in 1895 in a British court, Oscar Wilde made the following statement. "I do not believe that any book or work of art ever had any effect whatever on morality" (Linder, 2020). While Wilde's statement was simply an attempt to defend his writing, media influence is a topic audiences have worried about and studied in the U.S. since the early 20th century.

Movies were viral from the beginning. "By 1910 some 10,000 movie theaters—'Nickelodeons'—drew 26 million people weekly; by 1927 it was 57 million; by 1930 movies with sound drew over 100 million a week" (Doherty, 2019). U.S. advertising and public relations industries came into being around the same time, applying the new

---

[9] For the sake of those who may study us a thousand years from now, I suggest we stick to facts in our "documentary" movies. Only the facts, ma'am. Let's hear it for historians who set the permanent records right.

scientific theories of psychology to influence the masses. People concerned about cultural standards believed that new communication technologies—widespread advertising, radio, and motion pictures—would strengthen lowbrow behavior. In 1930, the Motion Picture Production Code (Hays Code) addressed these concerns by censoring filmmakers' productions.

However, studies found that the effects of media were not as direct as people feared they were. Still, a direct consequence occurred when Orson Welles narrated H. G. Wells' *The War of the Worlds* in a live radio broadcast in 1938. It panicked audiences across the country. Afterward, Princeton psychologist Hadley Cantril tried to understand why individual listeners took different meanings, thus had different responses to the same message.

> Neither education nor the circumstances in which they heard the radio broadcast could explain the different 'standards of judgment' displayed by individuals (p. 68). Rather, he argued that a combination of psychological personality traits—self-confidence, fatalism, or deep religious belief—predisposed audiences to uncritically believe what they were hearing. (O'Neill, 2011)

Further progress came from Katz and Lazarsfeld's book, *Personal Influence* (1955), which claimed that public information gets filtered when transmitted to audiences in ways that depend on the communication source. News media re-present what has transpired historically, interpreting what people have said, e.g., during an election, which may sway audience members' voting decisions (O'Neill, 2011). Opinion leaders act as message filters by explaining media content to their mass audiences. Individuals and groups filter messages according to their beliefs and social norms.

Other communication media and art forms can also change us with their subtle, and sometimes not so subtle, influence. As "not-so-subtle" influencers, politicians influence biased connotations by re-interpreting and re-mediating information apart from original sources.[10] Social networks act as additional filters and interpreters as people negotiate meanings among interpersonal and group relationships. In total, other influencers shape about 99.9 percent of all our decisions (Berger, 2016).

Following Katz and Lazarsfeld's work, a later study described media influence on public opinion as even more complicated (Klapper, 1960). Media influence varies among individuals based on pre-existing views and preferences, experiences, emotional and intellectual capabilities, education, and cultural backgrounds. For one thing, audience members with their pre-existing opinions and preferences tend to look at sources they understand and agree with. Understanding this discriminatory mental process isn't always straightforward. Theories of selective attention and cognitive dissonance suggest people may skim past or dismiss what they hear or read when it doesn't fit or make sense.

During the 1960s, when the Hays Code became less restrictive on movie content, filmmakers increasingly depicted stories with heightened realism. As a result, audiences again became concerned about the medium's impact on socialization and morality as they watched realistic violence. Indeed, research on pornography and

---

[10] The process of creating a media article is an interpretation of facts for readers or viewers—a mediating process. Re-interpretation offers a new or different meaning or reading. To achieve greater relevance, re-mediating places visual messages into newer media, which changes its context but re-forms and re-enacts earlier media environments. Putting old wine into new skins? See: Bolter & Grusin (1999).

violence shows that prolonged exposure to sexual abuse depictions has detrimental effects, including "emotion desensitization to violence and its victims" (Ball-Rokeach, 2001).

Media influence remains on people's minds today. The wide world of the Internet is a conduit for low-cost mass communication and widespread distribution of propaganda. We wonder about new media's instrumental roles in changing humanity—among gamers, and audiences bullied and polarized in social networks, adults obsessed with pornography. We all limit our brainpower by using computers to store phone numbers, facts, and events, using cameras continuously to capture and store experiences. This behavior may be dulling memory functions and emotions. The relationship between media and the mental health and well-being of youth is a growing concern.

With some younger children also addictively engaged, what are the consequences of media use during early formative years? What un-expected mental and physical outcomes will appear when they're grown? Humans with new neuroses, with spine, hearing, and eye-sight alterations?[11] Depending on the application—reading, chat-ting, playing cooperative games—maybe they will simply be a whole lot smarter and able to think more critically.

Critical Thinking Can Revise Prevailing Views

In discussing media influence, disinformation, and persuasion methods, we became more aware of the value of critical thinking.

> The essence of critical thinking is suspended judgment, and the essence of this suspense is inquiry to determine

---

[11] For insight on physical problems related to childhood experiences, *see* tangible effects on brain development related to trauma (Harris, 2015).

the nature of the problem before proceeding to attempts at its solution. This, more than any other thing, transforms mere inference into tested inference, suggested conclusions into proof. (Dewey, 1910)

Today, with our limitless sources of facts and commentary, we rely on traditional media (TV, newspapers) and social media (online interaction platforms) to inform us about current events. And, as always, the media sources interpret the meanings of conflicts and controversies.

In contrast, our group questions film portrayals, ponder whether they accurately present facts, and discuss whether they reflect or influence social norms. Finally, we focus on movie narratives to explore sociological concepts of culture, social class, gender, and identity.

Studying these concepts requires a broader way of thinking. In his famous book, *The Sociological Imagination* (1959), sociologist C. Wright Mills talks about this. He suggests looking at individual practices from a group and societal level to understand how different parties and practices interrelate and influence each other. Using a sociological imagination, one must step away from a personal circumstance to see it from a "big picture" perspective.

For example, one might notice biased TV reporters and wonder about their ethics and values. Mills would advise that we think about their employers' position in the U.S. or the world instead of focusing on reporters. Rather than considering the bias as an individual issue, view it as a public issue. I will try to do this.

Many changes have come with the Internet's growth and new media development. For example, we recently noted paper publications shrinking as organizations fight to survive in a digital world. Our

Atlanta Journal-Constitution newspaper is now much smaller and has fewer pages. What other changes can we see?

Think about the much-discussed bias in *Fox News* and the large following it gained (thus increased advertising dollars) by presenting conservative views without other perspectives. From research on media influence, we know that people tend to stay with familiar sources they understand and agree with. They may "skim past or dismiss what they hear or read when it doesn't fit or make sense."

In earlier times, *NBC* and *The New York Times* received honors for their adherence to journalistic ethics of independent and unbiased reporting. Now, maybe survival is more important than ideals since both organizations take a left-leaning view. Following *Fox*'s lead, public relations firms may be advising them to abandon their former obligation to general audiences in favor of higher ratings.

I am sure there are other possible answers, bearing in mind our current environment of misinformation and disinformation. My attempt at a broader view may or may not explain what is happening. In truth, I need other facts, opinions, and perspectives to make sense of it. As Mills advises us,

> Both the correct statement of the problem and the range
> of possible solutions require us to consider the economic
> and political institutions of the society, and not merely the
> personal situation and character of a scatter of individuals.

Further, whether any truth exists in what they're saying, today's political and extremist rhetoric presents general negativity toward individuals and groups. Someone somewhere is continuously stating an opposing idea or perception about Black lives, White lives, gay lives, fossil fuel workers, capitalists, communists, socialists, rich people, poor people, corporate and government employees, educated, uneducated, law enforcers, criminals, clerics, religious followers, nationalities—Americans, Syrians, Mexicans, etc.— immigrants, activists, and politicians.

Practicing critical thinking with a sociological imagination can help us reduce our prejudices and polarization and increase our investigative power to understand issues relevant to peaceful activism and positive social change. Moreover, by directly accessing facts for ourselves, evaluating information sources, and discussing with others, we can establish our own views and make better decisions. This idea brings us to the third element of our collaboration, group discussion.

Group Discussion Fosters New Ideas

At Movies on Chatham, we are all about groups. Movies enable our community. We screen and discuss movies in our private group setting. We watch movies among groups of spectators in movie theaters. We study movies in classes. We attend Zoom lectures about movies populated by groups online. We attend film festivals. We collaboratively write about films.

How would it be if group members communicated directly with each other but expressed no differences in ideas or observations? No conflicts among our beliefs, and no clashes of opinion? Sounds dull to me. We think a respectful argument is valuable, where people can listen, learn, and share. The following are our assumptions about the value of group discussion.

★ We learn more by group discussion than by solo investigation.

★ Group discussion enables synergy for grappling with something different from what any of us could experience alone.

★ Trying to view the world from others' perspectives stimulates the imagination and develops compassion.

* Disagreement is healthy. How can we arrive at better ideas
  and solutions for problems if we always agree? If we contend
  with controversial topics that engage our foundational beliefs
  and experiences, we get better at critical thinking.

* We can learn by listening to other perspectives without
  feeling forced to adapt.

To follow the train of thought in Movies on Chatham's
collaborative foundations, the chapter content in this book can
facilitate discussion and debate. In addition, the movies' contexts
enable consideration for relevant historical public concerns and
influence.[12]

Chapter articles are the authors' independent expressions and
responsibilities. They include facts, research from reputable sources,
and combine content curation with their own and others' opinions.
Thus, readers can watch the movies with background knowledge
and develop ideas that may disagree with or add to the writers' ideas.

We used this method in our group. Under each of our themes, we
drew from close readings of a small selection of movies as sources
for studying meaning. Before screening the films, the contributors'
articles, which we include here, were published on the *Movies on
Chatham* website so that group members could read them
beforehand if they wished. Those earlier versions have now been
changed to incorporate our audience's input and conform to the
book's chronology.

We have since concluded that, in this series, the portrayals we
observed from film history reinforced social discrimination in

---

[12] To follow the timeline of laws and policies mentioned in the chapters, please
consult page 204 in the Appendix.

keeping with the prevailing ideologies. In future volumes, we will cover other themes our group has studied over our time together.

We enjoy what we do, but the idea of exploring culture and the arts may not be high on everyone's list. Yet, there are good reasons that it should be. Maybe you haven't had an opportunity to think about movies until now because of other pressing obligations. Perhaps you have an interest and studied the topic of cinema long ago; for you, it is high time to revisit and update your lessons. The films and their contexts are changing continuously. As for me, I am late to the conversation, running to catch up to a swiftly moving sidewalk.

—Pam Hassebroek

Atlanta, 2021

Key Terms

Cognitive dissonance

Cognitive dissonance theory suggests that we attempt to reduce conflict between our attitudes and behaviors because it creates psychological stress. Encountering circumstances or information contradictory with what they believe, people may ignore or avoid it to eliminate the stress.

Critical thinking

Critical thinking is careful thinking—evaluating and analyzing "facts" before using them to guide beliefs and actions. Critical thinking means considering all sides before making decisions, whether it aligns pro or con with our prior observations.

Gender

Gender traditionally refers to the male or female sex (called the gender binary), based on the appearance of external reproductive organs at birth. However, understanding gender as a cultural creation, newer concepts recognize more than two. For example, *Facebook* now offers dozens of options for gender identity.

Gender identity

Gender identity is a personal awareness of one's gender. Most societies have used sex and gender interchangeably to represent biological sex and an associated gender norm. Yet, not all people identify with every associated gender trait. The broad categories disregard characterizing sexual orientation, gender identity, and gender expression.

Identity

Identity consists of an individual's unique characteristics, including psychological and physical attributes that set them apart from others. Personal identity also represents an individual's perception of where they belong and who they match with, compared to others in the world.

Media

Media are sources of widespread communication: books, newspapers, magazines, television, radio, film, and Internet-based websites.

Motion Picture Production Code (Hays Code)

The Motion Picture Production Code was a set of moral guidelines for censoring content in U.S. motion pictures. Known informally as the Hays Code,[13] it restricted words, images, and storylines in movies from 1934 to 1968.

Non-binary gender

Non-binary gender is a term that widens the concept of male and female, those traditionally strict gender categories held to represent alternatives of human sexual identity and behavior.

Selective attention

The theory of selective attention suggests that people look at sources that agree with them or align with their understanding.

Sexual orientation

Sexual orientation is an enduring experience of sexual attraction to people of the opposite sex, same-sex, or both or neither.

Sexuality

Sexuality is a broad term for a person's sexual experience and expression, a fundamental human characteristic. Ideas about

---

[13] I include detail about the Hays Code elsewhere in the book, including in the Appendix beginning on page 205.

sexual activity and reproduction were tightly bound together in the past. However, changes in ideology and technological interventions allow valuing the two events separately, enjoying sex without reproduction and reproduction without sex.

Social construction

Groups of people with a particular worldview develop (construct) and agree on thought and behavior standards. Then they evaluate ideas, practices, and people accordingly.

Social norms

Social norms define acceptable distinctiveness for people in a group or a society. Elements that identify people in social classes include attitudes and behaviors, ideas, body types, and dressing styles. For example, norms define the accepted behavior, grooming, and dress for women as a gender class.

Sociological imagination

A sociological imagination develops as one seeks to consider broader meanings in experiences and observations.

Straight

In the gendered body sense, straight means heterosexual or sexually attracted to a person of the opposite sex.

Transgender

Transgender is an adjective describing people whose gender identity or gender expression differs from what is typically associated with their observable sex at birth.

INTRODUCTION

EXPLORING THE WORLD THROUGH FILM

Mary Reed and Pam Hassebroek

There is no greater educator of the public in our day than the motion picture. It has covered almost every phase of life and imparted knowledge good and bad on a wholesale scale.
—*The Indiana Catholic*, 1915[1]

We know that anything to do with looking is complicated.
—DAVID CAMPANY, Tate Britain

I N OUR SEARCH FOR MEANING in movies, the Movies on Chatham group explores what movies communicate and how society's popular culture and public rules influence filmmakers' stories and audiences. Here we interpret what movies say about diversity, equity, individuality, and identity.

This introduction describes the contributions of early filmmakers and the structure of the book. Included are brief readings of selected films that illustrate human differences and show how social attitudes and customs have changed over time. These summations foretell our views and their pertinence to our conclusion. While we found evidence of societal discrimination, the films show positive

---

[1] Quoted in Doherty (2019).

trends and give us a reason for optimism.

Over history, our nation has received a world of people into this emergent culture. The diversity of these individuals—with their differences in language, age, skin color, sexes and sexualities, skills and capabilities—has produced the strong fabric of America. However, this fabric becomes warped and weaker when people with particular characteristics are considered unworthy of full inclusion. As we have recognized and openly expressed these inequalities, we have come together to lift one another to higher places of strength and participation. We see this reflected in our movies.

Movies provide endless illustrations of human experiences. Similar to books and other media, museum visits, and travels, the stories accessible to film audiences can expose broader worldviews than they might otherwise encounter. With this idea in mind, our group set out to discover new ways of exploring the world from the comfort of our movie room.

Down the road, we began to examine film history and our culture by investigating movies according to topics. We met our first challenge when looking into depictions of historically marginalized members of our diverse humanity—women, gay men and lesbians, and transgender persons.

Science Means Making Sense of Observations

We noticed changes in role portrayals and chronological environments related to these depictions while watching and discussing a series of British and American films. Audiences can benefit from our observations and use them to forge paths to future discoveries.

Filmmakers make our work possible, their repertoires relying on the camera's observational and recording powers. With increasingly complex cameras, filming, and editing techniques, each movie represents a filtered version of the world, a creative interpretation as the filmmaker has constructed it.

Consequently, the audience sees life in the world through writers' and filmmakers' minds, that life realized using multiple technological devices. Therefore, questioning a film's narrative and finding the meanings in its messages requires investigation and critical thinking.

Investigation is one of the reasons filmmakers tackle the arduous task of bringing a movie into being. In truth, the motivations are countless: the interest and challenge, education, innovation, the money, a calling to create, document, influence, or propagandize, and sometimes to answer a question that requires evidence beyond what one can see directly. Some facts in the world cannot be observed or processed by the naked eye.

For example, in the 1870s, people questioned whether all four horse's hooves were ever off the ground simultaneously while racing. They couldn't see this by watching the legs directly. So Leland Stanford, breeder of Standardbred horses at his California farm, commissioned a photographer, Eadweard Muybridge, to find an answer. Stanford tasked him to carry out scientific studies of horses' gaits (Eadweard Muybridge exhibition, 2010–2011).

Muybridge decided to place several cameras at points along Stanford's racetrack, where each camera could photograph a different position of a galloping horse as it progressed around the track. The idea was to assemble the individual pictures to see a continuing view of the motion.

The experiment worked. Muybridge successfully photographed a horse named Sallie Gardner in fast motion using a series of 24 cameras, "their shutters triggered by the horse's movement over tripwires" ("Stopping time," 2010–2011). In the sequence of photographs was indisputable evidence that all four hooves were off the ground at the same time.

This event in 1878 was the first spark of motion photography. The Muybridge movie captured the horse's image at different places and points in time, moving forward. This method is, in effect, the way we have approached the present work. Instead of the horse, we have put movies in place at various points in time to see what changes we can notice in portrayals of diverse individuals in their social contexts.

Others Advance the Science

Others began new experiments that confirmed the process following the momentous Muybridge success at the Stanford racetrack. Then by the end of the 19th century, motion photography had progressed to real-time continuous shots. In 1888, Louis LePrince made *Roundhay Garden Scene* at Roundhay, Leeds in northern England—the oldest known motion picture. It lasted 2.11 seconds.

In January 1894, William Kennedy Laurie Dickson directed the five-second *Edison Kinetoscopic Record of a Sneeze* in Edison's West Orange, New Jersey laboratory. That same year, the 21-second film, *Carmencita* (Dickson), brought negative attention to a popular vaudeville performer. Watching Carmencita dance in a swirling motion in the movie, people were troubled when her swaying long skirt revealed a little too much ankle. She was the "first woman to appear in front of an Edison motion picture camera" and the first woman in a U.S. movie (Paghat the Ratgirl, n.d.).

The Edison experiments appeared over a year before the Lumière Brothers' cinématographe films (Geiger, 2011). A café audience watched the Lumière Brothers' *Arrival of a Train at La Ciotat* in 1895. The 50-second French movie shows a train arriving at a depot and reportedly terrified viewers on that first night. The story has it that people jumped from their seats and ran screaming into the street, afraid of being run over by the train.

That motion picture indeed may have frightened its audiences at the time; yet, the movie aroused their curiosity, ingenuity, and creativity. It motivated minds that propelled filmmaking technology forward from one generation after another. Today, we celebrate almost 150 years of film.

Given the depth and breadth of their stories and imagery, whether presented within seconds, minutes, or hours, movies offer a gold mine of opportunities for discovery and dialogue. Our anthology of essays and background articles provides a foundation for fruitful discussions about the films we watched and the social identities they highlight.

Recording Our Exploration

This mission's record consists of 20 essays that stage the patterns we saw in movies. This book explains how popular culture and public policies influence filmmakers and the ways filmmakers' creations have resonated in society. The contexts we write about reflect, in general, the values American communities judged as vital for their times.

We structured the book's content in two parts, each under the theme of diversity, Part I: Changing Women and Part II: Celebrating LGBTQ. In the selected movies uniting this topic, we noted generational changes in feminism, gender roles, social and policy influences, gender inequality, and expressions of sexual orientation and gender identity across the many years of cinema.

5

Each of the ten chapters presents a single movie and begins with a summary page that provides a short synopsis, along with essential movie details, credits, and awards. Please note that while each of the featured films has acquired an abundance of praise, the list of awards shown in each chapter is brief to conserve space. Following many of the chapters' essays, we define terms and concepts to clarify and underscore their preferred and intended meanings in the associated critique.

In Part I, the films begin with Peter Glenville's *Summer and Smoke* (1961), an adaptation of Tennessee Williams' play set in the early 20th century. Then, they progress chronologically by historical setting to the present day with Bill Holderman's *Book Club* (2018) and its depictions of four contemporary American women. The following list unveils our interpretation of the features' storylines.

★ *SUMMER AND SMOKE:* Women repress their sexuality while men remain free of such social and psychological burdens.

★ *MR. AND MRS. BRIDGE:* A woman's role is to marry, serve her husband and family. Nothing more.

★ *PEYTON PLACE:* A promising writer tells a fictional story about discrimination and violence in a patriarchal community, setting off alarms worldwide. Its movie adaptation is milk toast.

★ *CHARADE*: A woman may be independent, adventurous, paint the town red, and still be virtuous and appealing.

★ *BOOK CLUB:* Women assert themselves as they pursue romance, their lives' depicting advances in male-female social equality.

In Part II, the focus shifts to movies featuring human sexual orientations and identity variations that are not exclusively heterosexual. The films deal with a range of subtopics that allow us to observe how our Western culture has adapted to a broader perception of humanity over time. Our chapters describe how roles for gay men emerged from the filmmaking closet and why their backstories are a sad reflection of human history. Further, while recent changes in laws are encouraging, the lack of social acceptance in some places reveals what remains woefully missing in today's norms.

* *THE CELLULOID CLOSET:* A pioneering advocate for equal civil and human rights, Vito Russo describes depictions of gay men in films.
* *WILDE:* A famous writer's talent lifts him onto a pedestal until his sexual orientation and egotism cause his downfall.
* *THE DANISH GIRL:* A couple's discovery of the husband's gender identity leads to an early case of human sex reassignment surgery.
* *BEHIND THE CANDELABRA:* The flamboyant Liberace leads a scandalous private life during a wildly successful career.
* *THE BIRDCAGE:* A comedy that features a gay couple's farcical predicament helps us envision human similarities.

Our theme allowed the group to observe progress in understanding our diversity, to recognize and celebrate individual lives' value regardless of reproductive capability, sexuality, or gender. We, thereby, witness the move toward equal rights for all.

However, this appreciation came with a greater awareness of failures in human relationships as reflected in expressions of discrimination, microaggression,[2] and underlying attitudes that prevent beneficial

---

[2] Microaggressions are often discussed with respect to unhealthy attitudes
Footnote continues on the next page ...

changes for everyone. Each of us has the power to advance respectful interaction with all of our world's people.

It's a Wrap

After just a few more words of encouragement, let's wrap this up and move on to our movies. We are confident that watching and discussing movies with others offers benefits. Listening brings other minds' perspectives and provides new ways to gain empathy, think critically, and expand ideas. Further, because it helps to employ a competent guide when exploring new territory, please allow us to take on that role for you. Our unique collection of articles and essays in *Movies on Chatham Presents* can serve as your reference as you watch.

---

toward different races, but individuals can fall victim based on almost any of our observable human identifiers, e.g., gender, sexual orientation, native language, disabilities, religion, political affiliation, employment status. See: Sue & Spanierman (2020).

PART I

CHANGING WOMEN

★ *Summer and Smoke*

★ *Mr. and Mrs. Bridge*

★ *Peyton Place*

★ *Charade*

★ *Book Club*

ABOUT CHANGING WOMEN

The selected films confirm women's spaces and places in 20th-century America. We notice dramatic changes in women's status beginning in the 1960s compared with movies released from the pre-code era of the 1900s–'30s through the censored 1940s–'50s. Observing these earlier times gives us a reason to celebrate today.

CHAPTER 1

SUMMER AND SMOKE (1961)

Summer and Smoke is an amazing work of art by Tennessee Williams—but the most amazing art is the performance of its star, Geraldine Paige. She is absolutely luminous and magic. One of the greatest performances by an actress ever captured on film!

—RON, *TCM* user review

DIRECTOR	Peter Glenville
SCREENPLAY	James Poe and Meade Roberts
CAST	Lawrence Harvey ~ John Buchanan, Jr. Geraldine Page ~ Alma Winemiller Rita Moreno ~ Rosa Zacharias Una Merkel ~ Mrs. Winemiller
AWARDS	ACADEMY AWARDS
	Best Actress in a Leading Role: Geraldine Page
	Best Actress in a Supporting Role: Una Merkel
RUN TIME	118 min
RATING	NR

SUMMARY

Set in the American South at the turn of the 20th century, a repressed young woman is in love with a handsome medical student but cannot return his affections. Thus, he romances the dance hall girl. The movie is adapted from Tennessee Williams' Broadway play of the same name.

REPRESSION, REJECTION, AND REVISION

Lucy Cota, Mary Reed, and Pam Hassebroek

T HE FIRST IN THIS MOVIE SERIES is *Summer and Smoke* (Glenville, 1961), one of the five we selected to explore American women's circumstances over recent times. Ordering the chapters by historical context puts *Summer and Smoke* first because of its setting in the 20th century through 1916.

The story, written by playwright Tennessee Williams, occurs in a small community shortly before World War I. Miss Alma Winemiller and John Buchanan, Jr., the main characters, illustrate the differences between the freedoms and opportunities available to men and women of this era.

Social class distinctions and unequal privileges between men and women were part of Victorian-era culture. For example, before the 19th Amendment in 1920, women had no right to vote, therefore, no power to express their discontent. Further, in keeping with cultural norms, specific topics of human experience were eliminated from polite conversation, thus ensuring general and widespread ignorance about them.

Author and Miss Alma Sweat in Parallel Closets

As lead character Alma demonstrates, the psychological effects of the repressed language and thought processes resulted in significant disabilities for women.

Other social groups felt similar discrimination, especially those whose sexual orientations didn't fit neatly into expected and acceptable binary gender assignments. Writing from within that cloaked group, Tennessee Williams suffered from repression too.

Miss Alma Winemiller reflected Williams' psyche. He describes this connection in an interview for *Playboy Magazine* in 1973.

> Alma of *Summer and Smoke* is my favorite—because I came out so late and so did Alma, and she had the greatest struggle, you know? I didn't even masturbate until I was 27. I only had spontaneous orgasms and wet dreams. But I was never frigid like Miss Alma, not even now, when I most need it. (Jennings, 1986)

Through Miss Alma, Williams presents unconsummated longings, forbidden sexual desires, and fantasies in an era of taboo. In addition, she gives voice to his stifled feelings of rejection.

> Williams has an obvious affection for all the flawed people populating his plays. 'I have always been more interested in creating a character that contains something crippled. I think nearly all of us have some kind of defect, anyway, and I suppose I have found it easier to identify with the characters who verge upon hysteria, who were frightened of life, who were desperate to reach out to another person.' (Stang, 1965)

Both the character and her creator had endured the agony of rejection. Art known to imitate life, Alma came directly from Williams' family experience in small-town Mississippi. Alma's behavior mirrors the social environment surrounding her (where she lives, how she was brought up, and the time's social norms).

In her mid-twenties, Alma is a virtuous, talented, and intelligent woman who displays the high standards of behavior she was taught.

But, unfortunately, that same stable background that dictates how she behaves also restricts her from a complete experience and expression of her emotions.

Her father is domineering, openly critical of Alma and her mother at a fourth of July celebration. What other evidence shows her struggles? In contrast, how does the movie present another woman in the story, Rosa, a flirtatious dance hall girl? Is she one who commands respect? What does the film communicate by casting a Latina in this role?

Throughout the story, Alma has had an opportunity for a loving romantic relationship right in her hometown of Glorious Hill, Mississippi, but cannot seize it. However, John Buchanan, Jr., her love interest, a young man who had been her friend from childhood, freely experiments in relationships and acts on his desires and feelings openly without much concern. These attitudes came from Victorian-era ideology that understood men as sexually active and women as passive.

Alma can't let herself feel the emotions and instincts that could allow her to respond more naturally to others. Thus, the object of her romantic desire slips away into the arms of another woman. Left behind, Alma sits dejectedly in the park at the movie's closing scene. Still, before the final credits appear, a man arrives to sit on the bench near Alma. Her earlier rejection does not end her story.

Summer and Smoke's Audience Rejection

As a play, *Summer and Smoke* opened first in Dallas, Texas, and performed its first Broadway run at the Music Box Theatre in New York City. When it closed much earlier than expected, Williams interpreted it as an audience rejection. However, it turns out that Williams so deeply engaged his emotions in this play that after the disappointment of its short run, he continued to revise and rename the story throughout his career. His attachment to Alma and her circumstances implies that she is responsible for his deep feelings about it. Especially so if he had used her to communicate his own psychological, social, and political distress.

Williams expressed this anguish in correspondence with Elia Kazan, following their trip to Rome after the play closed. Williams' openness about it likely relates to the fact that his previous production, *A Streetcar Named Desire* (directed by Kazan), had been so well received.[1] *Streetcar* was named the 1948 Pulitzer Prize winner in drama ("Prize Winners in Drama," 2020).

Kazan's Advice to Williams

Back in New York in the summer of 1949, Kazan responded to a letter from Williams (Kazan, 2014), which included the excerpt below. He describes Williams as a "misfit," a term that applies to Miss Alma, too, in her own way.

> It seems to me that the very things that make it uncomfortable for you here in the states are the things that make you write. I've seen it with a lot of writers (Cliff Odets,[2] for instance) that once they had dough and the power to live in a comfortable environment (as who doesn't want to) the NECESSARY quality in their writing disappeared. It seems to me that the things that make a man want to write in the first place are those elements in

---

[1] *A Streetcar Named Desire*, opening a year earlier, ran for 855 (Dec 03, 1947–Dec 17, 1949) (Williams, 1947). *Summer and Smoke*'s Broadway run was 102 performances (Oct 06, 1948–Jan 01, 1949) (Williams, 1948).

[2] Playwright Clifford Odets. For more information, *see* Lahr's article (2006) in *The New Yorker*.

his environment, personal or social, that outrage him, hurt him, make him bleed. Any artist is a misfit. What the hell would he go to all the trouble—if he could make the 'adjustment' in a 'normal' way. You get to Rome or whatever and you can perfectly well remain silent. You are not really Tennessee Williams in Rome. That fellow is a misfit, in his own way a rebel and a not-at-home in our Essentially Businessman's Society. Your very identity is in the quality of misfit and protest and rebellion (all in personal terms, not as conventionally thought of). In Rome, in North Africa, in Mexico, etc., your essential identity is lost. That's why I've always thought that, whether you like it or not, and in a way, especially since you do not, you should stay here in the States. I think you'd soon have some new plays writing that NO ONE could turn you off.

LOVE,

Gadg[3]

Williams Revises the Original Script

Whether Tennessee Williams read his wise friend's consoling words is unknown. However, his self-pitying yielded to writing a new play presented at the Circle in the Square Theatre in 1952 and starred Geraldine Page. Then Glenville's movie, *Summer and Smoke*, came nine years later, recasting Page in the starring role. Her film performance led to an Academy Award and a Golden Globe award for Best Actress–Drama and a Best Actress award from the National

---

[3] "Gadget, or the diminutive Gadg, became a trademark, as it were, that bespoke Kazan's remarkable success in theater and film, especially highly publicized collaborations with Williams" (Devlin, 2014).

Board of Review. Hence, just like Miss Alma, ultimately, Tennessee Williams did not let failure define him.

While Williams had revised the story over the years, the movie and subsequent plays retained his intriguing concept of Alma. She was shaped by her surroundings, then behaved accordingly. So what does this movie communicate about her? It's not a good idea to be like Alma, but better to be a dance hall girl?

No, that's not how it ends. Instead, Alma is a striking presentation of a woman of her era who is a "late bloomer." The Victorian era and its strict repression of language and emotion had kept her in silence and frigidity. However, she is bright enough to continue growing and evolving while becoming more alert to her unique self—both a physical and spiritual revision. Yes, she suffered setbacks, but that's life, and attempting to escape it is not the way to grow. Isn't that what Elia Kazan writes to his friend, Tennessee Williams, in his letter? Timing and luck are a lot of it too.

TENNESSEE WILLIAMS, WHO KNEW?

Lucy Cota and Mary Reed

LESSER KNOWN AMONG TENNESSEE WILLIAMS' REPERTOIRE is *Summer and Smoke* (Glenville, 1961), the movie adaptation of his 1948 play. The storyline juxtaposes a dutifully repressed young woman (Alma Winemiller) with a carefree dance hall girl (Rosa Zacharias) over the affections of a handsome young doctor (John Buchanan, Jr.).

Summer and Smoke's positive reception from the Movies on Chatham group led to questions about Tennessee Williams. Unfortunately, not everyone had had the privilege of exposure to his literary work in high school, college, or elsewhere. Thus in this overview, we fill in a bit of his history as a celebrated writer.

Writing Reflects Social Consciousness

Tennessee Williams' plays typically have a southern setting. They feature archetypes of overbearing mothers, absent fathers, and repressed or frustrated adult daughters. Themes tend to revolve subtly around topics awkward to address in the mid-20th century: mental health, unhealthy family dynamics, and sexuality.

Not surprisingly, these themes echo Williams' personal life. He struggled with depression, alcoholism, and insecurity—living openly as a gay man when same-sex relationships were illegal.

From his hardships, Williams gained a profound social consciousness that was ahead of his time. This heightened awareness, unusual for the era, gave him insight into human nature's nuances and tragedies, wherein his writing flourished. The plight of his sister Rose Williams, who lived to 86 years old, inspired his story in *The Glass Menagerie*.

In the late 1930s, Williams' parents had forced Rose to undergo a lobotomy, a neurosurgical operation they believed would ease her schizophrenia. Tragically, the surgery produced irreversible brain damage and required her to live in an institution for the rest of her life.[4] Williams never forgave his parents for their decisions. To support his sister, he willed his estate for her lifelong care.[5] After she died in 1996, the remainder went to the University of the South in Sewanee, Tennessee ("Rose Williams," 1996).

Beyond family relationships, Williams felt compassion toward others who, like himself, had been marginalized because of their human genetic characteristics. Though many were unaware of the modern Civil Rights Movement[6] until two decades later, Williams joined with others who protested on behalf of Black Americans in the 1940s. In 1947, the policy of the National Theatre in Washington DC barred Black Americans from attending. When *The Glass Menagerie* was scheduled for performance there, *The New York Times* published Williams' objection:

> I want to state that I have protested bringing *The Glass Menagerie* into Washington but have no legal power to prevent it. I can only express my humiliation that a play of

---

[4] Portuguese neurologist Antonio Egas Moniz developed the procedure in 1935 and won the Nobel Prize in medicine for this work in 1949.

[5] President John F. Kennedy's sister, also named Rosemary, similarly suffered a prefrontal lobotomy in 1941. As with Rose Williams, Rosemary Kennedy remained institutionalized until she died.

[6] The Civil Rights Movement is a term for the activism that sought political, social, and economic rights for Black Americans from 1946 to 1968.

mine should be denied to Negroes in the nation's capital. Any future contract I make will contain a clause to keep the show out of Washington while this undemocratic practice continues ("Protest by Williams," 1947).

Broadway and Hollywood Tributes

Honoring a very talented and courageous advocate for human and civil rights, America's highest echelon of writers includes a prime spot for Williams, who made profound contributions to literature. His life spanned the 20th century from 1911 to 1983. It was highlighted with not one but two Pulitzer Prizes: the first in 1948 for *A Streetcar Named Desire* and the second in 1955 for *Cat on a Hot Tin Roof* ("Prize Winners in Drama," 2020).

> Jessica Tandy, the original Blanche DuBois in *Streetcar*, said of Williams, 'If you wanted to place him in the American theater, you'd have to place him at the very top. The very, very highest.' (Singleton, 1983)

Williams was inducted into the American Theater Hall of Fame in 1979 (Johnston, 1979). In 2014, in the Castro neighborhood of San Francisco, Williams was an inaugural honoree on the Rainbow Honor Walk. This sidewalk tribute recognizes LGBTQ individuals who have made significant contributions in their fields of work.

Actors gave legendary performances of Williams' plays. And while plays are intended for stage presentation to live audiences, those penned by Tennessee Williams proved lucrative to Hollywood. In an article for *Entertainment Weekly*, Sollosi (2016) describes the adaptations. These movies accumulated boatloads of Academy Award nominations and an abundance of Oscars. *A Streetcar Named Desire* became the inspiration for Woody Allen's *Blue Jasmine* (2013). Fifteen films is an unofficial accounting of those adapted from

Williams' work. A glance at the casts is akin to a walk among the stars of Hollywood's Walk of Fame.

Celebrated Actors Perform in Williams' Movies

We know about Geraldine Page, who performed in both the stage and screen versions of *Summer and Smoke*. The table below includes other celebrities who have played roles in movies based on Williams' plays. Many in this brief, alphabetized list of names from Hollywood's storied past would credit Williams for their successful careers.

ACTOR	TITLE
★ Carroll Baker	*Baby Doll* (1956)
★ Warren Beatty	*The Roman Spring of Mrs. Stone* (1961)
★ Marlon Brando	*A Streetcar Named Desire* (1951) *The Fugitive Kind* (1959)
★ Richard Burton	*The Night of the Iguana* (1964) *Boom* (1968)
★ Montgomery Clift	*Suddenly Last Summer* (1959)
★ James Coburn	*The Last of the Mobile Hot Shots* (1970)
★ Kirk Douglas	*The Glass Menagerie* (1950)
★ Jane Fonda	*Period of Adjustment* (1962)[7]
★ Lawrence Harvey	*Summer and Smoke* (1961)
★ Katherine Hepburn	*Suddenly Last Summer* (1959)
★ Arthur Kennedy	*The Glass Menagerie* (1950)
★ Burt Lancaster	*The Rose Tattoo* (1955)
★ Gertrude Lawrence	*The Glass Menagerie* (1950)

[7] This was one of Fonda's first major roles.

★	Vivien Leigh	*A Streetcar Named Desire* (1951) *The Roman Spring of Mrs. Stone* (1961)
★	Lotte Lenya	*The Roman Spring of Mrs. Stone* (1961)
★	Anna Magnani	*The Rose Tattoo* (1955) *The Fugitive Kind* (1959)
★	Karl Malden	*A Streetcar Named Desire* (1951) *Baby Doll* (1956)
★	John Malkovich	*The Glass Menagerie* (1987)
★	Una Merkel	*Summer and Smoke* (1961)
★	Paul Newman	*Cat on a Hot Tin Roof* (1958) *Sweet Bird of Youth* (1962) *The Glass Menagerie* (1987), Director
★	Geraldine Page	*Summer and Smoke* (1961) *Sweet Bird of Youth* (1962)
★	Robert Redford	*This Property is Condemned* (1966)
★	Lynn Redgrave	*The Last of the Mobile Hot Shots* (1970)
★	Maureen Stapleton	*The Rose Tattoo* (1955)
★	Elizabeth Taylor	*Cat on a Hot Tin Roof* (1958) *Suddenly Last Summer* (1959) *Boom* (1968)
★	Eli Wallach	*Baby Doll* (1956)
★	Natalie Wood	*This Property is Condemned* (1966)
★	Joanne Woodward	*The Fugitive Kind* (1959) *The Glass Menagerie* (1987)
★	Jane Wyman[8]	*The Glass Menagerie* (1950)

---

[8] Wyman was former U.S. President Ronald Reagan's first wife.

Literary Festival Attracts Scholars

The dedicated study of Williams' literature ensures that his poignant writing will survive time's passage. Today one is likely to encounter current scholars of the playwright at the Tennessee Williams/New Orleans Literary Festival, a five-day celebration of literature and theater held in New Orleans, Louisiana.[9] The city of jazz, rhythm, and blues is also the city where America's renowned playwright lived for over 40 years and wrote his famous plays.

Williams died in 1983 in his suite at a New York hotel. Even though in poor health, his death came accidentally from a combination of drugs and alcohol.

Key Terms

Lobotomy

A lobotomy is a psychosurgery performed to treat brain dysfunction. Now considered barbaric, doctors lobotomized around 40,000 people in the U.S. between 1936 and the 1950s (Faria, 2013).

Schizophrenia

Schizophrenia is a chronic and severe mental disorder that affects how people think, feel, and behave. People with schizophrenia may appear to have lost touch with reality.[10]

---

[9] See: https://www.tennesseewilliams.net

[10] See: https://www.nimh.nih.gov/health/topics/schizophrenia/index.shtml

CHAPTER 2

MR. AND MRS. BRIDGE (1990)

Oh my gosh, he is just like my dad!
   —A Movies on Chatham member in a post-screening discussion

DIRECTOR	James Ivory
SCREENPLAY	Ruth Prawer Jhabvala
CAST	Paul Newman ~ Walter Bridge Joanne Woodward ~ India Bridge Margaret Welsh ~ Carolyn Bridge Kyra Sedgwick ~ Ruth Bridge Robert Sean Leonard ~ Douglas Bridge
AWARDS	ACADEMY AWARDS
	Best Actress nomination: Joanne Woodward
	GOLDEN GLOBE AWARDS
	Best Actress nomination: Joanne Woodward
RUN TIME	126 min
RATING	PG-13

SUMMARY

During World War II, a privileged American family deals with social expectations and three grown children's changing values. Ruth Jhabvala adapted the screenplay from the notable books by Evan S. Connell.

TWENTIETH-CENTURY VALUES LIMIT MRS. BRIDGE'S ROLE

Mary Reed

1777 – All states pass laws which take away women's right to vote.
—SUSAN MILLIGAN, *U.S. News*

SHOW ME A "FIRST-WORLD" COUNTRY, and I'll show you a Mrs. Bridge—one of the title characters in the movie, *Mr. and Mrs. Bridge* (Ivory, 1990). First-world countries offer capitalism, industrialization, and technological innovation as gravy trains that carry opportunity far and wide, thus creating a robust middle class. Mrs. Bridge and her husband represent middle-class roles that mid-20th-century America expected them to fill in the family and community. Mr. Bridge stoically complies with his career, while Mrs. Bridge resigns herself to their home's constraints with no outlet to release her intelligence or creativity.

For women of her time, patriarchal and paternalistic were the societal characteristics that defined their middle-class status. Yet, these exact circumstances prevented Mrs. Bridge and others from escaping the limiting gender roles of the past. Director James Ivory and the seasoned and talented actors in the movie's lead roles present this era in America with spectacular accuracy.

Humanity's story is one of ensuring daily survival, which, for most of recorded history, no one took for granted. Because our ancestors' existence depended on it, they dedicated themselves entirely to foraging, farming, or toiling in a trade to have food and shelter for survival. A life of prolonged leisure was an unheard-of concept exclusive to the highest echelons.[1]

Twentieth-Century America Enables a Middle Class

In the late 19th and 20th centuries, astounding progress enabled a middle class to enjoy weeks away from work for relaxation and recreation—under the right conditions, that is. The "right conditions" refers to a government that gives people religious liberty and the freedom to prosper.[2] Thus, Mrs. Bridge is a product of the prosperous constitutional republic that is the United States of America.[3]

Upon America's creation in the 18th century, founding father John Adams surmised in a letter to his wife (1780),

> I must study Politicks and War that my sons may have
> liberty to study Mathematicks and Philosophy. My sons
> ought to study Mathematicks and Philosophy, Geography,
> natural History and Naval Architecture, navigation,
> Commerce and Agriculture, in order to give their
> Children a right to study Painting, Poetry, Musick,
> Architecture, Statuary, Tapestry and Porcelaine.

Now, before we jump all over President Adams for excluding his daughters from his dreams of academia, keep in mind that he lived in the 18th century. A woman's place was strictly home and hearth. We should easily forgive him because his famous letters to his wife Abigail show great respect for her intellect. This very attitude about

---

[1] Highest echelons include a ruling class, the nobility in feudal systems.

[2] One is hard-pressed to find a class of Mrs. Bridges under communism or dictatorships, e.g., in Russia, China, Afghanistan, Iran, or Cuba.

[3] Some call the U.S. a democracy. Democracy or republic or is a matter of personal preference.

education created a country that, by the 20th century, established itself as the land of opportunity. Shelter, clothing, and essentials of life were readily accessible to the resourceful. For those with means, food was available without hunting, plowing, or gathering.

In the 1930s and '40s, hiring employees and service companies to help in household maintenance was widely affordable by the middle class, which included Mrs. Bridge. All she and other women of the era had to do was marry a responsible man with the ability, motivation, and opportunity to earn money.

Husband Defines Female Identity

Throughout history until the 20th century, a woman's quality of life depended on her husband. Mrs. Bridge lives well, not because of her education, but because she married a successful lawyer who provides for the family. Unless they were fighting in a war, men were necessarily lifelines for their families.[4] In these early feminist times, lest she acquires the spinster's derogatory brand, a woman's husband established her identity.[5]

By the mid-20th century, rapid technological advancements and innovation had extended into the home. As a result, they reduced the time-consuming, backbreaking effort of household duties. Yet, as we mentioned in an earlier article, "Are Psychiatric Issues Side Effects of Civilizing?" (Reed, 2016), such advancements don't always

[4] For a brief period while American men were off fighting the Third Reich in Europe, women took over much of the workforce in the U.S. This ended as soon as World War II was over and the men came home.

[5] At St. Jude's Women's Circle at Christ the King Church in Atlanta in the 1960s and '70s, a woman introduced herself by giving her name and her husband's occupation. "My name is Lucy Cota and my husband is a manufacturer's representative."

bring more freedom from household chores.

> As immigration dropped sharply during World War I and
> many native-born women left domestic service for
> wartime jobs, middle-class women lamented the shortage
> of domestic workers. This spurred efforts to reorganize
> housework and fostered a new breed of home economists
> who argued for 'scientific' housekeeping. ("The New
> Housekeeping," 2018)

Still, and especially for households with employees, these changes
generally freed up more of a woman's workday.

With all of her physical needs met, Mrs. Bridge has ample time on
her hands. Still, while Mr. Bridge occupies himself with his career,
Mrs. Bridge is home with no guide or role model on how to fill all
the empty days of her life. It is not a stretch to believe she is among
the first generation of women in such a predicament. And indeed,
this unique role of "suburban housewife" crossed all socioeconomic
boundaries. Mrs. Bridge and her country club set have counterparts
among homemakers in the blue-collar population.[6]

Cowan's study of household technologies (1983) argues that

> modern conveniences—washing machines, white flour,
> vacuums, commercial cotton—seemed at first to offer
> working-class women middle-class standards of comfort. It
> became clear that these gadgets and gizmos mainly
> replaced work previously conducted by men, children, and
> servants. Instead of living lives of leisure, middle-class

---

[6] In *A Woman under the Influence* (Cassavetes, 1974), Mabel Longhetti,
homemaker and mother, is driven to insanity by society's neglect of her as an
individual. See: Hassebroek (2016).

women found themselves struggling to keep up at ever-higher standards of cleanliness.

A variety of sitcoms from the 1950s to the 1970s showcased this new type of woman created by 20th-century changes. June Cleaver of *Leave it to Beaver* made this look easy—and even fun! As did Carol Brady of *The Brady Bunch*.

Mr. and Mrs. Bridge Are Connell's Parents

While TV idealized the suburban housewife, writer Evan S. Connell shined a light of realism through Mrs. India Bridge, portrayed in this adaptation. Though he neither married nor fathered children, Connell understood the dynamics of a 20th-century nuclear family.

He grew up in a Midwest family, observing his parents' attitudes and surroundings with a critical eye. As a result, he captured the nuances of his parents' marriage, deemed typical of upper-middle-class America. With his mother firmly in mind, Connell wrote *Mrs. Bridge* in 1959; he followed it ten years later with *Mr. Bridge*, about his father.

In the novel *Mrs. Bridge* and this movie, Connell highlights

> the plight of married American women, whether in the
> 1930s or 1960s, who hadn't much life outside a kitchen
> full of the latest appliances. It might also be thought of as
> a documentary of the repressed, compliant spouse,
> dependent for her opinions on her husband's authority,
> and subservient to his will. (Pritchard, 2013)

Remember Paula Alquist, Ingrid Bergman's role in *Gaslight* (Cukor, 1944)?[7]

---

[7] While the *Gaslight* story has a sole male villain, it also demonstrates how an
Footnote continues on the next page …

In her commentary on *Mrs. Bridge*, Grodstein (2009) describes her spending her days shopping, lunching, and trying to figure out how to ease her feelings of inadequacy.

> The maid cooks and cleans, the laundress launders, and the kids are self-sufficient. Though she wants to learn new things—she studies painting, picks up books—in the end, she always retreats to the place where she is most comfortable, behind her husband's opinions.

Gosnell (2013) added in her book review,

> Yet just as Mr. Bridge can't vocalize his feelings, nor can Mrs. Bridge make demands, least of all emotional ones. Everything she says is qualified, hesitant, for fear of offending, annoying—or simply standing out. 'It does seem too bad,' 'Well, yes, I expect that's true,' or 'I'm sure you're right' are her constant and endearing refrains.

> Mrs. Bridge is a pleaser, a woman trapped by her own vocabulary. And while her heroic attempts to make the best of situations are often very funny—'I do get so sick of crowds,' she says brightly, as they arrive at empty tables in the country club—she is a tragic figure.

Keeping the American Dream Intact

Since she has economic security and good health, Mrs. Bridge can afford to let her mind drift to the image her family presents to society. Attention to the family image seems frivolous, but the

---

entire social system can work together to ensure a woman's victimhood. See: Hassebroek (2017).

culture required it. When interviewed for *People Magazine*, Connell shared that his mother's "'principal concerns, for my sister and me, were that we have nice manners. She was terribly concerned with eccentrics and outrageous behavior'" (Wadler, 1990).

When image consciousness is sharp, "nice manners, a pleasant disposition, and cleanliness" (Schwarz, 2010) are essential values. (Don't we wish everyone could practice such consideration for others—and not merely to display an image?) Mrs. Bridge has all of the above, as she exudes social graces everywhere she goes.

Along with her concern for outrageous behavior, any confrontation of an active kind threatens serenity, so Mrs. Bridge avoids it at all costs. It would not do to blemish her reputation or complicate her life with conflict and anxiety.

Confrontation as the husband's turf, Mr. Bridge handles all external aspects of contention—haggling with the real estate agent or car dealer and negotiating bills. He makes all major economic decisions because *Father Knows Best* (Another TV sitcom depicting a 1950s family). Additionally, in Mrs. Bridge's era, much of a family's discipline was left to the husband ("Wait 'til your father gets home!").

Mrs. Bridge has a comfortable place in society. And, no different from most other parents, she naturally wants the same for her children. America doesn't guarantee a family's wealth and status across generations. Yet, women of Mrs. Bridge's era instinctively knew what the "American dream" required.

It required daughters to be refined, gracious, and well-educated enough to attract the right man to marry. In general, women were expected to pass directly from their fathers to their husbands. Consequently, Mrs. Bridge and her contemporaries have little chance to see what they can do independently.

Keeping the American dream intact required sons to be well-connected and maximally educated so they could assume their fathers' roles—and possibly go farther. But, of course, as with everything else, some children cooperated, and some rebelled. Evan Connell was among the latter. In his *People Magazine* interview, he told how his conservative upbringing made him feel "stifled." He ultimately rejected the conventional path laid out for him, deciding to strike out on his own.

> Expected to study medicine and take over his father's practice, he instead dropped out of Dartmouth after two years and embarked on a solitary bohemian life. Yet, while drinking a martini in Santa Fe's La Fonda Hotel, Connell said, 'I understand perfectly how those people feel. Everything was geared towards economic security. "Don't rock the boat; we've got a good thing."' (Wadler, 1990)

Yet, Connell acknowledged the work ethic it took for families to achieve success. "[My father] also taught me to do the best work I could, whatever it was. He was thoroughly honest. I don't think he ever shortchanged anyone in his life" (Wadler, 1990).

No Woman Is Immune to Rigid Standards

While Mr. Bridge has a purpose in keeping his family afloat, Mrs. Bridge veers dangerously close to the fine line between purpose and boredom. Without purpose, as without water, we all simply shrivel up and die. Literally or psychologically. Mrs. Bridge has little meaning to her life. Sure, she has children and that gave her purpose and kept her busy for a while. However, they grew up.

Still in force through later decades, the era's rigid standards decreed a woman's life plan. Dr. Luci Baines Johnson Turpin, former President Lyndon Johnson's daughter, credited a school for giving her "meaning and purpose." Still, she abandoned that purpose and left it behind in the mid-1960s.

She was pursuing a nursing degree at Georgetown when her boyfriend proposed. Forced to choose between accepting his proposal and staying the course to earn her BSN degree, Luci Johnson chose marriage.[8] When push came to shove, she knew she was giving up a nursing career, since

> in Johnson's time, 'many women understood that marriage was a life-changing decision, to have babies, not to work and to commit oneself to one's spouse,' said labor historian Alice Kessler-Harris.
>
> This was especially true for nurses, whose roles were considered to be 'vocations' more than professions. Georgetown's no-marriage policy was not unique. Many nursing programs, then run by hospitals rather than universities, required women to live in convent-like dormitories and be on-call at any time of night. Sex out-of-wedlock was grounds for dismissal. (Contrera, 2018)

"First World Boredom" Drove Women to the Edge

The "first world boredom" experienced by Mrs. Bridge drove some women to the brink. In extreme cases, their lives were so devoid of significance that they resorted to shoplifting to create excitement. In 1981, Oklahoma City police reported that shoplifting was becoming the crime of bored, middle-class housewives (Hopkins, 1981). According to a detective, women commit more than half of all shop-

---

[8] Johnson had earned a bachelor's degree in communications at age 49. As their 2018 commencement speaker, Georgetown University's School of Nursing and Health Studies awarded her an honorary doctorate at age 70.

lifting.

First-world boredom permeated to other family members as well, particularly children. For most of humanity's existence, children quickly crossed the bridge from childhood to adulthood with no transition period due to the need for survival. However, because of upward mobility in the U.S., a transition came into being, and teenagers became a new concept.

American society is still adjusting to these young adults who aren't children and aren't full-fledged adults with responsibilities. Teenagers with a lot of time and energy on their hands confound their parents with their ways of passing time: alcohol, drugs, sex, among other risky endeavors.

In the movie *American Animals* (Layton, 2018), we witness the true story of four privileged college students. They concoct a plan to rob Transylvania University's library of the extremely rare folio, Audubon's *Birds of America*. Lee (2018) suggests that what drove the students' actions was not a quest for cash but "an urge to escape the suburban torpor of their privileged upbringings."

With Title VII, Women Gain Opportunity

While Mrs. Bridge had gained the right to vote with the 19th Amendment, decades would pass before women were actively involved in business and politics. (Politics, in particular, is practically a synonym of conflict; and remember, conflict was a man's turf for most of the 20th century).

Pam Hassebroek had graduated from college with a degree in mathematics and computer science in the 1960s; however, she encountered roadblocks for women pursuing technical career paths in some companies. Then, after earning a master's degree in engineering,[9] she suddenly found a red carpet paving her way to a better future. Regrettably, as she noted, this dramatic policy change came late from some of the same companies that had earlier turned her down.[10] By the end of the 1960s, many large organizations had begun responding to the federal law prohibiting gender discrimination (Title VII of the Civil Rights Act of 1964) by considering job applications from qualified women. Some just took longer to adapt than others.

We fast-forward to note that my former employer, the consulting company Accenture PLC, is now led by a woman, "one of the most powerful women in corporate America" (Gelles, 2019). When the company began in the late 1960s as a division of the Arthur Andersen & Co. accounting firm, women in the professional ranks were almost unheard of. Today, Julie Sweet, Accenture's female CEO, runs one of the most valued companies globally with over 500,000 employees worldwide, in 317 office locations across 51 nation-states, serving clients in more than 120 countries. "She has made promoting women a top priority, setting aggressive targets for gender parity across the company and pushing to move more women into the executive ranks."[11] Her goal is to have 50 percent female employees by 2025. Sweet is board chair in September 2021.

---

[9] Pam was the first woman to earn a graduate degree in Petroleum Engineering from the University of Texas at Austin.

[10] She became the first female engineer at Exxon Production Research Co. in Houston. I won't mention what companies had turned her away.

[11] Accenture's focus on women began in 1995, when Jerry Hassebroek, Managing Partner in the Atlanta office, authorized a founding sponsorship (alongside BellSouth, Georgia-Pacific, and Delta Air Lines) of the "Georgia 100" women's mentoring program (now called "Pathbuilders").

Jacqueline Welch became executive vice president and chief human resources officer at *The New York Times* in January 2021. She oversees all aspects of hiring, career development, compensation practices, and diversity, equity, and inclusion. At the same time, Dr. Janet Yellen was appointed U.S. Treasury Secretary, the first woman to hold the position. Among other prior influential roles, Yellen served as Federal Reserve chair from 2014 to 2018, another first for women.

Also, in 2021 Dr. Sharon Wood advanced at The University of Texas at Austin from the dean of the Cockrell School of Engineering to executive vice-president and provost. In her position in one of the world's leading research universities, she is in charge of 18 colleges and schools that serve more than 51,000 students and support over 3,000 teaching and research faculty members.

Pope Francis appointed French Sister Nathalie Becquart to a leadership position in the Synod of Bishops' office in Rome in February 2021 (Lamb, 2021). In the Catholic Church, a woman now has the right to vote. Two women scientists, Dr. Jennifer Doudna and Dr. Emmanuelle Charpentier, jointly won the Nobel Prize in Chemistry in 2020 "for the development of a method for Genome editing." In 2018, Jody Singer was appointed director of the Marshall Space Flight Center in Marshall, Alabama.

With all of these notable advancements, not all is rosy still for women in the workplace. For example, women are losing jobs in clear cases of age discrimination. Some by younger female bosses, some job losses benefit hiring less-experienced and less-qualified new employees at lower salaries (Rikleen, 2016). At the same time, a law in California attempts to force placing more women onto company boards (Gharry & Molla, 2018). Still remarkable, there is no amendment guaranteeing equal rights for women. After all these years, gender discrimination in positions and salaries continues.

But, women are speaking up. Today, women seem to have no qualms about political confrontation. Four million women gathered in early 2017 to advance the #MeToo movement against sexual harassment and assault. Owing to the swift news propagation on the Internet, it was the single-most massive one-day rally in U.S. history. Astounding, considering it was just one or two generations ago when women like Mrs. Bridge left everything political to their husbands.

One hundred years ago, Susan B. Anthony and other suffragists struggled and successfully advocated for women's right to vote. Since then, American women have filled every kind of elected office and nominated seat except for the Federal Executive branch. That single exception has not been for lack of trying.

A Woman Is U.S. Vice-President in 2021

In January 2021, Kamala Harris became the first female vice president in U.S. history—the highest-ranking female elected official, the first American of African descent, and the first with Indian heritage to serve in that position.

In 2016, Hillary Clinton became the first female candidate for the U.S. presidency from a major political party.[12] Simultaneously, Kellyanne Conway ran her opponent's campaign, becoming the first woman employed in that position to win an election. Carol Moseley Braun was the first Black woman elected to the U.S. Senate, serving from 1993 to 1999. She was the first Black senator from the Democratic Party, "the first woman to defeat an incumbent U.S. Senator in an election, and the first female U.S. Senator from

---

[12] In 1964, Margaret Chase Smith became the first woman nominated for U.S. President at a major party's convention.

Illinois" (Wikipedia, 2021). Women have arrived on the political scene, and they are here to stay.

It will happen. A woman will be sworn in as President of the United States. It's just a matter of whether she will be a Democrat or Republican (or other). This momentous occasion will culminate a 250-year journey from 1769 when the British colonies decreed that women could not own property or keep their earnings. One hundred thirty-one years would pass before every state had approved these fundamental civil rights.

In 1890 Wyoming led the way in granting women the right to vote. Every state followed by confirming the 19th Amendment in 1920. Feminism was slow going until momentum started gathering in the 1960s, and it then gained strength through the 1970s.

A significant milestone was cleared in 1980 when "Paula Hawkins of Florida, a Republican, became the first woman elected to the U.S. Senate[13] without following her husband or father in the job" (Milligan, 2017). Whether women know it or not, that was the point where the playing field was truly beginning to equalize.

Mrs. Bridge's head would be spinning by the time many more women kept pushing feminism forward through the 1980s. Supreme Court Justice Sandra Day O'Connor, Vice-Presidential candidate Geraldine Ferraro, and astronaut Sally Ride are visible

---

[13] Hattie Caraway was the first woman elected as a U.S. Senator. Re-elected twice, she served from 1931 to 1945. Margaret Chase Smith was the first woman to serve in both houses, serving in the U.S. House from 1940 to 1949, re-elected four times. Elected Senator in 1948, reelected in 1954, 1960 and 1966, Smith served from 1949 until 1973. Shirley Chisholm was the first Black woman elected to Congress, representing New York's 12th district from 1969 to 1983. ("Women in the Senate," 2020; Michals, 2015).

examples. Moreover, feminism continued an upward trajectory through the 1990s and 2000s in ways that would make Mrs. Bridge's head spin even faster.

> The congressional freshman class of 2019 was perhaps best described in superlatives. It is the most racially diverse and most female group of representatives ever elected to the House, whose history spans more than 200 years. (Edmondson & Lee, 2019)

Then two years later, Blazina & Desilver (2021) report

> Women make up just over a quarter of all members of the 117th Congress—the highest percentage in U.S. history and a considerable increase from where things stood even a decade ago.

Dizzying progress, indeed. Feminists have not just broken ground but torn it up. Twenty-first-century girls are growing up in a society that allows them to compete as central players—as politicians, engineers, doctors, lawyers, actuaries, in sports—the sky's the limit. And, these girls know it. Recent Halloweens had mini Ruth Bader Ginsburgs trick-or-treating across America.

Ending 27 years as Supreme Court Justice, Ginsburg's death in 2020 deeply affected Americans who were inspired by her outstanding law career. Her diligent work dramatically changed gender-based laws, gaining rights and future opportunities for women. Three female justices currently sit on the nation's highest court: Justice Sonia Sotomayor, Justice Elena Kagan, and Justice Amy Coney Barrett. An abundance of female role models for America's daughters bodes well for our country's bright future.

Women Still Balance Work and Family Life

Yet, with the world literally at their fingertips, women still struggle with long-standing balance issues. The balancing act between a career and family creates stress for women. It takes a village to raise a child, yet at issue is who plays the primary role during the workday. If she has the option, a woman may play the role herself and defer her career until the children are older. Alternatively, a spouse or other family member, a nanny, or a teacher in a daycare center may be the caregiver while she attends to workplace duties. It is a choice that can create agonizing guilt.

Able moms still manage households with or without help, whether they work outside or solely inside their homes. The family's needs intensify daily life, and women expect to handle the pressure with aplomb. Plus, for many women who aspire to make the American dream reachable for their families, the world is busier, much busier, and more competitive than at the time of Mrs. Bridge. As a result, many present-day women fill their days, evenings, and weekends with full- or part-time jobs, maybe more than one.

They then exert more energy into charity projects, sports, yoga, and Mahjong or book clubs. Besides managing today's work and social lives, those moms remain involved in their children's education and supplemental activities. They spend abundant volunteer hours in schools and their children's extracurricular interests. One mother remarked to me, "I volunteered my head off [for my children's school]."

Some moms are even driven to outdo one another in what can be a very competitive mom world. For example, a local youth soccer league celebrates the end of the season with a parade organized by moms. For a show that only goes around a soccer field, floats resemble Macy's Thanksgiving Parade for the "Soccer Moms." They enthusiastically throw themselves into creating the perfect costumes for their children.

Never before in the history of civilization has the opportunity been so great for women to shine. Yet, to today's women, it would behoove us to remember to stand shoulder to shoulder with support, encouragement, and praise for each other. So, let's start with Mrs. Bridge.

Please Do Contain Your Criticism of Mrs. Bridge

Before we rush to write off Mrs. Bridge and her persona, we must contain our criticism and elicit respect for her tact and coping skills. Neither should go out of style, no matter the heights feminists achieve in the future. Writer Christina Schwarz, who captured the essence of Mrs. Bridge in an article for *The Atlantic* (2010), delicately points out that we may be unjustified in ridiculing her behavior to

> reassure ourselves that she's a relic of the past. Anyone, however, who has limped through a dull dinner party, offering up chipper observations because it's the socially decent thing to do; anyone who's baffled by her own grown children, who finds herself mindlessly agreeing with the political opinions of her friends, who suspects there's something better to do with her time—but has somehow neglected to develop the internal resources to figure out what; anyone who occasionally fears she may someday die 'without ever having been made to see all [life] may contain' and then allows daily trivialities to distract her, will realize otherwise.

It seems tragic, the unique and undiscovered talents Mrs. Bridge possesses that never see the light of day. May we study history so that our daughters and granddaughters never take for granted that they are free to choose their places in the world. And so they never take for granted their freedom to use their talents to prove their own identities without anybody else doing that for them.

Key Terms

Capitalism
Capitalism is a social system based on private ownership and the voluntary exchange of goods and services.

Communism
Communism is a government system with a state-controlled economy. A single party holds power and claims to work toward a higher social order where people share all goods equally.

Dictatorship
A dictatorship is a government or social circumstance where a single person holds power, makes all rules and decisions, controlling both the government and the media.

Constitutional republic
A country is a constitutional republic if it has a constitution limiting government power. Thus, citizens choose their heads of state and other governmental officials.

Feminism
Feminism includes a range of social and political movements and ideologies that aims for political, economic, and social equality.

Paternalism
Paternalism is a system that restricts personal liberty without

consent, for reasons intended as beneficial. In relationships, a desire to help or protect overrides others' individual choices and responsibilities, thus rendering them incompetent.

Patriarchy

Patriarchy describes a social system where men are the more powerful members. Men are the authority within the family and society, and power and possessions typically pass from father to son.

Spinster

A spinster is a negative description of an unmarried woman. The term first meant a woman whose occupation was spinning thread.

BLESS OUR MOTHERS, GRANDMOTHERS, AND JOANNE WOODWARD

Pam Hassebroek

In 1939 Elinor [Woodward Carter] took her daughter to the premiere of Gone with the Wind (1939) in Atlanta. Pulling up in a limo with the love of his life, Vivien Leigh, Laurence Olivier was shocked when 9-year-old Joanne hopped right into the limo and sat in his lap without any warning. —SKYE ROBINSON, *IMDb*

MRS. WOODWARD LOOKED ON AS her little girl claimed her place among Hollywood's elite. Joanne Woodward grew up to become one of America's most celebrated and enduring female actors, wives, and mothers. Among her 29 movies—and numbers of television and stage productions—Woodward has won praise for her performances, most as lead or co-lead. Her performance in *Mr. and Mrs. Bridge* (Ivory, 1990) is no exception; she earned an Academy Award nomination for portraying *Mrs. Bridge,* the female title role. Her vivid interpretation of Mrs. India Bridge lovingly brings to life the stoic generation of our mothers and grandmothers. Back then, married women had limited work opportunities. But, family loyalty and staying power were threads tightly woven into society's fabric.

> Joanne Woodward's exquisitely multilayered and nuanced performance as India Bridge, a frustrated, well-to-do WASP Kansas City housewife and mother … Woodward's humanization of her character actually improves on the original. Connell's imagination and compassion regarding this character have their limits, and Woodward

triumphantly exceeds them. (Rosenbaum, 1991)

"Ms. Woodward gives a finely tuned performance as Mrs. Bridge, evoking the character's habitual vagueness and confusion—as well as her positive qualities of friendliness, loyalty, and so forth—without a trace of condescension" (Sterritt, 1990).

A Georgia Native's Lifetime of Achievement

Born in 1930 in Thomasville, Georgia, Joanne Gignilliat Trimmier Woodward was among the first honored with a star on Hollywood's Walk of Fame in 1960. Her acting credits are abundant:

* ★ Four Academy Award nominations (won 1)
* ★ Ten Golden Globe Award nominations (won 3)
* ★ Four BAFTA Film Award nominations (won 1)
* ★ Nine Primetime Emmy Award nominations (won 3)
* ★ Two Independent Spirit Award nominations
* ★ Three Screen Actors Guild Award nominations
* ★ One Best Actress Award at the Cannes Film Festival.

As of this writing, she is the oldest living Best Actress Academy Award winner.[14] Marietta, Georgia, our Atlanta suburb where she attended high school, has named a public park for her. In addition, the Screen Actors Guild honored Woodward with a Lifetime Achievement Award in 1985, after which she continued to achieve and receive awards for over 20 years more.

Over the many years of her professional life, audiences have revered Joanne Woodward for her drama skills and her longtime marriage to Paul Newman. Woodward and Newman had an inspirational

---

[14] Woodward won the 1958 Academy Award for Best Actress for her performance in *The Three Faces of Eve* (Johnson, 1957).

marriage that lasted 50 years, from 1958 until Newman died in 2008. Parents of three daughters, middle daughter Melissa made them grandparents with the birth of her two sons. Their marriage stands out from so many in Hollywood who have divorced. Yet, what bonded them to each other and as a family must have been even more powerful than the passion they shared for acting.

From 1958 to 1990, Woodward and Newman co-starred in ten feature films—the first: *The Long, Hot Summer* (Ritt, 1958),[15] and the last, *Mr. and Mrs. Bridge (Ivory, 1990).*[16] This final joint film revisits an era of which they had intimate knowledge, both being products of the same 20th-century period in the movie.

Like millions of Americans, Woodward grew up loving the movies, but unlike most, she began performing in them at age 25. She majored in drama at LSU, studied acting in New York under Sanford Meisner,[17] and graduated from Sarah Lawrence College years later. In addition, Woodward has always been an advocate for positive social change. Because of that, it is fitting that Sarah Lawrence now lays claim to the Joanne Woodward Chair in Public Policy as a privileged faculty position.

Her early roles distinguished her from other female actors who played glamorous, frivolous, or dependent roles that were Hollywood's trademark (Blumberg, 2020). Instead, Woodward played more complicated characters, some psychologically distressed women, characters that include her role in *Mr. and Mrs. Bridge.* For

---

[15] Both had studied with director Martin Ritt at the Actors Studio.

[16] In television, their collaboration extended longer—her final performance with her husband was in the cable TV miniseries *Empire Falls* (2005).

[17] Like Elia Kazan, Meisner was a member of the Group Theatre in New York City, a collective formed the year after Woodward was born.

some, this role may evoke their mothers or grandmothers' presence if they lived during this era.

> *Mr. and Mrs. Bridge*, in which Paul Newman and Joanne Woodward give the most adventurous, most stringent performances of their careers ... set in Kansas City in those years between World Wars I and II ... when even people who had nothing were still obedient to the money and manners of others.

> There is a reserve, humor and desperation in their characterizations that enrich the very self-conscious flatness of the narrative terrain around them. (Canby, 1990)

Merchant Ivory Its Own Genre

Mr. and Mrs. Bridge records everyday events in an upper-middle-class American family from 1919 to 1944. Similar to other projects of Merchant Ivory Productions such as *A Room with a View* (1985), *Howards End* (1992), and *The Remains of the Day* (1994), *Mr. and Mrs. Bridge* is set in an earlier historical period and deals with social and economic class differences. Typical also are distinguished actors portraying refined characters who suffer distress and tragic situations.

Because of their elegant literary adaptations, spectacular cinematography, sets, and costumes, a Merchant Ivory film now forms a genre all its own. Loyal, dedicated, and creative business principals made Merchant Ivory successful. For most of their 44 films, Merchant produced, Ivory directed,[18] and Ruth Prawer Jhabvala scripted—she

---

[18] In 2018 at age 89, Ivory won his first Academy Award for the screenplay for *Call Me by Your Name* (2017). The win made him the oldest person to win an Academy Award for writing.

wrote 23 of them, including this one (Wikipedia, 2021).

> A favorite Jhabvala theme: people's powerlessness to escape their fate or to deviate from their essential character. As the writing arm of the Ismail Merchant-James Ivory filmmaking team, Ruth Prawer Jhabvala has a good idea of when and how literature can become cinema. She has written more than a dozen screenplays, all of them for Merchant Ivory—'We've been together 32 years,' she says. (Freedland, 1993)

Over a period parallel with Woodward and Newman, Ismail Merchant and James Ivory made a similar commitment as partners in business and as a couple from 1961 until Merchant died in 2005. Jhabvala, chiefly a novelist and a former German Jewish refugee, strayed from her main writing interest for decades to join their efforts.[19] She received an Oscar nomination for Best Adapted Screenplay for *The Remains of the Day*. In addition, she won Academy Awards for *A Room with a View* and *Howards End*. Jhabvala died in 2013 at age 85 (Róisín, 2018).

The Role of Married Women with Means

A few middle-class women in earlier generations may have been working moms, scout moms, or stage moms. Still, Mrs. Bridge would not have been among them. She was a Midwest product, a farming region similar to the South. New attitudes about roles for women of privilege were late to arrive there. In larger American cities, especially on the Northeast Coast, women had sought change from the Victorian period's restrictive sociopolitical rules.

---

[19] *See* Jasanoff (2018).

This significantly altered the attitudes and actions of women as they actively sought employment, created social lives away from the family, carved out autonomy within marriages and rediscovered the sexuality repressed during the reign of Victorianism. Many middle-class women became reformists and urged working women to join labor unions, fight for secure wages, and contribute to the financial security of the household to break free from the confines of male dominance. (Bishop, 2003)

Mrs. Bridge remained stuck. She had bought into older ideas of women's inferiority aligned with a strict biblical interpretation. Thus, she continued her submissiveness and couldn't articulate her needs. Moreover, the gradual changes in wifely duties that came with modernization hadn't moved her from this dependent position. A woman's place was at home, barefoot and pregnant, and the rules of society meant to keep her there.

Social norms and business practices demanded limits on women's opportunities and privileges, including those with talent and means. This was especially true for married women. My grandmother earned a college degree in education, one of the few tracks that would guarantee a job after graduation. She worked as a teacher as a single woman, but marriage required her resignation. Her job loss was unfortunate since hardships during the Depression forced the surrender of farming acreage to the bank.

During Mrs. Bridge's era, a married woman who needed to work to buy food for her family would be hard-pressed to find employment. Incredibly difficult to find one with adequate pay. For single women, technological advancements brought new jobs. Typing and answering phones allowed educated women—spinsters, unmarried mothers, orphans, and widows—to gain an income. But of course,

never in a management role.

Mrs. Bridge represented married women of financial means who could work only as volunteers, not in paying jobs.[20] They were otherwise required to stay in the home, serve their families, and manage the household and staff.

The upper or upper-middle-classes demonstrated their wealth by the leisure time they had. "Manicures and new outfits were luxuries that working, lower-class women could not afford, even if they had increased spare time" (Bishop, 2003). Bridge clubs, study clubs, and canasta games were ways to fill idle hours. After the children were grown, they lost the only jobs they had ever had.

In contrast, in America today, women can aspire to do so much more, whether single or married, wealthy or not. Women can earn a college degree in any discipline. They can run a business, contribute as professionals and parents, clergy in some religious organizations, or almost anything else within their capabilities.

Can Audiences Still Remember a Mrs. Bridge?

When *Mr. and Mrs. Bridge* was in theaters in 1990, many audiences likely recognized, empathized with, and appreciated Mrs. Bridge Joanne Woodward, raised during the Great Depression, probabl knew a Mrs. Bridge. Audiences 20 years ago could acknowledge th heritage while feeling grateful to live in an era where women ha choices and can pursue their individuality. Can today's young p ple identify, nearing a quarter into the 21st century?

American college students are emerging from childhoods that v bookended by 9/11 and the COVID19 pandemic—with na

---

[20] Of course, America runs on volunteerism. We benefit daily from the w millions who act compassionately with no compensation expected.

disasters, economic stress, political divide, and national unrest in between. College tuition has risen to such extreme levels that earnings from both parents are increasingly needed to support households. Thanks to pioneering women's work quality and work ethic in the generations that came after her, India Bridge's idleness is unfamiliar to most young adults.

Since many women who understand Mrs. Bridge's era are now grandmothers, great-grandmothers, or even great-great-grandmothers, recognition is disappearing. More rapidly, since grandmothers today are actively engaged in jobs of all types, as we note in Chapter 5.

Joanne Woodward's convincing performance as Mrs. Bridge is truly a gift to this generation and all future ones. It allows us to contemplate the limitations that women faced in the past and to celebrate the lives they lived. While silently enduring and pressing on, their dedication to family moved us to the benefits we have today. Thank you, Joanne Woodward. And, bless our mothers, grandmothers, and great-grandmothers indeed.

PEYTON PLACE (1957)

Is this Watergate or Peyton Place?
　　　—Sen. Lindsay Graham, Clinton impeachment hearing

DIRECTOR	Mark Robson
SCREENPLAY	John Michael Hayes
CAST	Lana Turner ~ Constance MacKenzie Diane Varsi ~ Allison MacKenzie Hope Lange ~ Selena Cross Arthur Kennedy ~ Lucas Cross Lee Philips ~ Michael Rossi Lloyd Nolan ~ Doc Swain
AWARDS	ACADEMY AWARDS
	Nominated for nine awards: 　Mark Robson for Best Director, 　Lana Turner for Best Actress, 　Hope Lange for Best Supporting Actress
	GOLDEN GLOBE AWARDS
	Won: New Star of the Year Actress: 　Diane Varsi
	Nominated for Best Supporting Actress: 　Mildred Dunnock, Hope Lange
RUN TIME	157 min
RATING	NR

SUMMARY

Disguised as a romantic drama, filled with euphemisms and innuendos, the revelations of discrimination, deceit, suicide, sexual violence, murder, and scandal shock an otherwise idyllic and charming mill town.

METALIOUS SHATTERS ILLUSIONS OF THE 1950s

Lucy Cota

I**N THE ERA AFTER WORLD WAR II**, a societal monotony swept across America that continued through the 1950s. After decades of wars and economic depression, America's eagerness for 'simpler times' was reflected in a newfound culture of wholesomeness. A high standard of morality was universally appealing but silently eluded universal adoption. In 1956, with the publication of her salacious book, *Peyton Place*, Grace Metalious thrust upon the world the stark reality behind the illusion. Yet, in the film *Peyton Place* (Robson, 1957), America's censors had prevented telling the story exactly as she wrote it.

Still, watching the movie serves to reflect on a time when social rules demanded that we keep large parts of our human experience hidden. Because society expected women to uphold a veil of innocence, a crushing blow fell to Grace Metalious for pulling the curtain back. Note that women were always vulnerable to being blamed for any of humanity's flaws.

In the early 1940s, over a decade before the book's publication, America had needed women in the workforce, with her men overseas fighting Nazi and Fascist regimes. Propaganda posters such as Rosie the Riveter, the iconic "We Can Do It," encouraged women to roll up their sleeves and keep America's motors running.

When World War II finally ended in 1945, our soldiers came home, took back the workforce, married, and settled down. Baby Boomers started arriving, and they kept coming throughout the idyllic 1950s when the only perceived blemish in the nation was the threat of Communism. People understood that secure, male-female family units were an effective defense against its spread.

The 1950s: a Decade of Conformity, Family, and TV

The phrase "family values" would not create buzz until decades later, yet that's what characterized the 1950s.[1] The decade's economic upturn, coupled with the housing boom, allowed Rosie the Riveter to leave her job, move into a suburban home, and turn into June Cleaver.

The 1950s was a decade of conformity among families as people clung to stability after years of depression and war. Television instantaneously became a dominant part of family life—TVs popped like popcorn in living rooms across America as families enthusiastically embraced the latest source of entertainment. TV ownership skyrocketed from three million at the beginning of the decade to 55 million toward the end (Wiegand, 2006).

Apart from Westerns, TV shows reflected the ideal of the traditional nuclear family with women in aprons. Among them were *Leave it to Beaver* (1957–1963), *The Adventures of Ozzie and Harriet* (1952–1966), and *Father Knows Best* (1954–1960).[2]

While *I Love Lucy* (1951–1957) had a twist of slapstick comedy, these shows impressed upon wide-eyed viewers their presentations of charming and perfectly functional families.

---

[1] In 1989, Vice President Dan Quayle criticized the glamorizing of TV sitcom character Murphy Brown in her decision to bear a child out of wedlock, citing its damage to "family values."

[2] Mary mentioned these TV shows in Chapter 2, pages 30, 32.

Writer Working at Home, Expected to Do It All

In these wholesome times in Gilmanton, New Hampshire, Grace Metalious, a writer and "stay-at-home mom," was not inclined to conform to television's teachings. Instead, she prioritized writing over child-rearing, housekeeping, and women's groups, which meant a troubled marriage.

> 'I did not like belonging to Friendly Clubs and bridge clubs.' 'I did not like being regarded as a freak because I spent time in front of a typewriter instead of a sink. And George did not like my not liking the things I was supposed to like.' (Quoted in Callahan, 2016)

She was said to lock her three young children outside when she retreated into her writing sanctuary—a corner of the living room with a desk and a treasured typewriter. Using town gossip fed by a local friend, Metalious worked obsessively on the book that she first titled, *The Tree and the Blossom*.

While feminism was dormant, Metalious actively sought to call her education and writing talent into service to support the family. But, since the feminist insurgence wouldn't happen for a decade later, she was way ahead and a real rags-to-riches story.[3]

Before *Peyton Place*, Metalious' family lived on her husband's annual salary of $3000. as principal of a local elementary school. *Peyton Place*'s publication enabled paying off creditors, buying her dream house outright, and, like Elvis Presley, purchasing a new luxury Cadillac car.

---

[3] In her 1963 book, *The Feminine Mystique*, women's rights advocate Betty Friedan argued that the suburbs were "burying women alive." This discontent contributed to the rebirth of the feminist movement in the 1960s.

In 1956, a time of church-going communities saturated with visions of purity and dignity among its citizens, *Peyton Place* shocked its readers with incest, rape, sex, lust, adultery, abortion, and family secrets. One of the novel's multifaceted plotlines is loosely based on an actual event that a local friend shared with the author.

A 20-year-old woman from Alton, NH, had shot and killed her father, then buried his body outside on their farm. The woman pleaded guilty to second-degree murder after revealing that her father had raped her and her sister for years, sometimes chaining them up in the bedroom for days.[4]

She had shot in self-defense as the abusive father chased his daughter, threatening to kill her.[5] This ghastly real-life story is stuff of writers' dreams, and Metalious seized the opportunity to incorporate the salacious details into *Peyton Place*.

Peyton Place Stays on the Best Seller List

One can't overestimate the shock waves the book created. It was a blockbuster of astounding proportions. *Peyton Place* sold more than 10 million copies—the bestselling novel of its time, second only to the *Bible*. Not even Margaret Mitchell's *Gone with the Wind* sold as many copies (Clark, 2019; Richardson, 2004). Following *Peyton Place*'s reign on the bestseller list for a year and a half, the movie adaptation received nine Academy Awards nominations. *Peyton*

---

[4] In *Peyton Place*, the fictional stepfather rapes the teenager. Publisher Kitty Messner instinctively knew that it would be too overwhelming for Americans to read that a biological father was capable of committing such a heinous act.

[5] The young woman was exonerated, likely aided by the journalists' coverage of her story—including that of Ben Bradlee, reporter for the *New Hampshire Sunday News* (New England Historical Society, 2019). Bradlee later became editor of *The Washington Post*.

Place also became television's first nighttime serial in the 1960s.

The unfortunate thing about fame and money is that they can be fleeting, especially when there is alcohol abuse. Metalious died at the young age of 39 of cirrhosis of the liver. She left her estate in tatters, owing more to the IRS than her assets were worth.

Interestingly, Lana Turner, who played Constance MacKenzie in the movie, extended her fortune when *Peyton Place* revived her career. In her next film, *Imitation of Life* (Sirk, 1959), Turner agreed to a box office royalty instead of a one-time payment. This decision, combined with the movie's success, made her a wealthy woman.[6]

The Book Emerges from the Struggle

Long after Metalious' struggle and death, the legacy of her book endures. The scandalized citizens of Gilmanton had resented Metalious for exposing the shameful stories about their hometown. So when she died, some didn't want "that bitch buried in their sacred ground" (Kelly, 2013), i.e., the nearby historical cemetery dating back to the 1700s.

Metalious assured the last laugh when she used her *Peyton Place* money to buy a lot in that cemetery, and several surrounding it, as her final resting place. Thus, Grace Metalious deliberately set herself apart in death, as in life.

Though the town of Gilmanton has largely swept *Peyton Place* under the rug, people remember. Today, visitors leave coins on Metalious' tombstone to pay respect to her. A neighbor, Jeanne Gallant, continues to tend her gravesite. At least two professors in America teach

---

[6] The original *Imitation of Life* (Stahl, 1934) had trouble getting Hays Code approval because it featured a biracial character who tried to pass for white and an actual mixed-race woman played the role.

CHAPTER 3 ♦ PEYTON PLACE

and write about *Peyton Place*—Professors Emily Toth (2006) at LSU and Ardis Cameron at Southern Maine. Cameron sought reissue of the novel, writing an "introduction that casts Grace Metalious as a literary Joan of Arc, sword drawn, swinging at the oppressive social conventions of the '50s" (Callahan, 2016).

Peyton Place Contributes to Opening Minds

Some may look back at the 1950s as the halcyon years. Life seemed less demanding and less costly in the time of swirling poodle skirts, sock hops, and exemplary entertainment. Indeed, the decade was a nice respite from the nationwide troubles that had come before. Yet, things weren't always what they seemed to be. *Peyton Place* contributed to opening minds to the fact that *Leave It to Beaver* was not a documentary of the times.

There grew an increased awareness of an imperfect world for everybody and their mother reading the book—an essential realization for the tumultuous 1960s.

PEYTON PLACE THEN AND NOW

Pam Hassebroek

'To a tourist, these towns look as peaceful as a postcard picture,'
Metalious once said. 'But if you go beneath that picture, it's like
turning over a rock with your foot—all kinds of strange things crawl
out.' —New England Historical Society

Maybe she honestly believed that a scene meant to demonstrate the
sexual awakening of one of her characters required that this woman,
the fair-haired Constance MacKenzie, be forced into submission by a
violent, swarthy suitor, Tomas Makris, who 'slapped her a stunning
blow across the mouth' before he made her feel 'the first red gush of
shamed pleasure.' —MALLON & HOLMES, *The New York Times*

A COMPLEX TAPESTRY OF SMALL-TOWN LIFE in pre-WWII America
is on display in the movie *Peyton Place* (Robson, 1957). It's a multi-
story tale about women of different ages and social strata, both good
and bad—"women of virtue" and "fallen women"[7]—who contend
with gender discrimination, sexual exploitation, and violence in
their small community. Using color cinematography shot in
beautiful Camden, Maine, and an ensemble cast of gorgeous actors,
the movie veils the vivid descriptions and nasty storylines from
Grace Metalious' book (1956). With Franz Waxman's memorable
music score calming throughout, all was in tune with Hollywood's
Hays code.

---

[7] Typical of the battle of good and evil in melodrama, "fallen" is a mid-19th-
century term applied to a woman who had fallen out of God's or society's
favor. Proverbs 31: 10–31 in the *Bible* describes the virtuous woman.

What remains in plain sight is a story and set of characters that portray a binary moral stance and, as always, a happily-ever-after ending. Thus, we find stark contrasts by comparing this censored film to today's industry products. A trend toward greater authenticity in movies began in the 1960s, ushering in the more complex view of humanity that continues today.

A Box Office Success Despite the Censors

Despite the movie's tamer story versions, it was a blockbuster at its release and then earned nine Academy Award nominations.[8] The nine included all three principal female actors: Lana Turner for Best Actress in a leading role, as Constance, single parent of Allison;[9] both Diane Varsi as Allison, and Hope Lange as Allison's friend, Selena Cross, for Best Actress in a Supporting Role.

Clearly, the movie was a success on its own, even though undoubtedly many saw it because of the book's reputation and the sexual content that caused tens of millions to buy it. Even so, the stories Grace Metalious threaded throughout her book were significant—spot-on as societal critiques.

> The late Sinclair Lewis would no doubt have hailed Grace
> Metalious as a sister-in-arms against the false fronts and
> bourgeois pretensions of allegedly respectable
> communities and certified her as a public accountant of
> what goes on in the basements, bedrooms, and back
> porches of a 'typical American town.' (Baker, 1956)

---

[8] Earning $25.6 million in the U.S., *Peyton Place* is #52 in gross revenue.

[9] Although her character was part of an ensemble cast, Turner was nominated in a "leading role." This was her only Academy Award nomination—Joanne Woodward won that year for *Three Faces of Eve* (Johnson, 1957).

Did anyone even notice the social ills? Apart from its storied carnal pursuits, readers of the novel in the 1950s may have otherwise skimmed right over and blindly accepted the description of the town's misogyny and social disparities. They most likely considered those characteristics as simply how things were—and still are in America to some extent. The mill owners run the town, and many mill workers live in poverty. Most respectable women are homemakers and have no voice. Any woman who veers from the norm gets a raised eyebrow or gets run out of town.

Peyton Place emphasizes that America's male-dominated society has always judged women responsible for male-female sexual violence, extramarital affairs, and "out-of-wedlock" children. However, the sanctity of marriage was so widely established that, on one point, even men were considered slightly culpable. Their thoughts of sex with a woman (and always a woman, God forbid) were sinful if that woman was not his wife. Thus, former President Jimmy Carter's remarks in a *Playboy Magazine* interview created controversy across the country.

> Among those who gave serious responses, the prevailing view was that it was neither smart nor Presidential for Mr. Carter to have said: 'I've looked on a lot of women with lust. I've committed adultery in my heart many times,' and to have used some mild vulgarisms in referring to other people's sexual conduct. (Dembart, 1976)

Hollywood's Narratives in the Extreme

Audiences watching the movie today may find it easier to see the abuse and blatant discrimination against women in the Peyton Place community. Metalious undoubtedly described extremes of behavior in her interconnecting stories to enhance sensationalism and focus on America's social inequalities.

> The novel takes its small town to task for the ways in
> which it deals with, or more often than not, does not deal
> with the abuses of power that often constitute scandalous
> behavior. Its abuses of power, privilege, position, and
> prominence. (Hirsh-Dickinson, 2007)

Scriptwriters positioned women with unequal social status
compared to men, which aligned perfectly with the construction of
a woman's moral responsibilities.

> They were taught to pity the neurotic, unfeminine,
> unhappy women who wanted to be poets or physicists or
> presidents. They learned that truly feminine women do
> not want careers, higher education, political rights—the
> independence and the opportunities that the old-fashioned
> feminists fought for. (Friedan, 1963)

In reality, whether their intentions were noble or appalling, women
were powerless victims not only because of their lesser physical
strength. Often their typically lower socioeconomic circumstances
victimized them as well. However, illicit topics sometimes avoided
the film-cutting floor—in *Peyton Place*: suicide, extramarital affairs,
unwed pregnancy, and abortion; the movie just addresses them in
different language. Of course, the plot had murder too—which is
always okay in a script, as long as the bad guys get punished by the
end of the story.

Characters representing Good and Bad

Metallious' story structure just happens to sync with Hollywood's
filmmaking style under the Hays Code—the explicit and polarized
representation of good and evil. White hats and black hats.

On the good side, characters include administrators, teachers, and students in a local high school. Miss Elsie Thornton (Mildred Dunnock) is a valued, reliable, virtuous high school teacher. Another extremely respectable, responsible woman, Constance MacKenzie, runs a clothing shop in the town. Her daughter, Allison, earns the title of class valedictorian. High school student Selena Cross, Allison's best friend, has a boyfriend, Ted Carter (David Nelson), who hopes to become a lawyer.

On the bad side, Mr. Harrington (Leon Ames) is the patriarchy's keeper, making Miss Thornton a victim of job discrimination. Harrington passes her over for the high school principal's job and hires a male teacher from outside the community. The Cross family lives in sub-standard housing. The father figure is a violent, abusive alcoholic who terrorizes his wife and stepchildren and rapes his stepdaughter, which the book describes in graphic detail. The links among poverty, class, and violence suggest that no man who makes a sustainable living for his family would behave this way.[10]

Censors Concerned about Sexual Content

Of course, it was not the extremes of poverty and class but the sexual content that created the uproar over the book and put the censors in the business of restricting the movie. The Hays Code, authored by a Catholic priest, had effectively regulated trashy and disreputable movie content since the 1930s. Thus, no one worried about what children might see while attending a movie showing at a local theater. Producers knew the exact types of content, visuals, and language they couldn't use. For three decades, no major studio

---

[10] Reports about Harvey Weinstein, Jeffrey Epstein, Roger Ailes, Larry Nasser and many other prominent men show that this isn't always the case.

produced a movie with objectionable content.

The following is evidence that John Michael Hayes' screenplay had altered the book's content.

> The PCA had few criticisms of the screenplay.[11] In letters to the studio, the PCA advised that the use of the word 'abortion' be forbidden, and instructed the studio to tone down the brutality in the scene in which Selena clubs her stepfather to death. The studio was also cautioned to temper the rape scene. (*"Peyton Place* (1957)," 2019)

The PCA prohibited even a hint of sex with a 'child.' In the book, Selena is 14 when the sexual abuse begins, continuing for years until she becomes pregnant. Then, Doc Swain (Lloyd Nolan) performs an illegal abortion, first presenting it to the public as an appendectomy.

However, telling of 1950s attitudes, one of Doc Swain's lines didn't even make it into Metalious' book: "knowing Lucas was guilty of the crime of incest, a crime worse than child abuse between homosexuals, in the doctor's mind" (Toth, 1981). Americans couldn't talk publicly about sex crimes. But, Metalious' unpublished words speak loudly about social perceptions and biases toward gay men. The movie also left out Norman's domineering mother—the abuse she inflicts on her son, enemas at age seventeen.

In the book, Betty, a "gold-digging slut," gets an abortion after Harrington threatens to fire her father from his job at the mill. In the movie, Betty (Terry Moore) is simply a "flashy" girl.

> The film offers Hollywood's staple depiction of stereotypes and of virtue rewarded, and it generally washes out much

---

[11] The Production Code Administration (PCA) was the group that enforced the Hays Code censorship rules.

of the cynicism and corruption at high levels and ugliness at lower levels. (Sypher, 1993)

Readers criticized Metalious' portrayal of religious and ethnic minorities. Back then, serious discussion of diversity was virtually taboo.

> Though a contemporary audience would hardly find *Peyton Place* shocking today, what is intriguing about this adaptation is that audiences in 1957 would not have found it shocking either. Weaned on the near toxic rum punch of Metalious' filthy prose, the audience would find the film a glass of watery tea. (Bailey, 2004)

Afghanistan Akin to 20th-Century America

Although attitudes and consequences for women victims have changed to some extent in the U.S. today, the situation in 20th-century America was similar to that in many other strongly patriarchal cultures. For example, a 2016 U.S. State Department report sounds all too familiar. The following excerpt observes Afghanistan's human rights abuses:

> Reports indicated men accused of rape often claimed the victim agreed to consensual sex. Rapes were difficult to document due to social stigma. Male victims seldom came forward due to fear of retribution or additional exploitation by authorities, but peer sexual abuse was reportedly common. Female victims faced stringent societal reprisal.

Still, today in the U.S., rape is an underreported crime. Shame, stigma, fear of the rapist, fear of not being believed, fear of being blamed, and fear of consequences to future opportunities silence its victims. Rape victims are at risk of mental health issues that can linger for a lifetime.

> Whether sexual violence is influenced by biological or cultural factors, it has a major influence on the mental health and functioning of the victim, especially due to the social responses to the violence. Negative social reactions lead to higher levels of mental health issues in the victims. (Kalra & Bhugra, 2013)

Several college administrators expelled female rape victims who reported it, especially when the perpetrator was a revenue-generating, attention-getting male athlete. Indeed, the case of Erica Kinsman, who accused Jameis Winston at Florida State University in 2013, shows how a whole town can turn its back on the victim (Payne, 2015; Novkov, 2016). In an article for *Slate Magazine* (2015), Stahl writes,

> Kinsman's allegations became a huge national story—in the sports world and beyond—in no small part because of reporting in the *New York Times* that detailed how the Tallahassee police neglected their most basic investigative duties in the initial handling of the case. Kinsman's description of the night in question, as reported in police records, described in the documentary *The Hunting Ground*, is horrific. No charges were ever brought against Winston. Whatever headway has been made doesn't change the fact that Winston is now a major part of the NFL landscape, and the rape allegation against him will likely soon not be. 'We forgive and forget, and winning does that to us. That will happen with Winston. If he comes into the league and starts winning, no one's going

to be talking about what happened at Florida State. No one.'

Later allegations against Jameis Winston confirm Stahl's prediction. Winston was the No. 1 overall pick in the 2015 NFL draft. He had groped a female Uber driver a month before the Tampa Bay Buccaneers formally drafted him. Three years later, in 2018, the NFL suspended Winston for three games, judging that "Winston violated the personal conduct policy by touching the driver in an inappropriate and sexual manner without her consent and that disciplinary action was necessary and appropriate" (Rivera, 2021).

In a 2017 article, filmmakers Dick and Ziering reported,

> Something is terribly wrong at Florida State when football players can commit crimes of violence with impunity, knowing FSU's athletic and police departments will protect them.

> Jameis Winston has been identified in the sexual assaults of two women, and

> The Florida State Chief of Police and the Dean of Students colluded to stop the investigations of Winston.

> FSU's victim advocate office had 113 sexual assault reports over 2014, yet FSU's administration reported only 14 sexual assaults to the federal government.

During his five-year rookie contract with Tampa Bay, Winston made more than $46 million. He earned about $20.1 million in 2019 (Stroud, 2020), then the team let him go. The New Orleans Saints signed Winston to a one-year, $1.1 million contract in April 2020. Amazing money for most of us.

But we've come to grips with the significant edge athletes and other celebrities have over the rest of us in earning power. Further, especially in the case of stars, publicizing sexual misconduct is considerably less offensive for a national audience today.

Because of the commonplace nature of unwelcome acts and our relaxed moral environment, fewer people are outraged when such scandals occur. A 2018 *Vanity Fair* article (Filipovic) questions whether we have made any positive change from Justice Clarence Thomas's hearing in 1991. "How Far Have We Really Come Since Anita Hill?" states that we have allowed men considerable latitude in mistreating women.

On the positive side, increasingly today, we see married or committed partners genuinely sharing responsibilities. Either spouse (or both of them) contributes to household income. Many couples share household duties and happily share parenting the children. This partnership support is happening, whether opposite-sex or same-sex couples. Interestingly, *Peyton Place* depicts some women with positive identities and positions that require neither marriage nor domestic duties for social acceptance. This characterization is very different from women's roles in *Mr. and Mrs. Bridge*'s era and a departure from the reality surrounding Grace Metalious.

On the negative side, today's norms lower the bar for accountability and responsibility by increased acceptance of sex without commitment. Also, accepting this behavior in teenagers places responsibility for controlling procreation on children.

No longer viewed as immoral by their peers, schoolchildren freed from social judgment take high risks in trying sex. Risk-taking increases STDs and irresponsible pregnancies where poverty limits education and upward mobility for teens and babies. And deprivation increases child abuse.

Are the children raising the children, or are the grandparents and the foster care system? What's more, "CDC data show that lesbian, gay, and bisexual high school students are at substantial risk for serious health outcomes as compared to their peers" ("Sexual risk behaviors," 2020).

Did *Peyton Place* Change Behavior?

Did the book *Peyton Place* accurately reflect life at the time? We know that some of the stories were partly true. And some exposed social issues that are still with us. Was it instrumental in changing attitudes and behavior? These are challenging questions. The lack of public exposure put social problems out of mind and likely deceived our collective consciousness.

In truth, the book shocked people because it portrayed women who didn't conform to the acceptable norms of female gender behavior—and neither did its author. Metalious understood this yet dared to put women's issues out front. She also had the support of her publisher. "Not only was the novel authored by a woman and largely about women and presumably read by women, it was also produced by publishing houses headed by women" (Brier, 2005).

Whether or not the book was influential, no one will refute the notion that attitudes now are different from those of the readers and audiences of *Peyton Place* in the 1950s. Many of today's adults know this because they experienced this time first-hand.

I wonder if the French novel *Bonjour Tristesse* (1954) by Françoise Sagan influenced Grace Metalious. Metalious could have read it; she came from a French-speaking family. However, an English version was published too, in 1955. But striking that Sagan's life in France sounds so uncannily familiar, as does the novel's movie adaptation and publication revival experience.

From Williams' account in *The Guardian* (2014),

> *Bonjour Tristesse*, Françoise Sagan's 'amoral' story of a schoolgirl's summer romance, scandalized French society and made its 18-year-old author famous. But this early success led to a life of drink, drugs, and unhappy relationships.

Françoise Sagan (aka Françoise Delphine Quoirez, 1935–2004), a French teenager from a Catholic family, wrote *Bonjour Tristesse*, which gave her remarkable celebrity status overnight. This elevated status came mainly because of the book's scandalous story and descriptions of immoral sex, suicide, devious and corrupt behavior.

> It is an invocation of an era, of a time when young people were beginning to seek freedom from the strict bourgeois society of France after the end of WW2. (Godin, 2019)

Otto Preminger produced a film adaptation in 1958 that starred David Niven and Deborah Kerr and 19-year-old Jean Seberg as the teen. Intriguingly, reviewers wrote about it with words from praise to disdain, from "a masterpiece" to "a bomb." *Le Monde* listed the book at number 41 among its "100 Books of the Century" in 1999.

Sagan destroyed herself with gambling, drinking, fast driving, and unhappy relationships. She was married and divorced twice and subsequently sustained several lesbian relationships. After draining her resources, she died, leaving unpaid debts.

A former French literature lecturer at Glasgow University, Heather Lloyd, brought attention to Irene Ash's omission of over 100 lines of Sagan's text and wanted to restore them. (Ash translated the 1955 novel.) The sex scenes in the French version were considered too daring for 1950s Britain and were removed for English publication. A new translation was published in 2013.

If you are among the millions who read *Peyton Place* when it was all the rage, did you wonder about the life of Grace Metalious? Or, did you ever think about who else was reading it?

> As a young queer boy who felt a kinship with women shaking off the limitations of their milieu and trying to rise above the social narratives around their gender, *Peyton Place* offered me immense comfort. (Smith, 2016)

Watching *Peyton Place* today may stir nostalgia in some viewers. Yet, no matter how or if you experienced this earlier time, it benefits us to consider the greater transparency and acceptance in attitudes toward others that we see today. Still, we know that the decades since the 1960s have been an evolving cultural transition that hasn't been trouble-free.

Words We Couldn't Say in Public

Many of the words we now hear in informal communication, especially evident in today's movies, are examples of dramatic change from when the PCA enforced the Hays Code. This change in attitudes happens when developing shared communication rules—acceptable language and behavior—influenced by prominent people and media. The ways we use words and how we communicate in a social setting tell us how we perceive others (Krauss & Chiu, 1998).

We now agree to the use of many words that we couldn't say at the time of *Peyton Place*. For example, until the 1960s, U.S. network television would not allow the word "hell" in its broadcasts.

> Pennsylvania routinely cut any reference to pregnancy, a woman could not even be shown knitting baby clothes; after all, 'The movies are patronized by thousands of children who believe that babies are brought by the stork,

and it would be criminal to undeceive them.' (Doherty, 2019)

The 64th U.S. Attorney General Robert Kennedy's wife, Ethel, defied general perceptions about pregnancy when she played tennis until right before her delivery date (Plummer, 1984). At the time, women were encouraged to eliminate any physical activity and take it easy as they approached the due date. And, indeed, to dress in a way that hid their "condition." Back then, when showing evidence of pregnancy, most women certainly had to quit their jobs.

After I had accepted a systems analyst position at the U.S. Army Finance Center in 1970, HR barred me from onboarding until I could "prove" no pregnancy. If pregnant, I was unemployable. Of course, the proof required a pregnancy test at a medical facility and a wait time for the results.[12]

Lucille Ball became TV's first pregnant character in 1952 on her TV series *I Love Lucy*. Since no one could say the word "pregnant" in a public conversation, she announced her pregnancy with the then scandalous line, "Lucy is enceinte." ("I Love Lucy," 2013).

Fortunately, some of the words we now find acceptable allow open discussion about important topics. Unfortunately, we take the bad with the good—people also use many more expressions that disparage and dehumanize others. In the 1950s, parents instructed their children to keep their "dirty linens" behind closed doors. Metalious' book opened them wide to show the human failings of all. Some would likely argue that we would benefit by closing those doors back a little.

---

[12] A home pregnancy test wasn't available in 1970. The first approved by the FDA came to market in 1976 (Romm, 2015). Before that, a woman had to leave a urine sample at a doctor's office and wait up to two weeks for results.

We humans will always struggle to lift our behavior to higher standards. However, today, we can be thankful for our freedom to speak clearly and openly about our lives' problematic concerns.

CHAPTER 4

CHARADE (1963)

Of course, you won't be able to lie on your back for a while, but then you can lie from any position, can't you?
—REGINA (REGGIE) LAMPERT, *Charade*

DIRECTOR	Stanley Donen
SCREENPLAY	Peter Stone
CAST	Audrey Hepburn ~ Regina Lampert *Cary* Grant ~ Peter Joshua Walter Matthau ~ Carson Dyle George Kennedy ~ Herman Scobie
AWARDS	ACADEMY AWARDS
	Best Original Song nomination: *Charade*, Henry Mancini (music) and Johnny Mercer (lyrics)
	BAFTA AWARDS
	Best British Actress: Audrey Hepburn
RUN TIME	113 min
RATING	NR

SUMMARY

The movie's primary plot is a suspenseful, stylish crime caper, tracking down bad guys while keeping audiences in doubt till the end. Set in typical jet-set places with adored stars Audrey Hepburn and Cary Grant.

DID DONEN'S *CHARADE* FOOL EVERYONE?

Pam Hassebroek

*Yes, movies! Look at them? All of those glamorous people—having
adventures—hogging it all, gobbling the whole thing up! Hollywood
characters are supposed to have all the adventures for everybody in
America, while everybody in America sits in a dark room and watches
them have them! Yes, until there's a war. That's when adventure
becomes available to the masses! Everyone's dish, not only Gable's!
Then the people in the dark room come out of the dark room to have
some adventure themselves. Goody, goody! It's our turn now, to go to
the South Sea Islands—to make a safari—to be exotic, far-off!*
—TOM, *The Glass Menagerie*

BY THE EARLY 1960s, HOLLYWOOD movie audiences had
come to expect big-name actors wearing fabulous clothing
and locations that were exotic, unfamiliar places.
Predictable narratives presented glamorous women and their
exhilarating male relationships. *Charade* (Donen, 1963) has those
typical elements, yet there's a difference. Audrey Hepburn's
character, Reggie, is a departure from a vulnerable, dependent
female.

Charade deserved its numerous awards—three wins and nine
nominations, fulfilling all the movie-going public's expectations and
more. Audrey Hepburn and *Cary* Grant received Golden Globe
nominations for their leading roles. If you have seen the film, Henry
Mancini's soundtrack melody can quickly come back to your mind.

Peter Stone and Marc Behm co-wrote the movie's original screenplay based on Stone's novel, *The Unsuspecting Wife* (1961), which *Redbook Magazine* had published as a serial. But Peter Stone then tailored it specifically for Hepburn and Grant for the final movie script (Wikipedia, 2020).

Stanley Donen's Role in Hollywood Legends

Charade was director Stanley Donen's biggest box-office hit (Eder, 2010), no small feat in light of his productive career. He was the last surviving prominent director of Hollywood's Golden Age.[1]

Donen was first a dancer and choreographer on Broadway before moving to Hollywood. He grew up in a Jewish family in Columbia, South Carolina. In coping with prejudice in the Christian community, he often escaped to movie theatres. (He and Vito Russo might have become great friends—Lucy discusses Russo's similar boyhood movie experiences in Chapter 6.) He made 8-mm home movies, attended dance classes, and aspired to tap dance professionally (Barson, 2020).

And so he did. Donen was 17 when he made his first public appearance on Broadway, and he met Gene Kelly at the same time. Their later collaboration in Hollywood brought several now-classic films to the screen.

His noteworthy films include *On the Town (1949)*, *Singin' in the Rain (1952)*, *Seven Brides for Seven Brothers (1954)*, *Funny Face (1957)*, *Damn Yankees! (1958)*, and *Two for the Road (1967)*. Actors in those movies include Gene Kelly, Frank Sinatra, Donald O'Connor, Debbie Reynolds, Cyd Charisse, Rita Moreno, Howard Keel, Russ Tamblyn, Audrey Hepburn, Fred Astaire, Tab Hunter, Audrey

---

[1] Donen, one of the most influential directors of movie musicals in the 1940s and '50s, died in 2019.

Hepburn, Albert Finney, and Jacqueline Bisset. And again, Audrey Hepburn. But, like Hepburn's role in the movie, *Charade* was a departure from Donen's earlier blockbusters.

Charade's release date in late 1963 came between two James Bond movies *Dr. No* (Young, 1963) and *From Russia with Love* (Young, 1964). That same year, Peter Sellers stars in the British comedy/crime caper, *The Wrong Arm of the Law* (Owen, 1963). The legendary, unforgettable Elizabeth Taylor performs both off- and on-stage to make *Cleopatra* (1963) one of the most expensive movies ever created. *The Birds,* a Hitchcock horror/thriller movie, was in theaters in 1963. Alfred Hitchcock was a household name because of his earlier film and TV dramas. *Charade* came into the public sphere amid all of this extraordinary entertainment. It also arrived right after the horrors of the Cuban Missile Crisis and U.S. President John Kennedy's assassination.

Apart from the real-life circumstances globally, war movies and crime films had become popular in America, especially those with a twist. Therefore, *Charade* arrived in perfect company with a twisting story and surprise ending, a form that Hitchcock had made famous in his numerous espionage/crime/war films. *North by Northwest* (1959) is an example, and, like *Charade*, stars Cary Grant.

Even though *Charade*'s genre is comedy romance, the central focus is neither romantic nor comedic. Well, one might say yes and no. No doubt, it's a crime/spy drama. A U.S. Treasury official is attempting to recover stolen federal government property. We are told that the bad guys are an ex-military group that served in WWII. However, neither Hepburn's character nor the audience knows it all.

Hepburn as Reggie, a Grown-up Nancy Drew

Hepburn's role was innovative and detached from the Hollywood mold in many ways, some of it simply because of Hepburn's youthful, lively personality. Through her, we can observe that a leading female actor's "appropriate" behavior was changing from a typical goody-goody, subservient role to men. For example, in her first line in the movie, Reggie confidently asserts to her friend Sylvie that she has decided to divorce her husband. What, divorce!? Could she say that in a movie?

Reggie represents a woman transitioning from dependence to one who can look after herself. She shows that a woman can openly make independent decisions. Maybe Stone got his ideas from the books about Nancy Drew, the fictional sleuth who influenced many of today's prominent and successful professional women (Wikipedia, 2021).[2]

Mildred Benson, aka Carolyn Keene, wrote the Nancy Drew stories that would have been available to Stone. Some claim the feisty Nancy Drew "to be a lot like [Benson] herself—confident, competent, and totally independent" (Kismaric & Heiferman, 2007). Nancy is young, attractive, rich, and remarkably talented. She sure sounds like Hepburn to me.

A Story Full of Throwbacks?

A *New York Times* review of *Charade* warned about the excessive and "gruesome violence," suggesting that moviegoers bringing their children should expect to be shocked (Crowther, 1963). Except that, *Charade* is a "caper" film, a popular genre because of its cartoon-like

---

[2] Prominent women include Supreme Court Justices, former First Lady Laura Bush, and former Secretary of State Hillary Clinton.

depiction of crime as amusing or comical instead of a grim focus on injustice—not unlike the 1990s TV reality show, *America's Dumbest Criminals* or the *Tom and Jerry* animated shorts.

Still, in the interest of critical thinking, I kept wondering why George Kennedy's character, one of the movie's bad guys, is fashioned with a prosthetic hand. Someone consciously chose to create the notion that a prosthetic hand is a dangerous weapon. Then I decided that such a character may be simply a parody of a late '50s James Bond book (*Goldfinger*) with villains such as Oddjob, but minus Pussy Galore.[3]

A parody imitates another creative work by incorporating its characters or other elements in humorous ways. Throughout movie history, audiences have discovered in single films similarities with other creative works or other movies, whether in the same or a different genre and formula type. This intertextuality suggests that knowing the origin of a narrative or motif can establish how we interpret what we're watching. Thus, if I had seen *Charade* at the time of its release, I might have immediately thought about Ian Fleming's work. However, one can appreciate this story as funny without considering its influences. Besides, maybe another bad guy with a prosthetic hand will come to mind. Some may remember Captain Hook from J.M. Barrie's *Peter Pan*.

But, let's stay with James Bond. *Charade*'s credits and opening scene are reminiscent of the first Bond movie, *Dr. No*. The gun barrel

---

[3] *Goldfinger* was a daily serial and a comic strip in the *Daily Express*, beginning in 1958, before it became the book and the third James Bond movie. Pussy Galore is a liberated woman and a lesbian. Ian Fleming presented her lesbianism as a psychological condition, a "side effect" of rape (Fleming, 1959).

sequence became a signature device featured in nearly every James Bond film after that. A gun points at Reggie in the opening scene of *Charade*.

But then, perhaps the prosthetic weapon is just a gruesome detail in keeping with a story full of throwbacks to Hitchcock films. His movies often include wry humor and a character with psychological dysfunction. Indeed, discerning fans would undoubtedly notice a touch of Hitchcock that had become his unique signature—his "Where's Waldo?"[4] appearance in many of his movies.

> The screenwriter, Peter Stone, and the director, Stanley Donen, have an unusual joint cameo role. When Reggie goes to the U.S. Embassy to meet with Bartholomew, two men get on the elevator as she gets off. The man who says, 'I bluffed the old man out of the last pot—with a pair of deuces' is Stone, but the voice is Donen's. Stone's voice is later used for the U.S. Marine guarding the Embassy at the film's ending. (Wikipedia, 2020)

Ah, Romance Is in the Air!

From 1954, when Hepburn earned an Oscar® for Best Actress in *Roman Holiday* (Wyler, 1950), she was an international star until the end of her life. Almost all of her roles were romantic, and in nearly all of them, her love interest was an older man.

This May-December age difference was also the case in *Charade*. Hepburn was 33 during filming, while Cary Grant had turned 59. Having been in movies for 30 years and nearing retirement, Grant

---

[4] The intertextual reference here is to the children's books by English artist Martin Handford. His *Where's Waldo?* books incorporate the boy Waldo in intricately detailed drawings that make finding him extremely difficult.

was uncomfortable about the 25-year age difference (Eastman, 1989). As a result, the only time Hepburn and Grant worked together was when making this movie.

Hepburn also plays the female lead in a subsequent movie that has similar elements. Paris is the setting for the William Wyler-directed film, *How to Steal a Million* (1966). Her character is actively involved in family crime as the daughter of a wealthy art forger. And one of her suitors is much older.

In contrast, in 1961, before either *Charade* or *How to Steal a Million*, Hepburn played a role that was even more out-of-step with Hollywood tradition. Director Wyler cast her as a lesbian. Or so it might seem.

As a lead-in to Part II's focus on sexual orientation and gender identity depictions, we note that film censorship generally became less restrictive as the years advanced through the 1960s. Like *Charade*'s changes to women's behavior, other films brought change when stories with gay and lesbian characters and same-sex relationships began to enter the theaters. However, in keeping with the Hollywood tradition, the stories still left out any words like lesbian or gay and presented negative consequences for the LG individuals involved.

In *The Children's Hour* (Wyler, 1961), Hepburn and Shirley MacLaine play teachers in a girls' school. From Higgins (2015) in the *Hollywood Reporter*:

> *The Children's Hour* was Wyler's remake of 1936's *These Three*, an adaptation of Lillian Hellman's 1934 Broadway hit *The Children's Hour*. The play is about a true story from 1809, where two women running a girls' school had their lives ruined when a student accused them of being

lesbians.

The Children's Hour remake was a landmark film that influenced changes to the Production Code. Arthur Krim, United Artists president, threatened to release the movie without the Codes' seal of approval. He suggested that the MPAA censors amend the code to comply with the film.

Not wanting to give up their authority image, the MPAA amended the Production Code on October 3, 1961, allowing gay and lesbian portrayals, with the constraint of "conservative treatment" (Westbrook, 2000). The Children's Hour, adapted by John Michael Hayes, got five Academy Award nominations following its release.

Even though movies with LGBTQ themes had gained permission for screening in movie theaters, in 1968 such films would acquire an X rating. *Midnight Cowboy* (1969), starring Dustin Hoffman and Jon Voight, was the first X-rated movie to win an Academy Award.

> *Victim*, a British film released in 1961, was quite literally an open protest against Britain's anti-gay laws that, until 1967, prosecuted gay males. The film was the first English language movie to use the word "homosexual." And even the Motion Picture Production Code in the U.S. denied *Victim*'s seal of approval, meaning it didn't meet Hollywood's moral guidelines. (Gonzales, 2017)

Stanley Donen's creative projects became more varied with the film industry's lesser restrictions and movie musicals' lesser popularity. In one case, he ventured out to direct a seriously Code-provoking movie, *Staircase* (1969), casting Rex Harrison and Richard Burton as a gay couple (Barson, 2020). The movie was adapted from a two-character British play that first performed in London in 1966 and then on Broadway in 1968. Twentieth Century-Fox agreed to finance the film based on the stars playing the lead roles. The film failed by all accounts, both critically and commercially, "an example of how not to treat homosexuality on-screen" (Miller, 2007). No one could agree on whether the movie was a comedy or a tragedy.

A Dream Can Fill Your Heart

Still today, Donen's *Charade* remains a delightful vicarious experience for those who can aspire to (or dream about) the high-flying lifestyle it depicts. At the beginning of the 1960s, dreaming could be fantastic and expansive at a time of stability, unity, and peace in America. Indeed, the extraordinary stories of Hollywood inspired many women to more critical missions in life. Growing up as a farm girl in a rural area, I was far from any sense of the urban environment and its bright lights. I think my vision of being out in the world came straight out of these magnificent movies and from the books about Nancy Drew. I wonder now, is that why I still drive a roadster?

Thanks to our home network connections and audio/visual technologies, we can all get this same inspiration at any time. Because *Charade* didn't receive proper copyright when it was released, among other places, it is available for free download from the *Internet Archive*.

Key Terms

Caper film

A caper film is a whimsical crime film with shrewdness, wayward adventure, or quirky humor.

Hollywood's Golden Age

In the Golden Age of American film, Hollywood studios developed a distinctive narrative and visual style that became the most pervasive filmmaking style worldwide. The studios developed this style between the 1910s and early 1960s, though some say it ended in the '40s.

Intertextuality

Intertextuality is the interconnection between similar or related texts. "Texts can influence, derive from, parody, reference, quote, contrast with, build on, draw from, or even inspire each other. Intertextuality produces meaning" (Nordquist, 2020).

CHARADE'S DAZZLING AUDREY HEPBURN

Mary Reed

AUDREY HEPBURN ENDURED STARVATION during World War II before becoming one of the movies' most iconic stars. Her strength and compassion, along with her beauty and dignity, survived to brighten people's lives worldwide. Hepburn's on-screen presence still captivates us today as we watch the delightful movie, *Charade* (Donen, 1963).

Charade features an exquisite actor dressed in magnificent Givenchy, matched with a debonair leading man in the glamorous City of Lights. This unassailable trois of Audrey Hepburn, Cary Grant, and Paris makes for a gem of a film over which audiences have swooned. One should watch it at least twice: first, to admire the clothes, and a second time to absorb the plot.

Charade as Lightweight Comic Relief

The auspicious timing of the movie's release may have contributed to its success. Its silliness may have attracted American audiences shocked by JFK's assassination. It was "lightweight comic relief" and "the undeniable appeal of its two stars" (V, 2014). However, not everyone was eager to see it. Film critic Pauline Kael wrote,

> 'I couldn't persuade friends to go to see *Charade*, which although no more than a charming confectionery trifle, was, I think, probably the best American film of last year.' For Kael, the film's invisibility was a sign of the times, a refusal of all that was vibrant and vulgar and wonderfully

frivolous in movies. (Newton, 2013)

Charade was among a cluster of 1950s–60s light-hearted romance films starring sought-after style icon Audrey Hepburn. To name a few: *Roman Holiday* (1953), *Sabrina* (1954), *Breakfast at Tiffany's* (1961), *My Fair Lady* (1964). Mere adjectives in the English language are not enough to describe how perfectly fashionable, utterly charming, alluringly elegant, and impossibly graceful Hepburn was in her prime. Her enchanting onscreen presence lifted her to a pedestal that enabled all women to admire and strive to emulate her.

Hepburn Revolutionizes the Female Body Image

Hepburn's stressful childhood included ballet and malnutrition, each contributing to her developing a slender frame. However, when she entered the entertainment field, she started a trend in which the slender-framed female figure became desirable.

> Her very slender silhouette was undeniably ahead of the curve as the exact physique that would become the most desirable in the realms of fashion and on-camera entertainment in general. (Collar, 2017)

Hepburn's ethereal figure left the curvaceous Marilyn Monroe far behind when unintentionally ushering in a torturous era of slenderness that continues today. Since that time, society has pressured women to be thin.

Twiggy and her younger counterpart, Kate Moss, made careers out of this ideal body type. And unfortunately, following their lead, women have resorted to unhealthy diets, dangerous weight loss pills, and risky surgery, sometimes leading to anorexia and bulimia.

Fortunately, some have discovered healthier ways to achieve optimal body weight since then—reducing fat, sugar, gluten, dairy products, and alcohol. Still, an Audrey Hepburn figure is not attainable for most women. And it shouldn't be.

Hepburn's body was not genetically programmed to be that slim. Malnourishment did that to her.

Suffering in Nazi-occupied Holland

Born to Ella van Heemstra Hepburn-Ruston in Belgium in 1929, she was a mere child when World War II ravaged Europe. While trapped by Nazis in Holland, fear, fighting, and famine were her ever-present companions. Without food, the family drank water to ease their hunger and resorted to eating nettle leaves and tulip bulbs to survive (James, 1993; McNeil, 2015).

Hepburn's son, Luca Dotti, said this about her in his book, *Audrey at Home* (2015),

> She suffered from asthma, jaundice, and other illnesses caused by malnutrition including acute anemia and a serious form of edema, which Mum explained like this: 'It begins with your feet and when it reaches your heart, you die. With me, it was above the ankles when I was liberated.' (Quoted in McNeil, 2015)

After the war ended, Hepburn pursued ballet and modeling in London. Then the course of her life dramatically shifted when the right person spotted her beauty and talents at the right time.

French writer Sidonie-Gabrielle Colette noticed her and soon afterward insisted that she star in the Broadway presentation of her novel, *Gigi* (Loos, 1952). This decision led to acting in *Roman Holiday* (Wyler, 1953). While the rest of her history is success and glamour, starvation's effects stayed with her, as she remained an elfin 88 pounds.

Contrary to many people's thoughts, Hepburn didn't deprive herself of food. She ate with enthusiasm, and her favorite dish was pasta. Taking women's obsession with Hepburn up another level, a college student followed Hepburn's diet rules in Dotti's book and described her experience in a *Spoon University* article (Le, 2016).

> Here are the rules: Have a small breakfast, eat a lot of fruit, no snacking in between meals, a piece of chocolate a day (apparently she had a giant stash), eat pasta every day (Audrey loved pasta too), and only eat until 80% full.

She concluded that moderation was her secret.

Givenchy Made Audrey Hepburn a Style Icon

While Colette first noticed Hepburn, Givenchy made her a style icon for the ages. She was Hubert de Givenchy's muse and the one on which he staked his career in fashion. The devotion was mutual. Givenchy's obituary in *The Washington Post* (McDonough, 2018) quoted Hepburn, "His are the only clothes in which I am myself. He is far more than a couturier; he is a creator of personality."

Their professional relationship began during filming for *Sabrina* (Wilder, 1954). Their loyalty to each other was sealed in 1955 when the movie won the Academy Award for Best Costume Design. However, Edith Head, the lead designer for the film, conspicuously left Givenchy out of her acceptance speech. Furious that Head had taken all the credit, Hepburn aligned herself with Givenchy, ensuring that he received recognition in her future films.

For all majestic life on Earth, youth is temporary. Try as we do, not one of us can escape Father Time. Not you, not I, and not the beautiful Audrey Hepburn. Hepburn graciously accepted aging as inevitable and shunned plastic surgery.

According to granddaughter Emma Ferrer, a well-intentioned

photographer offered to Photoshop the wrinkles on Hepburn's face. She responded, "Don't you dare touch any of those wrinkles. I earned every single one of them. For her, the wrinkles were symbols of age, experience, and wisdom" (McNeil, 2017).

A Final Role: Ambassador for UNICEF

In her later years beyond acting, Hepburn answered a calling to serve as Goodwill Ambassador for UNICEF. Haunted all her life by what she saw and experienced during WWII, several times she had politely refused the role of Anne Frank, who was Hepburn's exact age. A lasting interval of "survivor's guilt," it was unbearable that the precocious Anne Frank had died while she lived.

However, in the 1980s, Hepburn contacted Conductor Michael Tilson Thomas on behalf of UNICEF. She asked him to create original music that would reflect Frank's spirit of optimism to accompany readings from her diary. Entitled "From the *Diary of Anne Frank*," she toured the world with the San Francisco Orchestra, performing to large audiences to raise money for UNICEF (Stein, 2018).

Sadly, Hepburn died from a rare form of cancer in 1993 before the tour reached Holland. In returning to Holland, she would have come full circle—where both she and Anne Frank endured the worst of that which humanity is capable.

CHAPTER 5

BOOK CLUB (2018)

I am the demographic for whom Book Club was made, and I hated this movie. There's a fine line between 'This is so fake swallowing it would be like swallowing plastic fruit' and 'This is fake, but its artistry seduced me, and I have been swept up in an alternate world thanks to my suspension of disbelief. Book Club is 'eating plastic fruit' level fake.

—DANUSHA_GOSKA1, *IMDb* User Review

DIRECTOR	Bill Holderman
SCREENPLAY	Bill Holderman, Erin Simms
CAST	Diane Keaton ~ Diane Candice Bergen ~ Sharon Jane Fonda ~ Vivian Mary Steenbergen ~ Carol
AWARDS	PALM SPRINGS INT'L COMEDY FESTIVAL
	STANLEY KRAMER MAD WORLD AWARD
	Best Comedy Ensemble: Erin Simms, Bill Holderman, Apartment Story
RUN TIME	104 min
RATING	PG-13

SUMMARY

Book Club is a light-hearted comedy about four friends who find romance while reading *Fifty Shades of Grey* as their book club selection. Masters of comedy give inspiring performances reminiscent of their earlier movies.

NO FEMINIST WITHOUT
A BOOK CLUB?

Lucy Cota

About the same time that Friends in Council was chartered in 1869, Sarah [Atwater Denman] also worked to get a national women's suffrage convention in Quincy. According to Paul R. Anderson in Platonism in the Midwest, *the women's clubs were considered part of the early feminist movement serving to provide organizational support for women.* —IRIS NELSON, *The Herald-Whig*

THE PRIMARY FOCUS OF THE MOVIE *Book Club* (Holderman, 2018) is an activity that has been ongoing for hundreds of years in America. Written evidence that women have gathered for support, companionship, and intellectual stimulation goes back to the 17th century. In the first recorded meeting for group discussion of literature and the day's issues, women began, in essence, a book club. For centuries after, book clubs have retained the same purpose and have served as springboards for women's advancement. Miss Alma was a book club member in *Summer and Smoke*.

When Movies on Chatham screened *Mr. and Mrs. Bridge*, a discussion about feminism and its evolution was unavoidable, especially in the context of our theme, Changing Women. In *Book Club*, we find a financially successful and entertaining movie representing women who have far surpassed previously constricting roles and have lives full of potential. No doubt, the four women in the ensemble cast—beloved actors Candice Bergen, Jane Fonda, Diane Keaton, and Mary Steenburgen—are torchbearers for feminism. The following summaries attest to their accomplishments:

★ **CANDICE BERGEN.** In *Murphy Brown*, the long-running *CBS* sitcom, Bergen portrayed a star reporter for a fictional news magazine, *FYI*. Bergen's character unquestionably broke ground for the social acceptance of single mothers. Her portrayal may also have inspired many women to pursue careers in news organizations.

★ **JANE FONDA.** First a model, Fonda is an Academy Award-winning actor. She built a prosperous business from her popular exercise videos encouraging women to be healthy and physically fit. Fonda actively involved herself in politics in the 1960s, an era in which women were just emerging in the political arena. She perhaps planted the early seeds of Hollywood's political activism.

★ **DIANE KEATON AND MARY STEENBURGEN.** These two are vital in paving the way for women in entertainment. Both have steadily demonstrated to future artists that success can extend beyond acting. In addition to their Academy Awards, Golden Globe Awards, and many others between them, Keaton and Steenburgen have flourished in singing/songwriting, movie production, real estate, writing, conservancy (Keaton), and humanitarian work (Steenburgen).

Literacy a Privilege, Requirement for *Book Club*

How appropriate it is that these accomplished women worked together to make a movie based on the very thing that's the impetus for all their endeavors: literacy. The ability to read and write.[1] Book

---

[1] Since some are thinking also about audio books, before going farther, note that I use "reading" to include all methods you may apply for this purpose.

clubs, arguably, would not exist without it.

Naturally stemming from reading is a desire to gather with other readers to share ideas and learn from each other. And, book clubs are a privilege and freedom that we should not take for granted. In her article on women's book clubs in *Vice Magazine*, Hunt aptly titles it "A History of Radical Thinking" (2016).

The timeline below2 shows that book clubs' advancement was just a step ahead of the progression of feminism. It all began with a father teaching his daughter to read.

Timeline of the Book Club in America

The 1600s

Most all women were illiterate during this era. Yet, an English Puritan father insisted that his daughter, Anne, learn to read. Anne Marbury Hutchinson traveled from England to the Massachusetts Bay Colony with her husband and their children to escape Anglican Church persecution. Onboard the ship, she began leading a group of women to analyze weekly sermons. She expanded later to study literature more broadly. Her activity garnered followers, threatening Colony elders as expected in the male-dominated era. Tried for heresy, elders excommunicated her despite a strong defense.

The 1700s

Domesticating wild land is hard work; thus, both men and women worked endlessly. In the latter half of the century, the

---

[2] Adapted from Otto (2009), "The Evolution of American Book Clubs: A Timeline." Otto's version of the timeline includes men's gatherings as well.

community had settled down to where some privileged women could read and write.

1760s Hannah Adams of Massachusetts was the first American woman to earn a living from writing. She was part of a reading circle that gathered regularly to discuss belles-lettres and share poetry.

1778 Hannah Mather Crocker formed a reading society in Boston. As one of the earliest feminists, Crocker voiced radical thought that the "formal study of science and literature was more suitable to women's dignity" than the routines society defined.

THE 1800s

The catalyst for a feminist movement came in the early 19th century when women in New England began meeting to discuss literature and new publications. These social and educational gatherings gave rise to the following milestones:

1826 An American lyceum is founded, launching the lyceum movement. Ralph Waldo Emerson, Henry David Thoreau, Frederick Douglass, Nathaniel Hawthorne, Susan B. Anthony, and Daniel Webster were participating lecturers and entertainers. Around 3,000 lycea began in the Midwest and Northeast within the decade.

1827 Black women formed literary societies in the 1820s and 1830s in Northeast cities. The Society of Young Ladies in Massachusetts was the first.

1840 Margaret Fuller's Boston shop was the site of the first known U.S. bookstore-sponsored discussion club.

1866 Sarah Atwater Denman started a study group in Quincy, IL, known as 'Friends in Council.' At first, they met in Denman's home; the group is now "the oldest continuous literary club in America."

The 1900s

By the 20th century, omnipresent literary societies had considerably enhanced women's literacy. They had set a foundation that would continue to lift feminism to new heights.

Longing for knowledge drove women to read. The more women read, the more they learned; the more they knew, the better equipped they were to advocate for themselves. As a result, reading books stirred the feminist movement more than anything did.

Literacy in the 20th century became so advanced that it may be incomprehensible to a girl born during its span that Anne Hutchinson's ability to read was the exception, not the norm. The 20th-century girl arrived amid a renaissance for readers.

Books in Mass Production

Literacy rates rocketed throughout the 19th century, demanding economic ways to print more books in every genre. "The driving force behind innovation in book manufacture was an expanded readership" (Ott, 2012). Printers responded in kind, producing innovative technologies to supply enough books for the rising boon of readers.

Because of the dramatic increase in book production, 20th-century readers, young and old, were inundated with more books than they could read in a lifetime. With a book for every interest, passion, and hobby, children grew up with their minds stretched to boundless fantastical places. Children explored Dr. Seuss' whimsical worlds, solved mysteries with Nancy Drew and the Hardy boys, vacationed with the Bobbsey twins, survived with the Boxcar children, went to school at Sweet Valley High, and endless others. Writers offering exciting adventures right out of their imaginations, books embodied infinite possibilities for all.

Toward the end of the century, talk show host Oprah Winfrey started her famous book club via TV, creating unprecedented excitement for reading. At around the same time, Jeff Bezos launched his bookstore, now a behemoth that's still called Amazon. Like all good billionaire technologists, he sold the first book online from his garage.

Expanding Readership through Technology

The pastime of reading stayed on a technology trajectory with the introduction of online book clubs (i.e., GoodReads) and electronic reading devices such as Amazon's Kindle, Barnes and Noble's Book Nook, and various other tools. In addition, when web developers created blogging platforms and other online media, new reading and writing opportunities became available.

Since social media are here to stay, let's count the positives. These network-based communication media can link people together in communities and groups. They can connect individuals to posts, comments, articles and websites, memes, advertisements, and a virtual sea of information. Some claim that one can read 200 books in the time an average person spends interacting with social media and blogs every year (Chu, 2017). Yet, like books, all online activity involves one thing—reading.

Through the analysis and discussions about *Mr. and Mrs. Bridge*, Movies on Chatham learned about the book, *The End of Men: And the Rise of Women* (Rosin, 2012). This book describes today's trends toward significant leadership roles for women in the workforce and higher numbers of women than men graduating from college. No coincidence that the "rise of women" correlates with an increase in book clubs in America.

There are more than five million book club members in the U.S. today, as just an estimate. "Most clubs have 10 or more members. 70 to 80 percent of clubs are all-female" (Otto, 2009). Why is that?

Women's fundamental nature has not changed since the 17th century when Anne Hutchinson took the initiative to gather women on the sailing ship crossing the Atlantic. Modern-day women continue the tradition of supporting one another in pursuing knowledge. We get together for social and intellectual stimulation, mixing discussion with the enticing combination of food and drink. Hunt (2016) reports that,

> Book clubs today are so synonymous with women sipping Pinot Gris as they parse Gillian Flynn that some groups charge wine penalties if you fall behind on reading. Others go straight to the source by meeting monthly in bars.

Do Book Club Stars Read for Pleasure?

Do I remember the four women in *Book Club* meeting in bars? It follows with a most natural inquiry to wonder if the stars genuinely enjoy reading in real life. The list below confirms they do.

What books are favorites? Indisputably, not *Fifty Shades of Grey*.

ACTOR	TITLE
★ Candice Bergen	*A Gentleman in Moscow* (Towles) *White Nile* (Moorehead) *Blue Nile* (Moorehead) *Old Filth* (Gardam) Nancy Drew books
★ Jane Fonda	*Bird by Bird* (Lamont)

★ Diane Keaton	*Rocks and Clouds* (Epstein) Architecture and picture books
★ Mary Steenburgen	*A Gentleman in Moscow* (like Bergen) Reading to her grandchildren: Pippi Longstocking books (Lindgren)

Key Terms

Belles-lettres

Belles-lettres is a class of writing, originally meaning beautiful. A current meaning is literary works outside traditional fiction, poetry, or drama. It is also a term for excessively flowery writing.

Literacy

Traditionally, literacy is the ability to read and write. The term also means knowledge and competence in specific areas.

Lycea

Lycea are groups that promote adult education, sponsoring lectures on current issues.

HONORING A REMARKABLE GROUP

Pam Hassebroek

BECAUSE PEOPLE AND SOCIETIES ARE continuously changing, it is easier to identify what has and has not changed if we look at evidence from a distant past. We watched a remarkable group of movies representing American women's lives from the last 100 years under our Part I theme. As we reflect again on the stories in earlier historical settings, we pause to honor those who made possible the opportunities women enjoy today. I know that my grandmother would jump for joy to imagine that women's lifestyles shown in *Book Club* (2018) were achievable during her lifetime.

Movies Reflect Changes in Ways of Life

Suppose we think about these movies with that enthusiasm in mind. In that case, we can all agree that films reveal positive changes in our culture. In the beginning, in *Summer and Smoke* (1961), we commiserated with Alma as she struggled against her romantic desires and instincts to remain faithful to the strict moral code of the early 20th century. She strained emotionally while her boyfriend quite effortlessly acted in open defiance of any rules of propriety for men.

In *Mr. and Mrs. Bridge* (1990), we watched Mrs. Bridge muddle through her 1940s life with all the privileges a human could want. Yet, she lacked a way to feel valued in her family and community. Instead, she followed the role required by society to present a positive image and to keep her mouth shut.

When we screened *Peyton Place* (1957), we first noted how the movie fared against the content of its infamous sourcebook. The book was expansively denounced following its publication the year before. It became scandalous because it used the most sordid and descriptive terms and unearthed what had been buried as unspeakable inside homes across America—and in author Grace Metalious' local community. The topics the book confronted—divorce, alcoholism, incest, rape, pregnancy without marriage, abortion—were not spoken about back in the day because they had no acceptable language for public discussion.

Many places banned the book, yet it was so widely read that Metalious amassed a fortune overnight. However, because her critics were so ruthless, she drank herself to an early death. Indeed, she experienced a social condemnation similar to what Oscar Wilde endured, a topic we discuss in Part II.

The release of the movie *Peyton Place* came only a short time after the book was published. Consequently, only euphemistic references to all those evils were present, as we confirmed. So do we even consider comparing *Peyton Place* to what we see in theaters today to believe it represents a demarcation in philosophy about what's fit for public viewing in a film? And compare Metalious' experience as an author with that of other women authors who have written on similar topics since then.

The *Book Club* Selection: *Fifty Shades of Grey*

In *Book Club*, their monthly discussion focuses on *Fifty Shades of Grey* (James, 2012), a self-published book by a first-time British author. From 2011, writing her stories online as vampire fan fiction about violence and eroticism (BDSM: bondage, discipline, sadism, and masochism), James made it to *Time's* list of the "World's 100

Most Influential People" in 2012. On *Time's* webpage that features her, writer Luscombe states, "six months ago she was Erika Leonard, a mother of two who dabbled in saucy stories for the Web" (2012).

Later that year, she became the first author ever to receive the title of "Publishing Person of the Year" by *Publishers Weekly*. Further, "as of Nov. 30, the books [now three of them] had sold more than 35 million copies in America and garnered more than $200 million for their publisher, Random House" (Driscoll, 2012).

I wonder, did anyone truly gasp at *Fifty Shades* as all of America did when reading pages from *Peyton Place* in 1956? In any event, the consensus is that the *Fifty Shades* trilogy, described as erotic romance, is smutty and poorly written.[3] Further, similar to the stories in *Peyton Place*, the book places its female lead in a victim role in a relationship characterized by unhealthy emotional abuse and sexual violence.[4]

It most likely gained traction and notoriety from its beginnings as an online serial with its beautiful, well-educated people as lead characters. Regardless, taking the criticism as Grace Metalious once did, James can laugh all the way to the bank. In 2015, she co-produced the movie based on her first book. "Despite receiving generally negative reviews, it was an immediate box office success, breaking numerous box office records and earning over US$570 million worldwide" (Wikipedia, 2020).[5]

---

[3] Even though the music from the *Fifty Shades* movies was nominated for awards, the movies themselves swept the Golden Raspberry Awards, winning in all other categories of "Worst."

[4] *Fifty Shades of Grey* was written and the movie directed by women yet it demeans women as weak, submissive victims, and some say glorifies rape.

[5] The three movies, including *Fifty Shades Darker* in 2017 and *Fifty Shades Freed*
Footnote continues on the next page …

Similar Creative Works Achieve Greatness

In that same vein, consider Austrian author Elfriede Jelinek who won the 2004 Nobel Prize in literature. Jelinek's notable works include *The Piano Teacher* (1988), a novel adapted for a feature film that the Movies on Chatham group screened in 2016.[6] *The Piano Teacher* (Haneke, 2001), an almost 20-year-old French-language movie, features a neurotic 38-year-old woman who first resists her 17-year-old male piano student's advances. Then she becomes the perpetrator of a sadomasochistic sexual relationship with him. The world condemned Metalious for broaching similar topics in *Peyton Place*. Jelinek, 50 years later, wins the Nobel Prize.

Whatever your feelings about the changes onscreen, we have observed progressively liberated female roles and audience attitudes over time. When comparing depictions in Haneke's *The Piano Teacher* to those in our movies set in earlier times, this attitude change is especially apparent. Think of *Summer and Smoke, Mr. and Mrs. Bridge, Peyton Place*, and *Charade* in that order. Like *The Piano Teacher*, the story in *Charade* incorporates violence and deception. Still, *Charade* is among the best representations of the Golden Age's glamorous women. And, the movie refreshingly departs from the typical in its light-hearted presentation of greater independence for a leading female role. Remember that Reggie can openly announce a pending divorce without shame and actively pursue a romantic relationship.

Yes, but most women didn't allow themselves such pleasures of

---

in 2018, grossed over $1.320 billion worldwide, making it the seventh highest-grossing R-rated franchise of all-time.

[6] We include this movie in a future volume of *Movies on Chatham Presents*.

independence because that behavior was outside social norms. Still, isolated as they were in the 1960s in disconnected communities across America, women could dream about leading dignified, adventurous lives and gaining the material success shown in *Charade*. The awe-inspiring Audrey Hepburn made it possible.

Book Club and New Roles for Older Women

We jumped forward 55 years after *Charade* to watch the women in *Book Club*. The remarkable women who play the roles of book club members are evidence all by themselves of how different our lives are in 2021. And, the movie itself is not the point. That four women, ages 65 to over 80,[7] are still working and have leading roles in a feature film is fantastic. Unfortunately, though, their experiences are not yet the norm.

A study at USC[8] (Smith, Choueiti, & Pieper, 2017) quantifies my usual assessment of movie roles for older women. The study examined Academy Award-nominated films from 2014–2016 for depictions of persons aged 60-plus.

2014	2015	2016
American Sniper	The Big Short	Arrival
Birdman	Bridge of Spies	Fences
Boyhood	Brooklyn	Hacksaw Ridge
The Grand Budapest Hotel	Mad Max: Fury Road	Hell or High Water
The Imitation Game	The Martian	Hidden Figures
Selma	The Revenant	La La Land
The Theory of Everything	Room	Lion

---

[7] Jane Fonda turns 84 in December 2021.

[8] USC Annenberg School for Communication and Journalism

Whiplash	*Spotlight*	*Manchester by the Sea*
		Moonlight

Of the 1,256 speaking roles among the 25 films, only 33 were women over 60 or 2.6 percent. Results also reveal that in this 60-and-over group:

★ Only one of the female characters held a high-clout position, a gender ratio of 33 to 1.

★ Not one portrayed a lesbian, gay, bisexual, or transgender character.

★ Six of the 14 films (42.9 percent) with a leading or supporting role included a comment that showed prejudice or discrimination against older age groups.[9]

Book Club's roles are unlike the older women characters of the past, which were, as in real life, typically supporting roles. The *Book Club* roles accurately represent everyday life for many older women today. Mary's article mentions an outstanding leader, former Supreme Court Justice Ruth Bader Ginsburg, who served in an influential position beyond the age anyone may have imagined. Of course, U.S. Treasury Secretary Janet Yellen, former Secretary of State Condoleezza Rice, House Speaker Nancy Pelosi, and others are in that category too. Staying in the workforce longer reflects that Americans live longer and are healthier in their later years. Donna Shalala of Florida became the oldest freshman in her House of Representatives class when she took office just before her 78th

---

[9] To that end, ageist comments about older people's adaptation to computer-based technologies have dominated ads and greeting card messages for decades. Why would we expect movies to be different? But, it's certainly time for change.

birthday in 2019.

A *New York Times* article (Bennett, 2019) quoted Susan Douglas, professor of communication studies at the University of Michigan, who said,

> 'a demographic revolution' was occurring—both in the number of women who are working into their 60s and 70s and in the perception, in the wake of #MeToo, of their expertise and value.
>
> Older women are now saying, 'No, I'm still vibrant, I still have a lot to offer, and I'm not going to be consigned to invisibility.'

These changes demonstrate new norms unimagined during our parents' and grandparents' working lives.

While we notice modernity in *Book Club*, other observations hearken back to earlier movies our group has watched together. For example, compare *Book Club's* multi-storyline to *American Graffiti* (1974) and *Crush* (2001). *American Graffiti* has its four high-school boys and their antics, *Crush*, its three professional women. And compare *Book Club's* "book focus" to *The Hours* and its focus on the novel *Mrs. Dalloway*. Can you think of other comparisons?

Now, let's move on in a celebratory mode, as we anticipate more examples of social progress in Part II.

Key Terms

Bisexual

A bisexual person is attracted to both men and women emotionally, physically, or sexually. The attraction may extend to all genders, yet a preference may exist for one gender over others.

Transgender person

A transgender person is one whose gender identity or gender expression is different from what is typically associated with the sex identified by their body's physical appearance.

PART II

- ★ *The Celluloid Closet*

- ★ *Wilde*

- ★ *The Danish Girl*

- ★ *Behind the Candelabra*

- ★ *The Birdcage*

ABOUT CELEBRATING LGBTQ

Hollywood censors banned LGBTQ-themed movies in the Golden Era. In the 1960s, films with gay and lesbian roles were released but rare, and carried X-ratings. Later representation is more natural and authentic, breaking significant ground in fostering recognition, inclusion, and acceptance of LGBTQ individuals.

★ CHAPTER 6 ★

THE CELLULOID CLOSET (1996)

It's entertaining and funny, feels like a good piece of gossip. Great
documentary! —A Movies on Chatham group member

DIRECTOR	Rob Epstein and Jeffrey Friedman
SCREENPLAY	Rob Epstein, Jeffrey Friedman, Sharon Wood
CAST	Lily Tomlin ~ Narrator
	★ Whoopi Goldberg ★ Armistead Maupin ★ Susan Sarandon ★ Tony Curtis ★ Tom Hanks ★ Shirley MacLaine
AWARDS	BERLIN INTERNATIONAL FILM FESTIVAL
	Best Documentary
	PEABODY AWARD
RUN TIME	107 min
RATING	R

SUMMARY

The Celluloid Closet, a documentary adapted from Vito Russo's 1981 book, surveys the 20th-century history of American film and Hollywood's depictions of LGBTQ individuals. Most of that time, filmmakers overwhelmingly misrepresented lesbian, gay, bisexual, and transgender characters as perverted or twisted.

VIVA VITO'S GAY RIGHTS LEGACY!

Lucy Cota

VITO RUSSO WROTE A LANDMARK BOOK, *The Celluloid Closet: Homosexuality in the Movies* (1987), that led to the film *The Celluloid Closet* (Friedman & Epstein, 1996). Russo was a "giant in the fields of gay and AIDS [human immunodeficiency virus] activism" (Tomlin, 2011) and the founding father of the gay liberation movement. Yet, there seemed to be no widespread mention of him on June 26, 2015.

This oversight is hard to understand because most would deem it the most important day in American LGBTQ history. On that day, the U.S. Supreme Court legalized gay marriage.[1] The world erupted in joy to celebrate gay rights—rainbow flags flew with pride, and the White House lit up in rainbow colors. Millions of *Facebook* users commemorated the occasion by adding a rainbow to their profile pictures.

Amid all this euphoria, where was the homage to the man whose groundbreaking work for the LGBTQ cause helped make this day happen? Forgetting Vito Russo is akin to ignoring Martin Luther King, Jr. when appreciating what the Civil Rights Movement achieved for Black Americans. Yet, when Russo made his indelible mark, many people may not have known much about him or his background because of the general prejudice against gay men.

---

[1] See: Obergefell *v*. Hodges in the Appendix pages 212, 215.

Born in the 1940s, Russo grew up in New York City and New Jersey. In his biography, *Celluloid Activist: The Life and Times of Vito Russo* (2011), Michael Schiavi describes Russo as a child, growing up in rough, urban macho neighborhoods where boys played sports in the alleyways. However, Russo never felt compelled to join them. He was more interested in literature and the arts, and his "favorite place to go was always the movies." By age five, Russo was spending all his free time in theaters. "Memorizing lines, gestures, and costumes, he could do a 'perfect imitation of James Stewart in *It's a Wonderful Life* at an early age'" (Gelbert, 2011). One Christmas in the 1950s, his dad gave him his own film projector, and he invited friends and family to watch with him at home.

Exploring Sexuality Creates Conflict

Russo began to explore his sexuality during his childhood, creating discord in his household. His mother was concerned that a priest had molested him. When this activity had gone on for quite a long time, Vito became defiant about it. As a good Catholic, he had often confessed the sin of his same-sex experiences.

> I went to confession and told this priest that I was having sex with this guy. And of course, [the priest] recognized my voice because, you know, every week he was hearing me say this, so he says finally, 'Look! Enough is enough! Next time I'm not giving you absolution.' (Schiavi, 2011)

That was a turning point for him because he resolved that being gay was not a sin. When being gay "'could be so natural to who he was, then it had to be okay.' For a working-class Italian Catholic teenager, this was a stunningly precocious conclusion to reach nearly a decade before Stonewall" (Schiavi, 2011).

Progressing into adulthood, he embraced his identity and urged other gay men to do the same. At NYU graduate school, he reached out through his passion for theater and film in "Cabaret Nights" and "Firehouse Flicks." These settings allowed camaraderie and total acceptance, qualities absent in the public sphere where employers and housing firms shunned gay men.

Cabaret Nights and Firehouse Flicks

Cabaret Nights was an opportunity for talented gay men to perform on stage. It was an instant success because it guaranteed good entertainment and gave performers an outlet to express their talents, thoughts, and feelings in a safe place.

Firehouse Flicks offered gay men an old firehouse[2] as a place to watch movies where Russo could also network. One movie they watched, *The Battle of Algiers* (1966), fired up the audience so much they stormed up and down Sixth Avenue shouting for civil rights.

At about the same time, Russo witnessed Dr. Martin Luther King, Jr. advancing the cause of equal rights for Black Americans. Dr. King inspired him to do the same for gay men. Consequently, Russo dedicated himself to improving the lives of LBGTQ individuals, becoming the first dedicated activist for civil and human rights in the gay community.

> He helped deliver what is still the most powerful statement about the AIDS crisis, 'Why We Fight' [Russo, 1988], a speech in which he set his sights on a culture and society which supports war, misogyny, racism and homophobia. (Shepard, 2011)

---

[2] In 2019, the Landmarks Preservation Committee declared the Gay Activists Alliance Firehouse as a New York City landmark ("LPC designates six," 2019).

Sadly, in 1990, Russo's life was cut short by the AIDS virus. Discovered in 1981 (Altman, 1981), the AIDS illness first spread among the gay community; it brought hostility from some very misguided and misinformed Americans in leadership positions.

> Dr. Paul Cameron of the American Psychological Association[3] called gay men 'worse than murderers.' Senator Jesse Helms demanded that HIV be among the list of excludable diseases preventing travel and immigration to the United States, and he was fervently opposed to federal funding of AIDS research and treatment. (Borders, 2012)

American Attitudes Show Progress

On American's attitudes at the time of Russo's death, UC-Davis psychology professor Dr. Gregory Herek (1991) stated,

> Although they show increasing willingness to extend basic civil liberties to gay men and lesbians, most heterosexual Americans continue to condemn homosexuality morally and to reject or feel uncomfortable about gay people personally.

Though Russo's activism ended early, others picked up the torch and carried on through the 1990s and beyond. There is no question that we have made progress in inclusion and acceptance since then. Today, many LGBTQ individuals no longer fear that their sexual

---

[3] Cameron, former President of the APA, now chair of the Family Research Institute in Colorado Springs, CO was stripped of his membership in the association in 1983 because of violation of ethical principles. Other professional associations have stated that he has consistently misinterpreted and misrepresented research on sexuality.

orientations will affect their jobs. It is now common for openly gay people to gain starring roles on TV and in movies; think of Ellen DeGeneres, Jane Lynch, Jim Parsons, and Neil Patrick Harris.

And, we have witnessed the most significant achievement—gay marriage. Two people in love and devoted to each other, no matter their sexual orientation or gender identity, can legally bind themselves to one another in marriage. This policy change is significant because gay couples have achieved equality, with the same rights and respect as all partners who make this commitment. Further, studies show no significant difference exists for children between families headed by same-sex and opposite-sex parents.

Schiavi, Russo's biographer, believes that gay marriage was so far beyond Russo's frame of reference that he would never have imagined this victory. For that reason, he doesn't know how Russo might have reacted. However, it is safe to say he would be enthusiastically waving a rainbow flag.

HUMAN DIVERSITY: STILL BLISSFULLY IGNORANT?

Pam Hassebroek

WE CAN LEARN A LOT about the movies' misrepresentation of gay men and lesbians in its first 100 years by watching *The Celluloid Closet* (Friedman & Epstein, 1996). This movie joins many others released before and since with LGBTQ actors and roles that spotlight the gay community. Not to mention the community's activism and celebrated achievements in the last 50 years. Thus, it seems strange that our understanding of human diversity is still so shallow, especially about our differences in sexuality and gender.

Since this film's release, our nation has become better acquainted with several other individual identities, mainly because of mass media depictions. America's media and advertising industries had previously excluded people who represented or expressed gender and sexual orientation differences just as they banned other groups. Today we commonly see people in media roles that were once disqualified because of appearance, skin color, nationality, and religious persuasion. Nonetheless, many Americans still harbor prejudices that can create conflict.

Gender-related Prejudice is Long-Standing

The bias related to gender and sexuality differences is a significant prejudice and long-standing. The problematic fact is that a person's sex does not always directly correlate with their[4] gender or identity.

---

[4] Because the English language lacks a gender-neutral third-person singular
Footnote continues on the next page ...

While Americans can agree on two sex classifications based on the appearance of external reproductive organs, ideas about sexual orientation and gender, i.e., the sociocultural aspects of being a man or woman,[5] are troubling to some.

Gender-related characteristics include physical abilities and behaviors, hobbies and interests, parenting approaches, emotional expressions, etc. Traditional aspects of gender identity relate to family dynamics, i.e., who goes to work, is allowed to run a business, does the housework, and raises children. The change in these practices "has contributed to changing the meaning of male and female and thus to changing the gender order, the social structures that in their turn shape gender practices. It has also contributed to the development of new identity categories" (Eckert & McConnell-Ginet, 2013).

According to a Pew Research study, among observers of gender-related practices, "there is no clear consensus about whether these differences are primarily rooted in biology or in societal expectations" (Parker, Horowitz, & Stepler, 2017). Unfortunately, we lack the knowledge to understand this in a thoroughly competent way.

Additionally, sexual orientation is a distinct physical and behavioral component different from other identified elements of sex and gender. Other elements include social gender and gender identity

---

personal pronoun, using "their" is now acceptable, even though it sounds wrong. In fact, "they" was voted "Word of the Year" by the American Dialect Society in 2015 (Guo, 2016; "Gender Pronouns," 2020).

[5] "Sex is a biological categorization based on reproductive potential, whereas, gender is the social elaboration of biological sex" (Eckert & McConnell-Ginet, 2013).

(the personal sense of being male or female, or both). "Research over several decades has demonstrated that sexual orientation ranges along a continuum, from exclusive attraction to the other sex to exclusive attraction to the same sex" (American Psychological Association, 2008). Scientific research on this topic has been ongoing for well over a century.

More to the point, apart from scientific investigation, obstacles to our general understanding have been around for a very long time. Some of these barriers, established in good faith by religious conviction and public policy, have kept us in fear, ignorance, and confusion about the facts of our human individuality. Under these conditions, groups of people have developed beliefs about others, leading to conflicts and horrific acts of violence.

Vito Russo also suspected that part of the LGBTQ community's problem was that many people kept their sexual orientations to themselves. That was a "catch 22."[6] If a person revealed their sexual orientation, they would put their survival at risk.

Deciding Groups Are Inferior Creates Conflict

Aalai (2018) notes that our differences don't inherently cause problems; conflicts arise when we collectively decide that a group is inferior. A significant factor in such decisions is where we were born or who we socialize with. The community around us defines particular labels for people, e.g., racially different, biologically or socially inferior gender attributes. Facts dispute many stereotypes about others that some people feel strongly about.

It is also the case that, instead of taking the time to learn more,

---

[6] A catch-22 is an ironic situation from which an individual cannot escape because of contradictory rules or limitations.

people often cover their ignorance about, or discomfort with, specific topics by laughing. Is that why roles played by gay men in early films were comical? General ignorance and prejudice caused the censors in the Golden Age to restrict content about same-sex attraction. And, unfortunately, that same ignorance allowed filmmakers to portray gay men as wimpy, laughter objects or even sinister villains ("*The Celluloid Closet*," 2016).

Using Comedy for Bullying or Inclusion

As we examined comedy in films in recent years, it was easy to see that comedians use it to poke fun at (i.e., bully) people. Thus, for groups that some consider social misfits, such as gay men and lesbians, comedy is further marginalizing. Lugowski (1999) describes stereotypical cross-gendered roles in early films and claims there are more than Russo's previous studies suggest.

> Queer men tended to appear as one of two types. The queer in his more subdued form appears as the dithering, asexual "sissy" sometimes befuddled, incompetent, and, if married, very henpecked and sometimes fussy and officious.

> The other type, the more outrageous 'pansy,' an extremely effeminate boulevardier type sporting lipstick, rouge, a trim mustache and hairstyle, and an equally trim suit, incomplete without a boutonniere.

Lesbian depictions usually meant she was

> clad in a mannishly tailored suit (often a tuxedo), her hair slicked back in a short bob. She sometimes sported a monocle and cigarette holder, invariably possessed a deep alto voice and a haughty, aggressive attitude toward men.

The roles that exaggerated LGBTQ characteristics were, in that way, similar to abusing Black Americans in old movies. Like blackface in comedy, they entertained those who accepted such depictions in accord with social attitudes.

Because of movies' extraordinary influence in shaping our culture, comedy can, on the other hand, be instrumental in teaching us about differences without disparagement. Instead of bullying, films can introduce us kindly to people and situations that might be awkward or unknown. They can provide education that leads to new knowledge and greater inclusion.

Russo's Contribution to Knowledge

But to our objective of tracking how movies have portrayed sexuality and gender differences over time, we imagined a difficult but not impossible challenge. How would we begin to uncover those trends in light of the historic censorship and social taboos associated with particular topics and types of people in movies? Yet, this task is precisely what film historian Vito Russo accomplished in his study.

Russo, the author of *The Celluloid Closet* (1987), presents evidence about gay, lesbian, and bisexual actors and storylines in Hollywood movies from the beginning of the movie industry. Schiavi (2009) claims Russo's sourcebook as

> indispensable to our reading of gender and sexuality on-screen. Vito Russo's *The Celluloid Closet: Homosexuality in the Movies* is approaching its thirtieth anniversary. Before its 1981 publication (and 1987 revision), there had been only two major critical works, Parker Tyler's *Screening the Sexes: Homosexuality in the Movies* (1971) and Richard Dyer's *Gays in Film* (1977), neither of which has enjoyed

the popularity or influence of *Closet.*

In his Russo biography, *Celluloid Activist* (2011), Schiavi ascribes Russo's twofold contributions—activist politics and film scholarship. His screenings of "camp" films, which were fundraisers for the Gay Activists Alliance (GAA),[7] helped him develop material for his book.

It is interesting to note that Russo, in his early days of activism, reported the same benefits that we promote that come from watching and discussing movies in a group. When he was

> curating the 'Firehouse Flicks' series at the Gay Activists Alliance, he became interested in the audiences. Screening everything from *My Little Chickadee* to *The Shop on Main Street* to *The Blob*, he noted that the crowds often 'pick[ed] up on things that straight audiences miss—an innuendo, the direction, the way a scene is played.'[8] (Kennedy, 2011)

Events in LGBTQ History

Because of Vito Russo's immense contribution to the LGBTQ community, in June 2019, he was one of 50 Americans installed on the U.S. National LGBTQ Wall of Honor at the Stonewall National Monument's (SNM)[9] inaugural. He joins other well-known names such as James Baldwin, Christine Jorgensen, Alfred Kinsey, Harvey Milk, Bayard Rustin, and Matthew Wayne Shepard. New York City

---

[7] The GAA was formed soon after the Stonewall riots of 1969.

[8] At Movies on Chatham, we learn so much more about all aspects of a movie by watching with the group.

[9] The SNM is 7.7-acres in Greenwich Village in Lower Manhattan near the intersection of 7th Avenue South and Christopher Street.

established the SNM at the Stonewall Inn,[10] where the Stonewall riots took place on June 28, 1969. Dedicating the monument at the riots' 50th anniversary, the Wall of Honor pays tribute to people who have influenced the struggle for LGBTQ human and civil rights.

Other events have contributed to LGBTQ scholarship and queer theory; the most important was the AIDS epidemic in the 1980s that devastated U.S. gay communities. It was similar to the COVID-19 crisis in its outbreak and its dilemma. Yet, in contrast, it first struck the gay community exclusively.

> For a short time, the new disease was called gay-related immunodeficiency syndrome (GRIDS), but by September of 1982, the CDC had published a case definition, using the current designation of acquired immune deficiency syndrome (AIDS). Before HIV [human immunodeficiency virus] was identified as the virus that causes AIDS, tracking the course of the epidemic depended on reporting AIDS diagnoses to public health departments. (Osmond, 2003)

Tracking the epidemic was essential to preserving our health. Yet, through the 1980s, most states with massive AIDS cases failed to report HIV test results. The Reagan administration offered an inadequate response to the health crisis because of the limited understanding of the disease and Americans' discrimination against gay men and lesbians.

Still today, no effective cure exists for HIV infection. The irrational hatred of gays slowed a treatment that might have prevented deaths

---

[10] 53 Christopher St. is the present location of the Stonewall Inn. In 1969, it occupied both 51 and 53 Christopher St.

that now number over a half million people.[11] Russo was a leader in the activist groups that brought media attention to the disease and helped attract and build interest in the scientific community.

Media attention included new representation for individuals once hidden from the movie-going public. The changes in MPA's film regulation in 1968 permitted many more feature films depicting LGBTQ topics and relationships than in earlier days. Their inclusion now inspires visions of improved understanding. We are grateful that we can easily watch, discuss, and learn from the movies we write about in this book section.

Key Terms

Asexual
An asexual person has no sexual feelings or associations.

Closeted (In the closet)
Closeted refers to a gay, lesbian, bisexual, trans* person, or intersex person who cannot disclose their identity or identities.

Coming out
★Coming out is a process within an individual to accept their sexual orientation, gender identity, or intersex status (to come out to oneself).

★Coming out also means sharing one's sexual orientation, gender identity, or intersex status with others (to come out to friends, etc.). This event can be a continual, life-long process for many people.

---

[11] As of Dec 31, 2000, 774,467 persons had been reported with AIDS in the U.S.; 448,060 of these had died.

Gay

* ★Gay refers to same-sex- /same-gender-attracted people as a whole or a personal identity for anyone not identifying as heterosexual.
* ★In some cultural settings, the term gay represents male-identified people attracted to other male-identified people in a romantic, erotic, or emotional sense.

Heteronormativity

Heteronormativity is the societal norm. This belief system classifies all people into distinct male and female categories and defines heterosexual as the "natural" sexual union.

The Motion Picture Association

The Motion Picture Association (MPA) is a trade association representing six Hollywood studios: Paramount (1912). Universal (1912), Warner Bros (1923), Disney (1923), Sony Pictures (Columbia, 1924), Netflix Studios (2019).

MPA film rating system

MPA's film-rating system ranks film content by its appropriateness for specific U.S. audiences. Designed and implemented under Jack Valenti's leadership, this rating system replaced the Hays Code in 1968.

CHAPTER 7

WILDE (1998)

Wilde is a film about a man's passions destroying his life.

—PEACH-2, *IMDb* review

DIRECTOR	Brian Gilbert
SCREENPLAY	Julian Mitchell
CAST	Stephen Fry ~ Oscar Wilde Jude Law ~ Alfred Douglas (Bosie) Vanessa Redgrave ~ Lady 'Speranza' Wilde Tom Wilkinson ~ John Douglas
AWARDS	SEATTLE INTERNATIONAL FILM FESTIVAL
	Best Actor: Stephen Fry
	EVENING STANDARD BRITISH FILM AWARDS
	Most Promising Newcomer: Jude Law
RUN TIME	118 min
RATING	R

SUMMARY

Wilde is a dramatized historical account of the adult life of 19th-century Irish poet and playwright Oscar Wilde. His love for a young man became an extramarital affair that destroyed him and his family at the peak of his career. Laws barring intimate same-sex behavior led to Wilde's imprisonment and early death.

WILDE VERSUS PUBLIC MORALITY

Pam Hassebroek

My dear boy, people who love once in their lives are really shallow people. What they call their loyalty and their fidelity is either the lethargy of custom or lack of imagination. Faithfulness is to the emotional life is what constance is to the intellectual life, simply a confession of failure. —OSCAR WILDE, 1890

We teach people how to remember; we never teach them how to grow. —OSCAR WILDE, 1907

A HISTORICALLY-ACCURATE ACCOUNT OF THE VERY PUBLIC personal life of Oscar Wilde is presented in the movie *Wilde* (Gilbert, 1997). A docudrama about a witty, prolific, and prominent literary figure who suffered imprisonment for his lack of discretion in a romantic sexual relationship. However, when one's livelihood requires popularity and acceptance, defying the rules is a stance that requires thoughtfully considering the risks.

Society's rules reflect collective beliefs about moral behavior and its conception (or misconception) of humanity. Wilde's choice to confront the law designed to protect the public against gay "predators" was what led to his early death.

And, the legal system was not foreign to Wilde. From the outset of his publications, he dealt with ethical and legal issues—censorship and allegations of plagiarism or "presumed unoriginality" (Bristow & Mitchell, 2016). Yet, he successfully defended the accusations and went on to achieve international fame.

Today's statutes show changes in perspective about human sexuality in many places in the world. However, some people's ideas have not changed. And, some of the negative attitudes and beliefs are close to home. In Wilde's case, the rules dictated that an intelligent, contributing person must be disguised, marginalized, punished, or destroyed.

Celebrity Image Created in America

Before formally publishing a single piece of literature, Wilde had strategically created his celebrity image by traveling to America in 1882 and making his name known among socialites, politicians, and literary giants (Friedman, 2014). Wilde demonstrated his intelligence and razor-sharp wit everywhere he could, from academic lectures to dinner parties. And with a pompous self-confidence that did not always endear him to everyone he met.

However, returning to the UK, he reinforced his reputation through the now-legendary works that extended his fame. His social comedies, notably *Lady Windermere's Fan* (1892), *A Woman of No Importance* (1893), and *The Importance of Being Earnest* (1895), are familiar to many.

His novel, *The Picture of Dorian Gray* (1890), was adapted for film (Lewin, 1945) and earned an Oscar for Angela Lansbury as Best Supporting Actress. The movie has had additional remakes over the years. However, over a century passed before the novel achieved full recognition. "Revised after it was condemned in the British press over 130 years ago as 'vulgar,' 'unclean,' 'poisonous,' and 'discreditable,' an uncensored version of Oscar Wilde's *The Picture of Dorian Gray* has finally been published" (Flood, 2011).

According to his background, Wilde came by his intellectual capacity and literary talent naturally. He was born in Ireland in 1854 to prominent Dublin intellectuals—his father, a physician, and proper "Renaissance man" (Walshe, 2014), and his mother, a writer. He attended Trinity College, Dublin, and Magdalen College, Oxford. In 1884, he married Constance Lloyd, who gave birth to their two sons in 1885 and 1886. His celebrity intensified after that, but some portions of the limelight were not favorable.

Fame and Privilege No Guarantee of Freedom

In 1895, Wilde took John Douglas, a marquess,[1] to court for defamation after publicly exposing Wilde's romantic relationship with a young man. The young man was Lord Alfred ("Bosie") Douglas, the marquess's son. Defending himself during the trial, Douglas made further statements accusing Wilde of soliciting men for sex.

Facing hostile public opinion from the press that damaged Wilde's reputation, his lawyers dropped the charges against Douglas. The court then turned the tables and indicted Wilde for "gross indecency." This court action came under Britain's 1885 Criminal Law Amendment Act, which allowed prosecuting gay men when no one could prove sexual contact.[2]

---

[1] Douglas was the 8th Marquess of Queensberry (a title in the Peerage of Scotland).

[2] The law was enacted to protect boys from adult predators, not to punish consenting adults. It is sad to note that British courts convicted brilliant mathematician Alan Turing (1912-1954) under the same law and sentenced him to chemical castration as an alternative to prison. He died at age 41 from cyanide poisoning. Turing, responsible for the software concept of modern computing, was featured in *The Code Breakers* (1996), *The Imitation Game* (2014), and *Enigma* (2001). Movies on Chatham screened *Enigma* in 2011. Queen Elizabeth granted Turing a posthumous pardon in 2014.

At the time, in polite British society, any public discussion of sexuality was considered inappropriate and, by association, tarnishing to middle- and upper-class status. Thus, "because the libel trial exposed the Victorian elite's dirty linen, contaminated the authorities, and thereby drastically increased the costs of not legally sanctioning Wilde," the court brought charges against him (Adut, 2005). Otherwise, his indiscretions might have remained merely gossip.

Despite his popularity and visible contribution to society, he lost his public court battle. While serving two years' imprisonment in Reading, England, Wilde wrote *The Ballad of Reading Gaol* and *A Letter to Bosie*, expressing his anguish. The letter, published later, was entitled *De Profundis* (Latin: *From the Depths*). Released from prison in 1897, he died in Paris in 1900.

Was Wilde Born at the Wrong Time?

One could certainly make a case for the notion that Wilde was simply born at the wrong time. If he were living today, he would be very welcome in the U.S. in countless prominent places. In literary circles, likely in movies, and most certainly at *Saturday Night Live* because of his wit. And, like Elton John, he might be publicly celebrated for his art instead of condemned for refusing to mask his infidelity to heterosexual norms. ... Or, maybe not. Other famous people join his circle of "misfits."

The Russian novelist Nikolai Gogol. The actress Charlotte Cushman.[3] The American poet Walt Whitman. Women's

---

[3] Cushman was a 19th-century American celebrity. Her stage-acting ability creating an enormous following, she became one of the most famous people in the world (Wojczuk, 2020).

rightist Karl Ulrichs. The author of more than 1,000 poems, Emily Dickinson. The novelist Henry James. The British General Kitchener, who brought peace to Sudan. Friedrich Krupp, the German Industrialist. The writer Marcel Proust. Novelist Virginia Woolf. [T. E.] Lawrence, the 'Lawrence of Arabia.' The philosopher Ludwig Wittgenstein. Pop icons Elton John, Freddie Mercury, Madonna, David Bowie, Lady Gaga. The classical composers Franz Schubert, Handel, and Tchaikovsky. Singer, songwriter George Michael. (Ganesan, 2018)

Today we are free to watch movies that include LGBTQ portrayals and relationships. But, this freedom has come over the course of a long and ongoing struggle. In Chapter 6, we noted that Vito Russo studied 20th-century filmmaking and Hollywood's depictions (and lack thereof) of gay men and lesbians. In Part II of this book, our quest has been similar—to explore movie interpretations of non-binary sexual orientations and gender identities while investigating their societal contexts. We can compare Russo's film history with present-day film arts and gender conflicts to note the differences.

What's Okay in Public Communication Now?

A few years back, I found myself startled a bit at the uncensored realism I noted while watching episodes of Amazon Studio's TV series, *Transparent* (Soloway & Sperling, 2014–2019). Not that I consider the series' content without value or utterly tasteless; I was simply thinking about children. Frontal nudity and realistic depictions of sexual intercourse are now acceptable for public viewing, period, no matter the transmission source. (On television, one must watch via cable or another streaming source.) Yet, it hasn't been all that long since George Carlin's "7 words" challenged what was permissible for broadcast—and they were just words after all (Carlin, 1973). No pictures.

Describing obscenity in broadcasting is challenging because the concepts vary in different places. Even so, the U.S. bans it entirely. And, the FCC (n.d.) says broadcasters can air indecent or profane content only at certain times of the day.

> It is a violation of federal law to air obscene programming at any time.[4] It is also a violation of federal law to broadcast indecent or profane programming during certain hours. The Federal Communications Commission (FCC) defines indecent speech as material that, in context, depicts or describes sexual or excretory organs or activities in terms patently offensive as measured by contemporary community standards for the broadcast medium.

> The courts hold that indecent material is protected by the First Amendment and cannot be banned entirely. FCC rules prohibit indecent speech on broadcast radio and television between 6 a.m. and 10 p.m., when there is a reasonable risk that children may be in the audience.[5] (FCC admin, 2017)

The FCC may revoke a station's license, impose a fine, or issue a warning if a station violates rules by airing offensive material.

---

[4] Obscene material has no First Amendment protection and the FCC prohibits it for cable and satellite services as well as radio and TV broadcasters.

[5] The FCC interprets this restriction as applicable to radio and TV broadcasters only. It has never extended it to cover cable or satellite operators.

How and When to Legislate for Public Morality

Thus, how and when to legislate for public morality remains as pertinent today as in Wilde's time. Tragically, same-sex couples who engage in consensual, intimate behavior are still considered criminals in some places. Today, 72 countries—in the Caribbean, Africa, the Middle East, and Southeast Asia—impose harsh penalties. In 11 nation-states, same-sex acts can result in the death penalty ("Map of countries," 2020).

In Brunei, the Islamic country's Shariah Penal Code states, "those found guilty of gay sex could be stoned to death or whipped." Further, they "apply to children and foreigners, even if they are not Muslim" (Associated Press, 2019).

In Cameroon, Egypt, Kenya, Lebanon, Tunisia, Turkmenistan, Uganda, and Zambia, men and transgender women accused of consensual same-sex conduct are forced to undergo anal examinations. A *Human Rights Watch* report (Ghoshal, 2016) presents the evidence of exams as an "illegal form of torture or cruel, inhuman, and degrading treatment." The practice is also a violation of international principles of medical ethics, including the prohibition on medical personnel participating in any way in acts of torture or degrading treatment. Some victims have lasting psychological effects from this form of sexual assault.

In 1871, Germany's Paragraph 175 outlawed sexual relations between men, and the law became more potent under the Nazi regime. It stayed that way in West Germany after WWII. Long before the war, a physician, researcher, and outspoken advocate for sexual and gender minorities, Dr. Magnus Hirschfeld, attempted to educate Germans about same-sex attraction and urged the law's repeal (Wikipedia, 2020).

Between the end of WWII and when West Germany changed the law in 1969, it had convicted around 50,000 men (Moulson, 2017). Even though Communist East Germany had decriminalized same-sex relations in 1968, they didn't abolish the law until 1994. Similarly, racism didn't end when Obama became U.S. President; as Steakley reported in 1999, "in Germany, despite more than 50 years of scientific research, legal discrimination against homosexuals continues unabated. May justice soon prevail over injustice in this area, science conquer superstition, love achieve victory over hatred!"

Poland decriminalized same-sex relations in 1932, but the rights of LGBT citizens are diminishing today. In texts regarding teaching in schools, they forbid "homopropaganda" that could lead to "depravation of children" (Iborel, 2020).

In Russia—think about what we've learned about the climate for gay men and lesbians in that country today. Same-sex relations became legal in 1993. In 2012, the St. Petersburg legislature passed a law to eliminate gay "propaganda" among minors, punishable by fines up to $17,000. Other legislatures in Russia have adopted similar rules.

> Open discussion of homosexuality was almost unheard of in Russia until just a few years ago. A Soviet-era law that punished same-sex relations between men with prison time was repealed in 1993, but the subject has long remained taboo outside a smattering of bars and clubs in major Russian cities. (Schwirtz, 2012)

In 2015, the Moscow New Drama Theater, a respected theater company, prepared to present the 1997 U.S. play, *Gross Indecency: The Three Trials of Oscar Wilde*, with a cast of Russian actors and directed by its creator, Moisés Kaufman. Regrettably, the Russian government canceled the play before it got off the ground (Paulson & Kishkosky, 2015).[6] But wait, lest we Americans get too critical, I point to the Cobb County Commission, a local government in the Atlanta area that did the same thing.

The Cobb County Commission in Marietta, GA

When our family first arrived in Atlanta, we learned about the similar fate of a play staged at the Theatre in the Square in Marietta, GA. A local had complained about Terrence McNally's play, *Lips Together Teeth Apart* (1992), its topic being the AIDS crisis. The play was essentially a conversation about people's responsibility to reach out to the gay community when so many were dying from AIDS. Otherwise, it had no LGBTQ content.

The play closed and then made international headlines when it led to a resolution. The "infamous 1993 Cobb County Commission condemning the gay 'lifestyle' prompted protests that eventually kept Cobb from hosting events for the 1996 Atlanta Olympics" (*Georgia Voice* editors, 2012).[7]

The following is an excerpt from a *Los Angeles Times* article, entitled "It's Time to Shuck the Corn in Cobb" (Downey, 1994):

> No, they said in Cobb County, GA, if gay people feel they
> absolutely must have equal rights, then let them have
> equal rights, but let them have equal rights someplace else.

---

[6] Kaufman, the author of numerous plays, has directed extensively on Broadway and internationally. Best known for *The Laramie Project* (2002), he received the National Medal of Arts award in 2016.

[7] The theater has since produced several gay-themed plays, including *Gross Indecency: The Three Trials of Oscar Wilde*. The theater closed in 2012 for lack of funding, re-opening in 2015 with the play, *The Birdcage*.

I guess every volleyball match in Cobb County, GA, will be supervised by a big old sheriff who makes sure that nobody does any of that patting-on-the-butt stuff after a great spike.

Even now, I can see Atlanta mounting those billboards: 'Welcome to the Host City of the 1996 Summer Olympics. Proud to Host Most of You.'

Maybe if they really want to show their contempt, Gordon [Wysong] and the Cobb County commissioners can do their tomahawk chops with limp wrists.

This attitude of Cobb County officials would be regrettable if it weren't that some still feel that hostile now. I call it simply hateful. However, in many places, people are adapting and trying to make amends. Bayard Rustin's case is an example.

In 1953, Rustin, who helped Dr. Martin Luther King Jr. organize the Montgomery bus boycott and the March on Washington, was convicted in California under discriminatory LGBTQ laws. In 1975, California repealed the law prohibiting consensual acts between same-sex adults. This action came long after Rustin had served time in jail and was required to register as a sex offender.

After many years of humanitarian work, Rustin died in 1987. In 2020, California Governor Gavin Newsom pardoned the prominent civil rights leader posthumously. "In the official pardon, Newsom says Rustin was jailed because of 'stigma, bias and ignorance'" (Cahill, 2020). President Barack Obama had honored him with the Presidential Medal of Freedom in 2013.

In Germany, same-sex marriage became legal in 2017. Then, Chancellor Angela Merkel's cabinet approved a bill to annul criminal convictions for thousands of gay men (Moulson, 2017).

Other countries have done this too. In 2016, the UK government officially pardoned over 50,000 men the government had convicted for being gay under an archaic law.

However, metro Atlanta got a national spotlight once again for its discrimination role despite all the restitution activities. In this case, officials in Clayton County, Georgia, fired Gerald Bostock shortly after he joined and promoted a gay softball league. He had been a ten-year employee with good performance. Yet, the county dismissed him for conduct 'unbecoming' for his choice of recreational activities ("Bostock *v*. Clayton County," 2020).

In 2013 when he was fired, the state had no law protecting our gay community from employment discrimination. Thus, Bostock began a public inquiry of the injustice, which led to a favorable U.S. Supreme Court decision. As a result, as of June 15, 2020, Georgia's workforce is protected from employer bias and unmerited humiliation.

Who's Troubled About Movies' Sexual Content?

Given the belief systems that some people still promote regarding sexual orientation and gender identity, where is the outcry in the U.S. today about sexual content in the movies, one might ask? Especially in light of our past movie censorship and the importance our society placed on firm standards of behavior. In earlier times, the Catholic Church and similarly-focused organizations railed against the display of cultural taboos. However, women's conduct was always the center of attention; and men, regardless of their sexual relationships or behavior, were not part of theirs or anyone else's concern. Gay actors were present in U.S. films from the start—they just kept their private lives private.

Different institutions have been warning us for

centuries—about the sexual, and therefore social, impact of Boccaccio and Chaucer and comic books, of women on the theatrical stage, of mixed-gender public schools, of radio and then of talking movies, and of legalizing 'rubbers.'

Today they're warning us about the increasing social acceptance of same-gender sex. And they're right. We're approaching the end of normal sex. (Klein, 2013)

In that same vein, let's go back to look at another source of America's 20th-century concerns. In the 1950s, *Blakiston's New Gould Medical Dictionary* (Hoerr & Osol, 1956) defined the word "amphigenesis" as "the capacity of a predominantly homosexual person to carry on normal sexual relations with the opposite sex." "When modern sex research began after World War II, many thought that 'normal' sex was limited to married heterosexual vaginal intercourse—with everything else suspect or 'perverted'" (Castleman, 2018).

Blakiston's also defined a homosexual as an "invert." In the same volume, "sexual deviation" is described as

> a sociopathic personality disturbance characterized by deviant or aberrant sexuality, which is not part of any more extensive disorder such as the schizophrenic or obsessional reaction. It includes the various forms and practices of homosexuality, transvestism, pedophilia, fetishism, and sexual sadism (assault and rape, mutilation).

"Sex-o-esthetic inversion" meant adopting the habits, manners, and costumes of the opposite sex. And, before that, at the turn of the 20th century, the *American Illustrated Medical Dictionary* defined "heterosexuality"—today's general term for "normal sex"—as an "abnormal or perverted sexual appetite toward the opposite sex," and represented "homosexuality" as sexual perversion toward those of the same sex (Dorland, 1900). No wonder people didn't talk about this. They wouldn't consider discussing it with a medical doctor, for sure.

The dwindling of Americans' sense of sexual morality since the early 1960s has made derogatory sex-related language increasingly acceptable. Maybe that decline, plus the Catholic Church's sex scandals, has lessened the righteous anger over movie content.

Sexuality Is Unique to Individuals

Today an estimated 11 percent of Americans (30 million) are not exclusively heterosexual (Meyer, 2019). However, the number of those who self-identify as LGB is much smaller.

> An estimated 19 million Americans (8.2%) report that they have engaged in same-sex sexual behavior, and nearly 25.6 million Americans (11%) acknowledge at least some same-sex sexual attraction. (Gates, 2011)

As it turns out, there is no standard for sexual thoughts or behavior. Sexuality is as unique as any other part of an individual. No two people have identical erotic feelings or preferences. Therefore, we should stop labeling a legal sexual activity as peculiar or deviant. If there is no standard, we can't call anything abnormal. As we discuss this topic further in the remaining chapters, our focus will be on other outstanding artists like Oscar Wilde, gay or transgender individuals.

THE RISE AND RUIN
OF OSCAR WILDE

Lucy Cota

THE 19TH CENTURY IS THE STAGE for events in Oscar Wilde's life shown in the biographical movie *Wilde* (Gilbert, 1997). Wilde's story is tragic and exposes the intolerance toward gay men in the Victorian era. Unfortunately, in our very modern age of information and greater understanding, this bias endures for some.

I recently attended a memorial service for a lifelong friend. One of the speakers stated in remembrance that a person dies three times. First, they die physically; they die again when memorialized and buried; they die the third death when nobody remembers them or mentions their name. Since the time of Wilde's death, appreciation for his works has not faded. Nor has interest waned in the man who took eloquent self-expression to a level reachable only by the brilliant.

It has been well over a century since his death. Yet, Wilde's name keeps popping up in enough cultural references that it seems every educated person today knows this renowned playwright by name and famous works, including *The Picture of Dorian Gray* (1890) and *The Importance of Being Earnest* (1909).

Oscar Wilde was a well-raised and well-educated Irishman who married a well-raised and well-educated woman with whom he had two sons. This description sounds like the picture of a stable life, yet his life was anything but.

'Sexual Perversion' Common Among Elites

During his young adulthood at Oxford University, then an all-male school,[8] he had lived among students who recognized his remarkable talent. About those students, according to a Wilde biography (Harris, 1916),

> For the most part, they were persons usually called 'sexual inverts,' who looked to the brilliancy of his intellect to gild their esoteric indulgence. This class in England is almost wholly recruited from the aristocracy and the upper-middle-class that apes the 'smart set.' It is an inevitable product of the English boarding school and University system; indeed one of the most characteristic products.

While Wilde never paraded his sexual orientation, it was common knowledge among elites. Because of his associations at Oxford, one may assume that he had no qualms about "sexual perversion," the name for same-sex behavior at the time. The characteristic is said to have been a "'Jacob's ladder'[9] to most forms of success" in London. "These admirers and supporters praised and defended Oscar Wilde from the beginning with the persistence and courage of men who, if they don't hang together, are likely to hang separately" (Harris, 1916).

Wilde's elevated position gave him access to all happenings in society, wherein both he and his writing continually thrived. Unfortunately, he became too comfortable in this position. He

---

[8] Wilde arrived at Oxford in 1874. Women first earned degrees in 1920 (Hughes-Johnson, 2020).

[9] Jacob's ladder is a biblical reference to a dream where a stairway/ladder rests on the earth, with its top reaching to heaven.

became romantically involved with Lord Alfred Douglas, a young man nicknamed "Bosie." When his father, John Douglas, the Marquess of Queensberry, objected vehemently to the relationship, Wilde jumped into the middle of the battle between father and son.

Common sense says that family conflict is a "no man's land" for outsiders, and Wilde knew that as well as anyone. "I choose my friends for their good looks, my acquaintances for their good characters, and my enemies for their intellects. A man cannot be too careful in the choice of his enemies" (Wilde, 1890). However, passion, anger, and of course, abundant family wealth and peerage make for compelling drama, and he stayed in, not out of it.

Wilde certainly made a formidable enemy out of Queensberry, a man who had the resources to do much damage. As mentioned in the previous article, Queensberry publicly accused Wilde of having a sexual relationship with his son and further accused him of soliciting men for sex. A court convicted him of the crime of "gross indecency" and sentenced him to two years of hard labor.

Wilde's superior talent and connections in aristocratic circles had exempted his gay behavior. Yet, when he could no longer display his abilities, his pedestal in high society came crashing down.

Wilde in Prison and After

Wilde was sent away to prison, where he was treated more like an animal than a human. There, when a fellow prisoner whispered into Wilde's ear that he admired his writings, he could not help but exclaim his gratitude out loud. Sadly, his response resulted in a horrible beating since speaking was not permitted.

While enduring hardships, Wilde found out his real friends were not the British aristocracy. After years of meaningless, soul-crushing labor, he came out a broken man. The ugliness of life had caught up with him, and he couldn't summon the ability to write as he had before. The insight and flourish with which he wrote about the ironies of society was gone.

Oscar Wilde would never be the same, and the rest of humanity was deprived of any future masterpieces he may have produced. Although his wife continued to send money, she otherwise abandoned him with their sons. To dissociate themselves from the scandalous man, she changed their surname from Wilde to Holland. Wilde died three years after his prison release.

As expected, Bosie eventually received his inheritance and moved on in comfortable style. Wilde, the man that came between his lover and his lover's father, was ostracized and left behind.

It seems to be one of life's truths that the one who walks willingly into a minefield between two warring parties is the one who gets punished. In contrast, the two opposing parties hold themselves unaccountable for that third person's fate.

Bosie and his father cared nothing about what their actions did to Wilde's life, but the playwright himself had chosen to get involved. He had actively perpetuated the drama, a fact that he recognized and for which he took responsibility.

> I must say to myself that I ruined myself and that nobody great or small can be ruined except by his own hand. I am quite ready to say so. I am trying to say so, though they may not think it at the present moment. This pitiless indictment I bring without pity against myself. Terrible as was what the world did to me, what I did to myself was far more terrible still. (Wilde, 1913)

Interestingly, in later years, Queensberry's great-niece took it personally that her family had ruined Wilde. Her feelings of family guilt were so strong that she made prisoner rehabilitation her life's mission.

Queensberry and Wilde's Legacy

Queensberry and his son, Lord Alfred? Today, we know little about them beyond what they did to silence the genius of wit in Oscar Wilde.

Wilde's legacy survives today when people read his works, watch movies about him, talk about him, and wish he could have written more literary masterpieces.

He hasn't died that third death. So may it be that he never will.

CHAPTER 8

THE DANISH GIRL (2015)

A beautiful love story with a tragic outcome.

—Movies on Chatham group member

DIRECTOR	Tom Hooper
SCREENPLAY	Lucinda Coxon, David Ebershoff
CAST	Eddie Redmayne ~ Einar/Lili Alicia Vikander ~ Gerda
AWARDS	ACADEMY AWARDS SCREEN ACTORS GUILD AWARDS
	Best Performance by an Actor in a Leading Role: Eddie Redmayne
	Best Performance by an Actor in a Supporting Role: Alicia Vikander
RUN TIME	119 min
RATING	R

SUMMARY

David Ebershoff wrote the novel, *The Danish Girl* (2000), based on the experiences of married Danish artists Einar and Gerda Wegener. This movie adaptation shows their struggle to adjust to Einar's female identity.

GENDER DIFFERENCES: WHY THE SUDDEN CONCERN?

Pam Hassebroek

A TRUE LOVE STORY UNFOLDS IN the movie, *The Danish Girl* (Hooper, 2015). It's about two artists who married, then suffered a relationship crisis that led to a separation. Ultimately, a gender difference was the problem. However, since the genders of a male-female couple are traditionally different, this doesn't sound like the real trouble. But in their case, the husband's gender identity had become confused, and they experienced a profound struggle in dealing with it.

The husband's gender was psychologically different from his male physical attributes. This story may help those who share similar self-awareness. It may also help explain the dilemma to people who consider that individuals born with a gender difference are a problem. How they define the problem dictates its solution.

Some years ago, gender differences were a front-burner concern for Mississippi, North Carolina, and Georgia citizens. They were possibly alarmed because of the 2015 Supreme Court decision that gave same-sex couples the right to marry (Liptak, 2015). Their fear of lesbian, gay, bisexual, and transgender people led to passing laws that drew reactions nationwide. Quoted from an article in *The New York Times*,

> In Mississippi, companies such as Tyson Foods, MGM Resorts International, Nissan, and Toyota, all major employers in the state, have raised objections to the law

signed by Gov. Phil Bryant. The far-reaching legislation allows individuals and institutions like churches, religious charities, and privately held businesses to decline services to gay people if doing so would violate their religious beliefs on marriage and gender. (Mêlé, 2016)

North Carolina Law Bars Use of Public Bathrooms

The article says that the North Carolina law "bars transgender people from using public bathrooms that do not match the sex on their birth certificates." Because Governor Deal vetoed Georgia's so-called "religious liberty bill," its citizens narrowly escaped state-sponsored bigotry as well.

To me, this underscores the ignorance and strange attitudes that exist about human particularities amid the wide-ranging spectrum of biological characteristics that make each person unique. To help me conceptualize individual differences, I first consider the possible variations in all human parts.

Imagine dividing each body system into sub-sets, perhaps based on functions such as seeing, hearing, breathing, intelligence, procreation, etc. Each element of a functional sub-set has a range of values and a vast number of possible values within that range. For example, under "seeing," each of our eyes can be countless colors and shades, have minute differences in shape, size, seeing ability, etc. In combination, those eyes can have untold differences from someone else's.

And, under "hearing," we can identify many details and variations. My son is one of those fortunate people to have ears that are so in tune with his brain that he has absolute pitch. Then there's Jory

Fleming,[1] a brilliant man with autism who recently earned a degree as a Rhodes Scholar at Oxford University. In an interview on *NBC Today*, he told Harry Smith that he could identify him by looking only at his ears. Of course, like all features of our faces, our fingerprints, voices, teeth, and hair strands are unique identifiers too. Still, apart from facial recognition surveillance, we don't worry much about any of that.

Under "procreation," I similarly envision a sub-set of cellular components, parts, and features with an enormous number of differences in function, appearance, and size in the human population. In a sex educator's book, *Come as You Are: The Surprising New Science that Will Transform Your Sex Life* (2021), author Nagoski affirms my intuition.

> Variety may be the one and only truly universal characteristic of human sexuality. From our bodies to our desires to our behaviors, there are as many "sexualities" as there are humans alive on Earth. No two alike.

However, when referring to sex and gender differences, most people classify all of these differences under two broad categories: female and male. Then after that, they subclassify people as gay or straight.

Instead, suppose I place the gazillions of unique sex-related measurements along a line between two extreme and opposite points. Where would we put the female and male markers? We could start with the most prominent division based on whether the person produces an egg or a sperm.

Then, where would we put the humans who make multiple eggs or no eggs, lots of sperm or a little, or something otherwise? How

---

[1] See: Fleming, J. (2021).

might we arrange those who have a group of parts that are both female and male mixed? Can a man who has adequate sperm to create another human also have female hormones in higher amounts than most? Which people have the measured characteristics that define an entirely feminine human? Or, toward the other end, "this person is fully masculine." We can't draw these lines because we don't know enough about this. Maybe DNA researchers will help.

> Part of the categorization problem is due to the fact that we do not have a well-established detailed theory—let alone a neuroanatomic/neurophysiologic model—of normal gender identity development that gives us clear guidance in distinguishing non-pathologic from pathologic. (Meyer-Bahlburg, 2010).

Today, as in the past, we define men and women broadly based on outward appearances.

Gender Differences Not Fully Understood

In truth, we are all naturally curious about other people, how they look and behave. We have observed or heard about all kinds of people in our lifetimes: those who seem to look like us and adapt well to everyday activities and conflicts. And people who are different and whose behavior is dangerous, problematic, or puzzling.

We have all formed opinions about others based on our own experiences, coupled with public opinion. What we consider appropriate or inappropriate mainly relates to public opinion. Over the years, any discussion of gender differences, especially those outside a worldview of heteronormativity, went underground because of public censorship, which of course, relates to public opinion.

Now, gender differences have suddenly become a critical social issue. On the front page, even though differences in sexual behaviors, sexual orientations, and gender identities have been around at least since the beginning of recorded history. Maybe for some, *The Danish Girl* contributed to this perceived public problem's urgency.

A couple of ideas may help us decide what about this human condition has suddenly become critical, 1) lack of familiarity and 2) the problem definition. First, we aren't familiar with all of humanity. Therefore, we may fear and distrust that person or group that is unknown to us or is outside our view of "ordinary" or "normal." We may think of them as irregular, unusual, or oddities, i.e., "queer." We then marginalize and label them as abnormal, scary, dysfunctional, or disabled.

Many variations in physical, intellectual, emotional, or psychological well-being can cause individual functional limitation or impairment. However, a deviation from normal won't lead to disability unless society fails to acknowledge and include all people regardless of their differences.

Defining a "Problem" of Gender Difference

Next, a human difference may be considered a problem because of exclusion or social segregation. Thus, the person with characteristics outside recognized norms is in danger of unjustified social limitations. Further, how you define the problem, or the tools you have available to manage it, dictates its solution. ("If your only tool is a hammer, then every problem looks like a nail.")

In *The Danish Girl*, Einar pursues consultation with medical doctors for help with gender identification. This course of action reveals that, in their context, Einar and Gerda have defined this distressing concern as a potential medical problem.

A medical problem is one of three ways that people typically define individual human systems differences or dysfunction:

1) **A medical problem:** Physical malfunction or physical disability. A medical model of disability defines a medical problem as a physical condition in the individual ("Medical Model of Disability," 2008). Medicalization is the social process whereby human characteristics and problems become medical conditions.

2) **A psychiatric problem:** Crazy, mental disorder, mentally disturbed. A group of attributes typically considered in defining a mental illness: differences in how a person behaves, feels, perceives, and thinks.

3) **A religious or spiritual/faith problem:** Sinful, acting against God's laws. A difference is a faith issue if it violates religious beliefs. The problem may then fall into a particular subset of evil: physical, supernatural, or moral corruption.

On terms and definitions, people in the LGBTQ community prefer some terms over others because of negative associations. For example, *The Associated Press Institute (API)*, *The New York Times*, and other publications restrict using the word "homosexual." Healthcare professionals callously misapplied the term when they believed that lesbians and gay men were dysfunctional or psychologically disordered. Anti-gay extremists use "homosexual" in a derogatory way more often than not.

Our contributors have established rules to guard against the use of inaccurate terms such as "sexual preference" and "gay lifestyle" (GLAAD, 2013). However, it would be a positive step for everyone to become familiar with and avoid negative connotations that may unwittingly promote hurtful prejudice.

The Problem Represented in the Movie

Now, let's look at how *The Danish Girl* represents the gender identification problem in Einar's diagnosis.

First, the couple seeks a medical solution. A physician treats him with radiation, but it is not clear why.

Then, the problem changes to a different dilemma. Again, physicians weigh in, this time psychiatrists, and the diagnosis becomes schizophrenia. He barely escapes the men in white coats pursuing him with a straitjacket in that scene.[2]

If, in the movie, he had consulted a priest, would the treatment have been exorcism to cast out his demons or evil spirits? If a pastor, would the procedure be to shun him until or unless he repents and remains celibate (Boorstein, 2014)?

Lack of information and misunderstanding can produce all kinds of responses thought to be helpful (or hurtful). Sadly, this fictionalized story calls attention to an unfortunate societal misunderstanding that still exists. "If America is reaching a turning point on transgender issues, so far it is strictly in terms of visibility—not, as one might hope, in terms of America's overall attitudes and laws" (Sasson, 2015).

Psychopathia Sexualis (Krafft-Ebing, 1886/1906) is cited as the first scholarly attempt to shed light on human gender differences. Thanks to the Guttenberg Project and the Internet Archive, the book is available online. Krafft-Ebing proposed a theory that "homosexuality" begins in the womb as "a 'sexual inversion' of the brain."

---

[2] Today, standard of care for a person seeking sex reassignment surgery includes a required diagnosis of gender dysphoria before beginning hormone therapy with a medical doctor.

The Fallacy of Assignable Gender (Bradford, 2007) is a more recent contribution from an author who has lived through the experience of gender identity difference herself. She explores this gender condition from multiple perspectives. "Whether the reader's interest is personal or professional, ending the social and economic scourge of suppressed gender identity will require a broad concerted effort. Its undertaking is long overdue." Brenda Bradford's book about her long struggle is a courageous and enlightening work.

Sex Reassignment History

In the next article, Mary discusses Caitlyn Marie Jenner, the former Bruce Jenner, who brought attention to LGBTQ issues in 2015. The news delivered mixed reactions when she publicly announced her intention to become female, just as when Christine Jorgensen revealed her sex reassignment in the 1950s. However, Jorgensen's experience turned out to be very positive for her.

She had grown up in the Bronx, NY, raised as a boy and named George by her parents, both Danish-born. After serving in the U.S. military at the end of WWII, George began to investigate medical options to relieve the stress of being a woman trapped in a man's body. Visiting with relatives in Denmark led him to Christian Hamburger, a Danish doctor known to be using hormone testing on animals in experiments for gender therapy (Hadjimatheou, 2012).

Hamburger and his team then helped her transform, acquiring the 1930s medical notes from a Berlin surgeons group. This same group had earlier attempted the transgender surgery depicted in *The Danish Girl*. George Jorgensen changed her name to Christine to honor Dr. Hamburger's work.

When she returned from Denmark in December 1952, neither the media nor the public expressed hostility. Instead, most people seemed to have a curious fascination. She made the news all over America; the Scandinavian Societies of Greater New York even named her "Woman of the Year" ("From GI Joe to GI Jane," 2020). That she was beautiful, blond, confident, and highly eloquent undoubtedly helped.[3]

Jorgensen lectured at colleges across the U.S. on gender identity. At a speaking engagement recorded at UCLA, she talks about how in the 1950s, "sex was not discussed. Problems of identification were not discussed" (Jorgensen, 1972). People stayed silent on TB and cancer topics as though they were "some sort of a terrible, terrible anti-social condition." People today [in the 1970s] believe in "telling it like it is" and "there is no subject today that is hidden." In the 1950s, no one could mention even an STD on television or anywhere else.

Nineteenth-Century Study of Sex Characteristics

Although historical records in many cultures describe people with varying degrees of sexual development, research to understand this and other associated human characteristics started only in the mid-19th century. The writings of European scientists Ulrichs, Freud, Kertbeny, Krafft-Ebing, and Hirschfeld were early influencers. However, when adding to discourses in the science community, some intentionally wrote in ways that created obstacles to public understanding. For example, in the Preface to Krafft-Ebing's first edition (1886), he states, "A scientific title has been chosen, and technical terms are used throughout the book in order to exclude the lay reader. For the same reason certain portions are written in

---

[3] Edward Small produced *The Christine Jorgensen Story* (Rapper, 1970); and Teit Ritzau, a Danish doctor, made a documentary film about her in 1985 called *Paradise Is Not for Sale*.

Latin."

Further, as stated in the Preface to the 12th edition, "The number of technical terms has been increased, and the Latin language is more frequently made use of than in former editions." Finally, he added, "The sale of the book is rigidly restricted to the members of the medical and legal professions."

Johann Friedrich Blumenbach, a German professor of medicine, played a significant role in elevating the scientific knowledge about human individuality above widespread ignorance and prejudice. By the end of the century, other prominent scientists followed Blumenbach, concluding that no taxonomy[4] was valid that places humans into simple broad categories of skin color. A sub-categorization of "human race" by skin color showed no other distinctive or significant biological differences.

Blumenbach strongly opposed the notion of European cultural superiority (Barber, 2008). Still, despite the contrary evidence, race classification stayed in place to become an ideology that served to elevate the prejudice to "universal truth."

Hirschfeld was very public in his belief that the erroneous typecasting of "race" formed the Western concept of white superiority. He was also central in the development of taxonomies of sexual identities.

Hirschfeld Establishes Institute for Sexual Science

Dr. Hirschfeld's 1914 book, *The Homosexuality of Men & Women*, was part of a research effort to show that same-sex attraction occurs in every culture. He established the Institute for Sexual Science in 1919

---

[4] A taxonomy is a classification system—the practice and science of classifying (organizing) things or concepts.

in Berlin, an active center for collaboration among scientists, activists, and people who wanted to know more about themselves. He co-wrote and acted in the movie *Different from the Others* (Oswald, 1919) to influence gay rights law reform. Conrad Veidt played one of the first gay characters ever written for cinema (Steakley, 1999).

Hirschfeld believed that restrictions on women's and gay men's rights were related problems; he pushed for the repeal of Germany's Paragraph 218 law that banned abortion. Oscar Wilde's trial affected Hirschfeld greatly; he often referred to it in his writings (Bauer, 2017).

However, after all the research efforts in Europe, U.S. medical professionals remained out of touch. By the mid-20th century, gender identity disorder (GID) was still considered a persistent mental dysfunction, even a form of psychosis.[5] In addition, they called it an illness by assuming the condition included "clinically significant distress or impairment" (Meyer-Bahlburg, 2010).

In 1965, Johns Hopkins was the first U.S. academic medical institution to study gender identity and offer sex reassignment surgeries.

> 'This program, including the surgery, is investigational,' plastic surgeon John Hoopes, who was the head of the Gender Identity Clinic, told *The New York Times* in 1966. 'The most important result of our efforts will be to determine precisely what constitutes a transsexual and what makes him remain that way.'[6] (Witkin, 2014)

---

[5] GID is a controversial label, but the American Psychiatric Association still uses it in treatment discussions.

[6] Transsexual is an older term from medical and psychological communities.

However, the clinic closed in 1979 because of ill-conceived theories and ideological clashes among the doctors.

> In 1968, *DSM-II* (the second edition of the American classification of mental disorders) listed homosexuality as a mental disorder. In this, the *DSM* followed in a long tradition in medicine and psychiatry, which in the 19th century appropriated homosexuality from the Church and, in an élan of enlightenment, promoted it from sin to mental disorder. (Burton, 2015)

DSM Editor Publishes Flawed Study on Gay Therapy

In 1973, the U.S. psychiatry board removed the term "homosexuality" from the *DSM* (*Diagnostic and Statistical Manual*), no longer viewed as a mental disturbance. However, one of the *DSM* editors that made this change, Dr. Robert Spitzer, later published an article (2003) promoting psychotherapy ("reparative therapy" or "conversion therapy") to change the sexual orientation of gay men and lesbians. Then in 2012, he publicly acknowledged the flaws in his "study," revealing that it was biased and unscientific, written only to create controversy. He now says, "failed attempts to rid oneself of homosexual attractions 'can be quite harmful'" (Lane, 2012).

In the last two decades, scientific communities have recognized transgender men and women's satisfaction with their adopted genders. They have shown neither impairment nor distress. However, because of failures and abuses in the medical profession regarding past diagnoses and treatment, mental health remains a sensitive topic among transgender people.[7] Mental health

---

[7] Labeling gender identity variants (GIVs) as "mental disorders" in the
Footnote continues on the next page ...

professionals' role in diagnosing related disorders remains controversial.

Today Transgender Medicine a "Free-for-all"

Horvath (2020) reports concern that the

> field of transgender medicine is like a reckless, 'Wild West' free-for-all in which activist clinicians run small, terribly biased observational studies and then, 'spin' narratives that seem to 'confirm' benefit. These practices will undoubtedly lead to harm.

"Psychologists and other mental health professionals who have limited training and experience in TGNC [transgender and gender non-conforming] affirmative care may cause harm to TGNC people" (American Psychological Association, 2015).

> LGBTQ people are being harmed by minority stressors such as stigma, discrimination, and lack of legal protection, prior to entering mental health services. Further, there is a profound lack of cultural competence, knowledge, and sensitivity among providers who are expected to work with them once they access services. (Mikalson, Pardo, & Green, 2012)

In the face of current controversy and her attempts to make a difference, Caitlin Jenner has decided

> to 'only try and change one person at a time' and views equality as imperative, regardless of who's in the White

---

Diagnostic and Statistical Manual (DSM) is highly controversial among professionals and persons so described.

House.

In recent years, she's awarded scholarships to trans students and her self-named foundation 'promotes equality and combats discrimination by providing grants to organizations that empower and improve the lives of transgender people, including youth, anti-bullying, suicide prevention, healthcare, housing, employment, and related programs.' (Ganz, 2020)

Key Terms

Celibate

Celibate describes a person who, for personal health, safety, or religious reasons, voluntarily abstains from sexual relations.

Exorcism

Exorcism is the spiritual practice of evicting unidentified objects or entities from a person others believe to be possessed by evil.

Gender dysphoria

Gender dysphoria is a controversial term for a conflict between biological sex and gender identity (Meyer-Bahlburg, 2010; American Psychiatric Association, 2020).

Gender identity disorder

Gender identity disorder is a term no longer used. The newer medical term, "gender dysphoria," describes a person's relentless discontent with their assigned sex and gender.

Gender non-conforming

Many people have gender expressions that are not entirely conventional or "conforming" to the typical expectations for males and females. For example, until later in the 20th century, women who pursued STEM careers would be considered gender non-conforming.

Medicalization

Medicalization is the social process whereby human conditions and problems become defined as medical conditions and topics of medical research, diagnosis, prevention, and treatment. A physical condition thus becomes a disease that needs treatment ("Medicalization," 2017).

Transgender and Gender non-conforming (TGNC)

TGNC describes people whose gender identity is a blend or alternative male or female gender. Being a transgender person does not make someone gender non-conforming, nor do all gender non-conforming people identify as transgender. Therefore, you shouldn't use gender non-conforming unless someone self-identifies as gender non-conforming.

Sex reassignment

Sex reassignment is associated with a physical and psychological transformation from the biological sex assigned at birth to the opposite sex characteristics.

OBSTACLES AND OPTIONS FOR TRANSGENDER PEOPLE

Mary Reed

A MOVIE ABOUT A TRANSGENDER INDIVIDUAL takes place in 1920s Copenhagen. The focus of the celebrated film *The Danish Girl* (Hooper, 2015) is a married couple, Gerda and Einar Wegener, who address the unsettling revelation that Einar's identity has changed from male to female. Nominated for four Oscars, Alicia Vikander and Eddie Redmayne won awards for their leading roles. The movie's success reflects our times' progressive march towards approval and acceptance for all the world's people. It also motivates us to survey the obstacles and options for transgender people today.

The Danish Girl producers chose an auspicious time to release the movie as 2015 was a banner year for the LGBTQ cause. Neil Patrick Harris hosted the Academy Awards ceremony; the Supreme Court legalized gay marriage; and Caitlyn Jenner made her début in a *Vanity Fair* spread (Bissinger, 2015).

Comedies and Thrillers Include Cross-dressers

Over the history of motion pictures, movie scripts in the comedy and action thriller genres have included cross-dressers, i.e., men dressing as women. Tony Curtis and Jack Lemmon endeared themselves in *Some Like It Hot* (Wilder, 1959). Dustin Hoffman impressed critics in *Tootsie* (Pollack, 1982), and Robin Williams charmed everyone by portraying *Mrs. Doubtfire* (Columbus, 1993).

The Crying Game (Jordan, 1992) surprised audiences by introducing a cross-dressing, transgender character in a serious role. This award-winning thriller explores themes of race, gender, and sexuality. Yet, as viewers reacted and then recovered from the major twist in the movie, they may have chalked it off as "alternative" because of its context instead of giving it serious thought.

Over 20 years later, we again encounter a movie featuring a person who exhibits a gender difference. However, *The Danish Girl* is not a comedy, nor a thriller, but a film based on a true story about gender misidentification and sex reassignment surgery.

The concept of sex reassignment surgery is uncomfortable for some audiences and may be unfamiliar to many. However, Caitlyn Jenner fully exposed the topic to American households in summer 2015. Multiple generations know about Caitlyn; grandparents remember cheering when Bruce Jenner won the gold medal at the 1972 Olympic Decathlon Competition. Parents enjoyed eating Wheaties at the breakfast table, with Bruce Jenner's picture on the cereal box.

Unlike most parents and grandparents, children associate Caitlyn with the Kardashian family and reality TV. However, when the time came for Bruce to become Caitlyn, it was a lot for Americans of all ages to take in. Caitlyn's sincere narrative in *Vanity Fair* opened many minds to the complexities and harsh realities of gender when accompanied by misunderstanding and discrimination. With the article fresh in America's minds, *The Danish Girl* came along at just the right time.

Complexities in Gender Identification

At the moment of conception, each of us acquires unique human characteristics—by God, science, or chance. Regardless of your view, external appearance at birth determines male or female. Yet, a person's sex is as complicated as other human attributes.

Females typically have XX chromosomes and males XY, each with a range of chromosome complements, hormone balances, and other variations that determine sex ("Sex, gender and genetics," 2019). Some variations are common thus have names, for example, XXY/Klinefelter syndrome, XYY/Jacob's syndrome, XXX/triple X syndrome, XO/Turner syndrome (the O denotes the absence of a second sex chromosome), and androgen insensitivity syndrome (AIS).

In the previous article, Pam describes sex and gender differences as a spectrum of characteristics, not the simplified categories we call male and female, gay, and straight. In her words, "To me, this underscores the ignorance and strange attitudes that exist about human particularities amid the wide-ranging spectrum of biological characteristics that make each person unique. To help me conceptualize individual differences, I first consider the possible variations in all human parts."[8]

As an example of complexity in sex and gender differences, consider the case of South African track athlete Caster Semenya. She presented a dilemma when her performances suggested a potentially unfair advantage over other female athletes. Semenya reportedly has testosterone levels above the typical female range. Thus, people have questioned a possible sex misassignment. And, according to Longman (2016) in *The New York Times*,

> The questioning of Semenya's success led to a policy enacted in 2011 by the IAAF,[9] the sport's governing body, that restricted the permitted levels of testosterone, which occur naturally high in some women. That condition is

---

[8] *See* page 155.

[9] The Int'l Amateur Athletic Federation (IAAF) governs track and field sports.

called hyperandrogenism.

An article in *LetsRun* (Johnson, 2019) stated, "She is believed to have internal testes and lack a womb or ovaries," in addition to a high level of testosterone. And, "the problem is, human biology doesn't always neatly divide into male or female. Some people—intersex people—have traits of both sexes."

Longman (2020) questions this account,

> It is not known for certain what, if any, procedures were undergone by Semenya, who won a silver medal at the 2012 London Olympics. Nor could it be verified that Semenya had internal testes and three times the testosterone level of a typical woman.

> Legal proceedings over this controversy concluded in September 2020 when Semenya lost an appeal at the Swiss Supreme Court to be able to compete in the Tokyo Olympics in summer 2021.

Those in book club circles will remember the book *Middlesex* (Eugenides, 2013). The main character has a mixture of male and female traits.

In *The Danish Girl*, Gerda prevails upon her husband, Einar, to be an artist's model. With Einar posing in female clothes and adopting female mannerisms, the model experienced an awakening that led him to transform into Lili.

Caitlin Jenner's Life Change

Caitlyn Jenner described the feelings that propelled her to make the drastic life change. "The uncomfortableness of being me never leaves me all day long. I'm not doing this to be interesting. I'm doing this to live" (Bissinger, 2015).

A gender-misidentified individual's inner turmoil can be unbearable, thus, the willingness to submit to sex reassignment. And it is not only the surgery. Caitlyn Jenner and other transgender individuals have undergone the transition's legal processes: the Social Security Administration, the driver's licensing bureau, changes to passports, credit cards, and other official documents. The bureaucratic paperwork alone should give one considerable pause before a permanent change. Navigating the Social Security office alone would do me in.

When pain reaches intolerable levels, one must address it, hence knee and hip replacements. The same applies to sex reassignment. The inner chaos of gender dysphoria can be that urgent.

Recent Policies Bring New Optimism

Because people are becoming more open about their identities, the transgender community is growing. Transgender individuals are present in every age group, religion, national origin, gender, ability, and sexual orientation. Awareness, understanding, and acceptance of this human uniqueness can help bring needed positive attention.

For example, within the transgender community, people of color suffer from poverty, violence, and incarceration at much higher rates than others do. In addition, LGBTQ individuals often have problems getting needed healthcare and can suffer worse health outcomes.

Medical providers' lack of awareness—partly because of the lack of training—can have severe healthcare consequences. Further, mainstream medical research may be scarce regarding LGBTQ-specific health needs. In 2016, a significant advancement offered healthcare improvement for the transgender community, which GLAAD had reported (2020).

The Department of Health and Human Services issued a rule stating that under the Affordable Care Act of 2010, individuals are protected from discrimination based on gender identity and sex stereotyping in health care settings that have a connection to federal funds, which includes the vast majority of health insurance companies.

Executive action in 2021 has reinstated these equal rights provisions that were rescinded in 2020.

President Biden signed an executive order providing anti-discrimination protections in federal law for the LGBTQ community in areas like housing, health care, and employment. The order also directs agencies to undo harmful regulations from the Trump Administration, such as a rule from the U.S. Department of Health and Human Services that removed anti-discrimination protections in health care for transgender patients. (Burnside, 2021)

May this attention bring renewed optimism to transgender people toward investigating their increasing life options.

Key Terms

Cross-dressing

Cross-dressing means wearing the clothing and accessories associated with the opposite sex. Note that cross-dressing does not necessarily indicate that someone is gay or transgender.

Gender misidentification

Misidentifying a person's gender means assuming incorrectly that their gender identity or expression is the same as their sex assignment at birth.

Hermaphrodite

The term hermaphrodite refers to an animal or plant—not a human—having both male and female characteristics.[10]

Hyperandrogenism

Hyperandrogenemia is a characteristic of women whose steroid hormones, known as androgens, are higher than average. Medications, tumors, growths, or androgen overproduction may be the cause (Chappell & Schutt, 2018).

Intersex

An intersex person is born with male and female sex organs and other related attributes ("What is intersex?," 2008).

Sex reassignment surgery

Sex reassignment surgery (SRS) is a procedure that alters a transgender person's physical appearance and existing sex characteristics to resemble those of their identified gender.

---

[10] Intersex, a disorder of sex development (DSD), is preferred over the term hermaphrodite, deemed inaccurate and derogatory ("What is intersex?," 2008).

SOME FACTS ABOUT THE REAL DANISH GIRLS

Lucy Cota

WE SEE A HIGHLY ENTERTAINING VERSION of the lives of Gerda Marie Fredrikke Gottlieb and Einar Magnus Andreas Wegener presented in the movie, *The Danish Girl* (Hooper, 2015). Both were Danish by birth; they met at art school, married in 1904, and moved to Paris, France to establish themselves as artists. However, during their 26 years of marriage, Einar, born male, discovered his identity as a woman.

With his wife's support, he transitioned officially to Lili Ilse Elvenes (Lili Elbe). Afterward, since he was legally Lili, there was no longer an Einar for Gerda to divorce. In 1930, King Christian X of Denmark annulled the marriage, which was the only way for Lili and Gerda to marry other partners in the future.

Sadly, in 1931, Lili died of medical complications from a uterine transplant, the last in a series of five operations that would complete her transition. Two surgeons at Dr. Magnus Hirschfeld's Institute for Sexual Science had performed the beginning surgeries (of a series of four or five). These procedures were among the earliest attempts at sex reassignment surgery (Schillace, 2021).[11] And, they were still experimental and dangerous even though physicians reportedly had

---

[11] Dora "Dörchen" Richter (1891–1933) was the first person known to undergo complete male-to-female sex reassignment surgery. Erwin Gohrbandt, a surgeon, and Ludwig Levy-Lenz, a gynecologist, performed the male-to-female surgeries in stages, only treating men at the Institute at that time.

performed many incomplete male-to-female surgeries over the years since the institute began in 1919. It would be over 20 years later, in the 1950s, when sex reassignment surgery was successful in Europe.

Before her death, Lili wrote *Man into Woman: An Authentic Record of a Change of Sex* (Hoyer, 1933/2004), a fascinating personal account of her experiences as a transgender woman.[12] It is historically significant as a rare perspective on gender identity differences.

The bittersweet story of Gerda and Lili caught the interest of writer David Ebershoff, who was inspired to write a novel based on Lili's book. Ebershoff's *The Danish Girl* was published in 2000; the movie version was released in theaters 15 years later.

Both Ebershoff's novel and the movie script added dramatic flair for enhanced entertainment. Thus, the movie is intentionally a tenuous line to the original story. We discovered the following differences between the film and the historical accounts from a century ago.

Research Highlights

1. While both were talented artists, Gerda Wegener's work earned more critical acclaim. For example, her paintings won awards at the 1925 World's Fair in Paris.[13]

2. Gerda became a portrait painter and a leading illustrator in high fashion, earning more than Einar from her work. Her other artwork was lesbian erotica.

3. After moving to Paris in 1912, the lifestyle advanced their artistic

---

[12] Dr. Renée Richards, an American ophthalmologist and former highly ranked amateur tennis player, gave credit to the book for inspiring her transformation in the 1970s (Herman, 1976). She was known before as Dr. Richard Raskind.

[13] *See* images of her art at http://www.artnet.com/artists/gerda-wegener/.

careers but reportedly changed their relationship from romantic to platonic. In contrast, the movie depicts sexual passion between the couple. Indeed, that may have been true; some have suggested that Gerda was bisexual.

4. In Paris, Gerda introduced Lili as her sister-in-law. In the movie, she presents Lili as Einar's cousin.

5. Elbe's physicians speculated that Einar Wegener had the Klinefelter syndrome. In this genetic condition, males have an X and a Y chromosome and an extra X. A typical consequence is a tall and thin body with low testosterone.

6. On her transition, Lili took her name from the Elbe River.

After grieving Lili's death, Gerda was briefly remarried, then gradually faded into obscurity. She illustrated Christmas cards and sold them for one Danish Krone apiece (the equivalent of 15 cents at today's rates) to support herself. She died alone in 1940.

Wegener's Paintings and the Fashion Industry

There is conjecture that Gerda Wegener's illustrations of women with androgynous body types contributed to the fashion industry's ideal female body.[14] Images of these fashion models banished the definitive female of the Renaissance forever. Botticelli's *Venus*[15] would now be considered plus-sized.

More than 40 years after her death, Wegener's art resurfaced in Copenhagen's junk stores. Now, there is no shortage of due recognition for her art ("Gerda Wegener," 2021). Today's articles

---

[14] In Chapter 4, Mary writes about Audrey Hepburn, who inspired the body type.

[15] *Birth of Venus*, the painting by Sandro Botticelli, is at the Uffizi Gallery in Florence, Italy. It is among the world's most famous and cherished artworks.

describe her significant contribution to Danish art history. In addition, exhibitions featured her work at the Arken Museum of Modern Art in Copenhagen and the Museum für Kunst und Gewerbe Hamburg (MK&G) in Hamburg.

Key Terms

Klinefelter syndrome

Humans have chromosomes, genetic material, in all body cells. Two chromosome types labeled X and Y determine the genetic sex. The X chromosome is present in everyone; it is not a female chromosome. Klinefelter syndrome is a genetic condition in males with a second X chromosome ("About Klinefelter Syndrome," 2019).

Sexual identity

Sexual identity and sexual behavior relate closely to sexual orientation but are different terms. Sexual or gender identity refers to a person's conception of themselves. In contrast, sexual behavior refers to actual sexual acts performed by the individual. Sexual orientation is romantic or sexual attraction— toward the opposite sex, same-sex, to both or more than one, or no one. Knowing a person's sexual or gender identity should tell us nothing in principle about their sexual behavior.

CHAPTER 9

BEHIND THE CANDELABRA (2013)

This was a fascinating story about a man who was in love with himself far more than he could have been with Scott or anyone else.

—LASTLIBERAL, *IMDb* user review

DIRECTOR	Steven Soderbergh
SCREENPLAY	Richard LaGravenese
CAST	Michael Douglas ~ Liberace Matt Damon ~ Scott Thorson Debbie Reynolds ~ Frances Liberace Rob Lowe ~ Dr. Jack Startz
AWARDS	GOLDEN GLOBES SCREEN ACTORS GUILD AWARDS Best Performance, Actor In A Motion Picture Made For Television: Michael Douglas Best Motion Picture Made For Television PRIMETIME EMMY AWARDS Outstanding Lead Actor: Michael Douglas Outstanding Directing: Steven Soderbergh
RUN TIME	118 min
RATING	TV-MA

SUMMARY

Behind the Candelabra describes a six-year romantic relationship between megastar entertainer Liberace and Scott Thorson, 40 years younger. Thorson's book, written after Liberace's death, was adapted for the movie.

SODERBERGH: ANOTHER HOLLYWOOD STEVEN

Mary Reed

S TEVEN SODERBERGH, THE DIRECTOR OF *Behind the Candelabra* (2013), can boast an impressive resume. He spun out movie-making magic with *Sex, Lies, and Videotape* (1989), *Traffic* (2000), the *Ocean's* series (2001, 2004, 2007, 2018), and *Side Effects* (2013),[1] among others. His movie *Erin Brockovich* (2000) won him a much-deserved Oscar, and *Traffic* won many more. *Behind the Candelabra* was released in the same year as *Side Effects*, but not in movie theaters. Soderbergh had moved away from Hollywood to explore other outlets. As a "Motion Picture Made for Television," this movie won awards in a different category. Yet, after all of his undeniable success in filmmaking, he is still not the best-known Steven in the movie-making business.

Spielberg Inspires Soderbergh

Soderbergh's inspiration came through his heightened exposure to movies from his movie-buff father, coupled with an awe-inspired viewing of *Jaws* (1975)—directed by Steven Spielberg, of course.

Spielberg is possibly the most recognizable name in Hollywood. He has entertained and educated America for decades with his films—*Indiana Jones* (1984), *Jurassic Park* (1993), *Schindler's List* (1993), and *Saving Private Ryan* (1998)—to name a very few.

Spielberg's resume lists one big-grossing blockbuster after another.

---

[1] Movies on Chatham screened *Side Effects* in 2016.

No other director, producer, or writer comes close to duplicating this record in a career that unquestionably goes beyond his wildest dreams. Indeed, he stands alone at the top of the "Ivory Tower of Hollywood,"[2] where he could now rest comfortably on his laurels.

Soderbergh's Calling, a Film on Liberace

Born in 1963 right here in Atlanta, Georgia, Soderbergh is among a generation familiar with America's flamboyant Liberace—an outrageous and exceptionally talented pianist, singer, and actor. Soderbergh had a calling to create a film about Liberace but struggled to frame the story.

When he came across the book written by Liberace's alleged lover, *Behind the Candelabra: My Life with Liberace* (Thorson & Thorleifson, 1990), he knew how he would preserve Liberace on film. However, finding a studio willing to finance a project is challenging for every Hollywood director with good ideas.

Some directors can quickly round up the best among available screenwriters, costume designers, actors, prop designers, etc. But coming up with the money to pay them all is the first order of business. As in many other cases, this was all about return on investment.

The concern was whether mainstream America would open their wallets to watch unsettling scenes of an older man romancing a teenage boy. Producer Jerry Weintraub,[3] another movie-making legend, said this about his attraction to the project:

---

[2] A term originating in the *Bible*, an ivory tower is used to describe a place where people pursue intellectual and esoteric activities, disconnected from practical concerns of everyday life.

[3] Jerry Weintraub died in Santa Barbara, CA in 2015.

What excites me is story and character. The other thing that excites me is working with people like Steven Soderbergh. He and I have a great relationship. Working with Michael Douglas and Matt Damon excited me. Working with Richard LaGravenese's script excited me. Working with Marvin Hamlisch excited me. The people involved are so creative and compelling; I'd be out of my mind not to do it. (HBO, 2013)

Weintraub interested HBO executives with Soderbergh's idea and eventually sealed the deal. For their perceived risky investment in *Behind the Candelabra*, the rewards were abundant—two Golden Globes and three Emmys among a plethora of awards.

Soderbergh Attracts Top Actors to HBO

Soderbergh attracted two big-name actors (Michael Douglas and Matt Damon) whose skills contributed enormously to the movie's success. For a film not destined for the big screen, this must have been a testament to Soderbergh's reputation—or his innovation.

Actors no longer consider the big screen a determining factor of success since streaming services such as Netflix and Amazon Video heavily influence our age. In the future, the same will apply to directors too.

Speaking of the future, according to *IMDb*, Spielberg is not resting on his laurels anytime soon; he has an endless stream of movie projects in the works ("Steven Spielberg," 2021). On the other hand, Soderbergh folded up his director's chair after *Candelabra*, only to unfold it with zeal three or four years later.

Soderbergh has since written a novel on *Twitter* called *Glue* (Kastrenakes, 2013). He experimented with shooting movies using an iPhone and completed two: *Unsane* (2018) and *High Flying Bird* (2019). And he helped to direct a plague. In May 2020, the Directors' Guild of America selected Soderbergh to lead a committee exploring options for movie directors' return to work after the COVID19 pandemic (Curto, 2020).

No Sudden Move (2021) is a recent movie released on HBO Max starring Don Cheadle. Soderbergh will likely continue to break new ground with his movie-making brilliance and creativity, taking filmmaking to unforeseen heights in the future.

PUTTING LIBERACE BACK IN THE SPOTLIGHT

Lucy Cota

IT'S A RARITY WHEN STARDOM ENDURES across multiple generations because, in most cases, as they say, fame is fleeting. Entertainers, musicians, movies, and popular cultural icons are highly susceptible to time. Liberace, for instance. His glorious spotlight faded away a long time ago. Yet, our LGBTQ focus gave the Movies on Chatham group an opportunity to visit the era when Liberace made his mark as a wildly entertaining pianist on TV and in Las Vegas.

Also known as "Mr. Showmanship," Liberace's fame spanned the mid-20th century when he, as a flamboyant performer, was the object of many a celebrity crush. Liberace's shows in Las Vegas were the stuff of legend, and rightly so, according to my husband, who had the good fortune to see one during a business trip. He also recalls when his mother's dressmaker replaced a framed picture of Cary Grant with one of Liberace, who had that special knack of making a woman feel like she was the most special person in the audience—that he was performing solely for her enjoyment.

Soderbergh Preserves Liberace's Fame

But, the opportunity for that experience did not happen for most people today. Recently, I was in a hospital visiting a patient. As a steady stream of nurses and techs entered the room, I asked all of them, each out of the blue, if they had heard of Liberace. Not one could give an affirmative response as facial expressions revealed

186

confusion at that unusual name. Liberace could be slowly but surely dying that third death in which no one speaks of him or remembers his name anymore.

However, there is hope for Liberace's name and fame to linger on for more years through this movie. In creating *Behind the Candelabra* (2013), director Steven Soderbergh made the wise choice to cast Michael Douglas as Liberace and Matt Damon as Scott Thorson. Both are renowned actors with multi-generational appeal and loyal audiences. Ironic that Liberace's protégé, Thorson, whose public story resonated with Soderbergh, may save Liberace from becoming obsolete.

Behind the Candelabra recounts an intimate and volatile six-year relationship between Liberace and Thorson, whose real name is Jess Marlow.[4] Approximately 40 years younger than Liberace, Thorson was 16 years old when their paths crossed. Yes, legally, that might be statutory rape, but the entertainment business is not exactly known for its high moral standards.

How did a boy who spent his childhood bouncing from one foster home to another end up personally involved with a world-famous entertainer? It started with Thorson's knowledge of animal care and a chance visit backstage where Liberace invited the teenager to care for his blind dogs at home.

Bedazzled by Liberace's Glittering Lifestyle

A psychology degree is not required to understand the value of a loving, caring, and consistent family foundation in defending

---

[4] The name change occurred in 1989 when he entered the federal witness protection program for helping prosecute criminal drug dealer Eddie Nash (Segal, 2013).

against being lured away by cults, gangs, and toxic individuals. But, unluckily, Thorson's family background was anything but. Even as his last foster family tried to create a loving home for him, he was a prime target for Liberace to pick up and play with exclusively for the next six years.

Liberace's glittering lifestyle predictably bedazzled Thorson, who fully consented to the twisted sexual/father-son relationship, including a chin implant and a nose job to look more like the entertainer. In 1982, after Thorson had become addicted to drugs and involved with organized crime, Liberace cast him aside. Without this relationship, Thorson fragmented in a tailspin that continued long after, evidenced by his 2014 imprisonment in the Northern Nevada Correctional Center (Associated Press, 2014).[5]

It seems that some who strongly come onto you leave just as strongly, so perhaps it was inevitable that Liberace would drop Thorson to move on to other relationships. However, after being discarded, Thorson did not go quietly. He sued Liberace for palimony, settling in 1986 for $95,000 and giving interviews about their relationship (Segal, 2013). In 1988, one year after Liberace's death, he released his tell-all book.[6]

Entertainment from Liberace Continues

Intensely private about his sexuality, Liberace would have denied all allegations and countered Thorson's claims. Yet, that same book caught Steven Soderbergh's eye and started the ball rolling toward a

---

[5] Sentenced to 8-20 years for failing drug tests while on probation for burglary and identity theft convictions, Marlow is scheduled for release in 2022.

[6] Liberace became infected with the AIDS virus and died at his home in Palm Springs, CA in Feb 1987. He was 67.

movie that sheds light on Liberace's private life. Thus keeping him in his favorite position—in the spotlight—more than 25 years after his death.

But, back to those nurses I mentioned earlier who had never heard of Liberace. Of course, he belongs to a time long past, yet Michael Douglas' performance should give them a reason to search for the real Liberace on *YouTube*. For the essence of the man, they would best start with his Christmas special from 1954.

Key Terms

Palimony

Palimony is compensation paid to a former partner in a romantic relationship, even though they lived together without a marriage contract.

CHAPTER 10

THE BIRDCAGE (1996)

What makes the film interesting is that [Robin Williams] must play against type, toning down his manic persona in the face of Lane's hilarious over-the-top turn. —CHUCK KOPLINSKI, *The News-Gazette*

DIRECTOR	Mike Nichols
SCREENPLAY	Elaine May Earlier: Francis Veber, Édouard Molinaro, Marcello Danon, Jean Poiret
CAST	Nathan Lane ~ Albert Goldman Robin Williams ~ Armand Goldman Gene Hackman ~ Sen. Kevin Keeley Diane Wiest ~ Louise Keeley
AWARDS	SCREEN ACTORS GUILD AWARDS
	Outstanding Performance by a Cast
	AMERICAN COMEDY AWARDS
	Funniest Actor in a Motion Picture (Leading Role): Nathan Lane Funniest Supporting Actress in a Motion Picture: Dianne Wiest
RUN TIME	117 min
RATING	R

SUMMARY

A gay couple—a cabaret owner and his "drag queen" partner—present themselves as straight when their son introduces them to his fiancé's moralistic parents.

LOOKING FOR A RAINBOW CONNECTION

Pam Hassebroek

You do an eclectic celebration of the dance! You do Fosse, Fosse, Fosse!
You do Martha Graham, Martha Graham, Martha Graham! Or,
Twyla, Twyla, Twyla! Or, Michael Kidd, Michael Kidd, Michael
Kidd! Or, Madonna, Madonna, Madonna! But you keep it all inside.
                                    —ARMAND, *The Birdcage*

BECAUSE OF THE COMEDIC PRESENTATION, storyline and celebrated cast in *The Birdcage* (Nichols, 1996), a popular means of communication can help change beliefs about LGBTQ individuals. In our investigation of LBGTQ-themed movies in Part II, we have noted the evolution in societal attitudes and public policies related to LGBTQ communities in the last century. Over time, films have increasingly exposed more realistic and diverse depictions, and *The Birdcage* is a striking example of that.

Today more Americans recognize and welcome greater diversity among fellow humans than they did during the early film days. Still, it's not easy to adjust to a new idea or perspective that is different from customary thought.[1] Moreover, it is incredibly thorny when a new finding challenges rock-solid beliefs about "other" people. In recent times, shining a spotlight on LGBTQ communities has been

---

[1] Remember that during the 17th-century Roman Inquisition, the Catholic Church persecuted Galileo for expressing support for Copernicus' 1543 theory that the Earth orbited the Sun.

unsettling for some because of deep-rooted ideas and opinions about sexual orientation and gender identity.

This movie created enormous controversy at the time of its release. It also led to some differences of opinion within our group when we watched it. Thus, I end the book with a qualification about our group discussion.

The Movies on Chatham group has not met for over a year because of the threat of COVID19 virus contagion. During this break, we all have had a chance to ponder the nature and impact of people's differing perspectives about the full range of gender-related issues—gender, sexual orientation, and gender identities.

And we have learned more, which may or may not harmonize the notions and beliefs that we found conflicting when we last met together. Therefore, our next book will begin with our collective reflection on this topic. Even though we have identified obstacles to change that may remain with us, I am optimistic that we can re-engage respectfully on this topic. I believe in rainbows.

When well-established social norms and associated societal and political systems have created foundational mindsets, they are firmly resistant to change. For example, when we think about sex and gender, I expect that most people have unwaveringly associated males and females in concert with behaviors and rules. Because no alternative way of thinking existed in the mainstream, these associations became solidly entrenched. The book *Paradoxes of Gender* (Lorber, 1994) offers an example of how our social construct of gender relates to our social practices.

> In our society, in addition to man and woman, the status can be transvestite (a person who dresses in opposite-gender clothes) and transsexual (a person who has had sex-

MOVIES ON CHATHAM PRESENTS

change surgery).[2] Transvestites and transsexuals carefully construct their gender status by dressing, speaking, walking, gesturing in ways prescribed for women or men, whichever they want to be taken for—and so does any 'normal' person.

The Birdcage (1996) features a "drag queen" and his life partner. Let's see how their story might change beliefs.

About *The Birdcage*

The American film *The Birdcage* (1996) began as the French comedy *La Cage aux Folles* (*The Cage of Madwomen*), a play written by Jean Poiret and first performed in Paris in 1973. Poiret's stage play became a movie (Molinaro, 1978) that won the Golden Globe award for Best Motion Picture–Foreign Language in 1979.[3]

Later, the French film became a Broadway musical, *La Cage aux Folles*, opening on August 21, 1983 ("*La Cage aux Folles*," 2020). It won the 1984 Tony Award for Best Musical, Book, and Score.

The 1996 English-language movie version, *The Birdcage*, was even more successful because Mike Nichols directed it. And because Nichols cast Robin Williams and Nathan Lane for its two leading roles. Williams plays Armand, owner of the Miami Beach drag nightclub called "The Birdcage," and Lane plays Albert, his drag queen partner.

Their straight son Val (Dan Futterman), from Armand's past one-

---

[2] Transvestite and transsexual are outdated terms. "Transgender person" and "transgender individual" are preferred terms respectively.

[3] The original French play ran for 1800 performances (1973–1978), at the Theatre du Palais-Royal in Paris, France. The movie ran for over a year at the 68th Street Playhouse Cinema in New York and at theaters across the U.S.

194

night heterosexual experience, is engaged to Barbara (Calista Flockhart), a woman from a family with conservative beliefs. This knowledge about her background inspires the couple's conspiracy as they plan their first meeting. Gene Hackman and Diane Wiest play Barbara's parents. *The Bird Cage* "opened at No. 1 at the box office and stayed there for four weeks. Ultimately, it grossed $185 million, about six times what it cost to make" (Peterson, 2017).

Using Comedy to Communicate

Apart from its robust financial success, the movie also took on a complicated topic and made it approachable for a broad audience by using comedy. Because of its light-hearted humor, it was a gentler yet more effective way to broach the topic of romantic relationships within LGBTQ communities than by other methods. Unfortunately, however, some were not paying attention, and others were intentionally tuning out.

I remember being in New York with a friend in the mid-'80s and discussing Broadway shows we might see while visiting there. Since I was not keeping up with current headliners, I didn't ask about the reasons for her preferences at the time. However, I clearly remember her stating that she would attend any shows except *La Cage aux Folles* because it was "about gays." Looking back, I regret that we unquestionably missed an outstanding performance.

Like all of the various script enactments before it, this movie required comedians in the cast, i.e., actors who can entertain audiences by making them laugh. So how do they do this?

We learned from our Movies on Chatham comedy series that they do this in a number of different ways, using social satire and slapstick, among others. Could playwrights and screenwriters so totally focus on what seems funny that the result is irresponsibly

195

mean? Chapter 6 discusses the dark side of comedy that makes fun of vulnerable people—the kind of humor that bullies people considered societal misfits.

Theorists from long ago, "Hobbes and Plato took the playground perspective, suggesting that making fun helps us feel superior to others. Kant, and later psychologists, thought it was about a cognitive shift that moves a serious situation into playful territory" (Khazan, 2014). Yet, for historically marginalized groups like women, people of color, gay men, and transgender individuals, comedy has incorporated stereotypical characters and roles that helped maintain their lesser social status.

Then again, screenwriters can use comedy to dispel prejudice against certain groups or specific human characteristics. But, of course, we now understand that any societal misfit is a socially constructed concept. It is not biological but practiced through observing, communicating, and learning from others.

Does *The Birdcage* show gay men in an unflattering light? Are the individuals presented as the "other"—not fitting the image of "real" men? Is the depiction of Armand and Albert's relationship or their cultural setting funny? Or is the humor confined to the movie's narrative? Finally, what impact does this movie have on those who struggle with their sexual orientations?

Alternative Personas Created for Celebrities

Dirk Shafer,[4] a man who self-identified as gay, posed nude as a *Playgirl* model in earlier decades and wrote about his experiences. Posing as a sex object for straight women, he had to present himself

---

[4] Shafer died in 2015 at age 52, from a combination of recreational drug use and cardiovascular disease.

as straight to keep his job (Stack, 2015).

Shafer produced his life story on film after *Playgirl Magazine* voted him "Man of the Year" in 1992. The movie is a comedy that shows the stress of being a gay man in a heterosexual world. Titled *Man of the Year* (1995), the film was a public coming-out for Shafer. Predictably, his nude modeling career declined after the publication. In a *New York Times* review (1996), Holden wrote this about the movie:

> On a deeper level, *Man of the Year* treats Mr. Shafer's modeling experience as a metaphor for the way society pressures gay people to act straight. After watching Mr. Shafer wriggle uncomfortably inside the role he has agreed to play, it comes as a relief when he finally abandons it.

After the demise of the studio system, people discovered that several film stars had hidden their sexual orientations to keep their jobs: Rock Hudson, Montgomery Clift, and others (Petersen, 2014). Although, did anyone really consider the sexual aspect of Liberace's life at all when he was at the peak of his career?

However, Liberace's life, as depicted in *Behind the Candelabra*, discussed in Chapter 9, is not a model for good relationships. It is difficult to compare the relationship between Liberace and a starry-eyed, drug-addicted groupie teenager with any other couple, gay or straight, in a committed healthy union. That relationship appears more like a view of same-sex couples as human psychopathology, but who knows?

For a long time, mental health professionals alleged that committed same-sex relationships were inferior to heterosexual unions regarding psychological health. In 2008, results from two studies compared gay male and lesbian couples with both committed (engaged and married) and noncommitted (exclusively dating) heterosexual couples (Roisman, Clausell, Holland, Fortuna, & Elieff, 2008). Otherwise comparable in skin color/ethnicity and age, the individuals in committed same-sex relationships were generally no different from their devoted heterosexual counterparts, for better or for worse.

Longing for Pure and Genderless Love

Examining relationships in such an analytical way bypasses the essential power that most people long to seek openly and acceptably—to love and be loved. An article in *The New York Times* (Als, 2019) discusses the heartrending struggle of gay Black writer James Baldwin as revealed through his novel, *Giovanni's Room* (1956).

> Baldwin's deepest longings as a gay man, to be cherished and held, and to be seen and not seen, all at the same time.

> Toward the idea that love may come attached with different ideas of what it should look like, feel like, but in the end, it's what you do with its responsibilities that renders you genderless—and human.

Giovanni's Room also revealed Baldwin's horror at what he learned about himself after traveling to Paris. "He hates himself, this searing prototype of the self-loathing queer person, yet no matter how he tries, he cannot escape from that simplest and most difficult of pursuers: his own desire" (Bellott, 2019).

> David's[5] self-lacerating tone is close, for example, to that of Oscar Wilde in 'De Profundis,' as Wilde, in prison, is trying

---

[5] David is the narrator in Baldwin's book.

to reconstruct what happened to him and his lover, what illusions, self-delusions, and failures of imagination were in place to wreak such havoc in their lives. Just as Wilde will compare himself to Christ in his suffering, David in *Giovanni's Room* will say, 'Judas and the Savior had met in me.' (Tóibín, 2016)

The Birdcage is not a sensationalist or disparaging view of societal outcasts. It is a personal experience of the lives and problems of two men in a committed relationship. Similarly, we can experience the lives of a President and First Lady through the Netflix series *House of Cards*. I pondered the term "virtual reality" to describe a film's immersive environment that transports an audience into the scene to experience the action firsthand. This exceptional movie experience should bring us all closer together.

Sesame Street's Kermit the Frog tried to teach us about diversity when he struggled with rejection because of his green skin color. He wondered out loud about the value of searching in the skies to help relieve his sadness—with enduring hope for a rainbow connection.[6]

Key Terms

Comedian

A comedian is a person who entertains by making audiences laugh. This might be through jokes or amusing situations, using prop comedy, acting a fool in slapstick.

---

[6] "Rainbow Connection" is the title of a song from *The Muppet Movie* (Frawley, 1979). Writers Williams and Ascher received an Academy Award nomination for Best Original Song at the 52nd Academy Awards.

Drag queen

A drag queen is a male performer who puts on traditional female appearance and attire for entertainment.

Homophobia

Homophobia is an irrational fear or disapproval of gay and lesbian people and their culture.

Misogyny

Misogyny is the extreme dislike of women as a sex and gender-defined human group.

Social satire

Social satire uses humor, irony, exaggeration, or ridicule in a text to expose and criticize social groups, often exploiting contemporary politics, customs, and popular trends.

Transsexual

Transsexual, an outdated and sometimes offensive term, has been used in the medical community to denote trans individuals who opt to "change their sex."

Transvestite

Transvestite is no longer an acceptable term unless someone self-identifies that way explicitly.

Virtual reality

Virtual reality is a simulated environment created using software. While employing a VR system, users can suspend belief and accept it as an actual environment.

APPENDIX

FILM HISTORY AND PUBLIC POLICIES CORRESPOND

Pam Hassebroek

W E REFER TO RELEVANT LAWS and policies in various places throughout this book, typically when describing a movie's historical context. These regulative codes pertain to freedom of speech, antitrust, psychiatric medicine, and human and civil rights. To minimize repetition in the chapters, the text below presents a brief overview of the policies. The table at the end lists them chronologically.

Over the history of film in America, the UK, and Europe, popular beliefs and concerns have prompted regulation and legislative actions that influenced the movie industry. And, generally, U.S. public policies have matched overall public sentiment.

As is the case now, motion pictures profoundly affected America's communication at the start of the industry. The revolutionary media industry worried many people because it threatened public values and the status quo. As Vaughn (1990) describes,

> By speaking to mass audiences directly, movies all too easily bypassed traditional agencies of socialization—the church, the school, the family. Fierce debates over the content and control of this new medium arose in the early days of silent film and intensified with the advent of sound.

The nation protested the industry's publicly viewable content—particularly sex-related concerns. Overall, people found erotic movies and gay portrayals offensive. Yet, if filmmakers thought anyone was interested in it, they produced it. "Directors such as Josef von Sternberg worked with Marlene Dietrich to create provocative explorations of sexuality and power. 1930s' *Morocco* even featured the first lesbian kiss in sound cinema" ("TV Tropes," 2020).

There were no real limits on any content until the 1930s, but this was not without government action long before that.

Nationwide Censorship

Setting up the possibility for federal censorship, in 1915, the U.S. Supreme Court decided in Mutual Film Corporation *v.* Industrial Commission of Ohio that movies didn't merit free speech protection. That ruling meant that filmmakers were no longer free to create and market just any film content they thought they could sell. The Court's unanimous decision came about by first rejecting film as a news broadcast medium. We are now over 100 years past that landmark event.

The U.S. has recently passed a similar milestone in celebrating the 19th Amendment. That landmark event in 1920 granted American women the right to vote. The Congressional vote, all-male, of course, changed the country powerfully. Then, just on the heels of that event, another happening was instrumental in changing the public's perception of movies and American life for the next 40 years.

In 1922, the Hollywood movie studios established an association of enterprises, the Motion Picture Producers and Distributors of America (MPPDA). The studios' strategy in doing this was to attend to their shared interests, but it was also to guarantee the industry's survival in the face of public concern. Initial member studios were Paramount (1912), Universal (1912), and United Artists (1919–

1982). Joining later were Warner Bros (1923), Walt Disney (1923), Metro-Goldwyn-Mayer (1924–1986), Columbia (1924), RKO Pictures (1928–1960), Twentieth Century-Fox (1935), and others.

After years of raging public complaints about movies' offensive content and fearing federal censorship, in 1930, the MPPDA produced the Motion Picture Production Code (the Hays Code[1]). The Hays Code then became the association's official guidelines for restricting film content during the Golden Age. The MPPDA began enforcing the Code in 1934, with compliance required for films released by the studios from 1930 to 1968.

No Indecent Material or Obscene Language

For the duration of the Hays Code, Hollywood studios produced movies, one after another, in what became a stereotypical movie format. No offensive language, sleazy topics, or evil characters that weren't "done in" or reformed by the end of the story.

Yet, Rhett Butler's disrespectful word in *Gone with the Wind* (Fleming, 1939) remained in the film, first because Margaret Mitchell wrote it in the original novel. It was likely less offensive in 1939 than it would have been later because censorship was relatively new. Profanity in movies then stayed off-limits until 1952, when the First Amendment protection status changed.

Under the Hays Code guidelines, women typically played subservient roles. They were all expendable, victims mostly powerless to protect themselves against abuses and unable to manage almost any circumstance without the help of a man. Women's roles covered the demographic and ethical range—rich and poor, bad and good. Still,

---

[1] William Harrison Hays Sr. was chair of the MPPDA from 1922–1945 and the source for the popular name of the policy.

a power position required inheritance or another back door. If in power, their skin color was always white, not black, brown, or any other. Most Black actors played servant roles, and openly gay characters didn't make it to the screen at all.

Marriage had to be shown as sacred—yet no depiction was allowed of, or reference to, any sexual behavior, gay or straight, that would come after marriage. Movies could express neither pregnancy nor childbirth. The word "virgin" was censored. Scripts couldn't discuss or depict miscegenation (interracial relationships). And needless to say, the Code banned nudity.

Shortly after enacting the Hays Code guidelines, a parallel landmark event came in 1934. Under U.S. President Franklin D. Roosevelt, Congress passed the Communications Act, which established the Federal Communications Commission (FCC) to manage broadcast (radio) communications. Reflecting an enduring public sentiment regarding content, the FCC, then as now, prohibits indecent or obscene language. Today, the agency's regulatory oversight includes television, wire, satellite, cable communications, and, in addition to radio, licensing of all wireless services.

Vertical Integration Key to Audience Ratings

The FCC had the power of the federal government to enable enforcement. The Production Code Administration (PCA), the group enforcing the movie censorship rules, had power because of the studio system's vertical integration. MGM, RKO studios, Paramount, Twentieth Century-Fox, and Warner Brothers owned theater chains, thus controlling people's movie choices.

Their ownership guaranteed that 1) the movie theaters would show the film, and 2) the theaters would rent their screens to them at a discount. Along with production efficiencies, these circumstances kept ticket prices low for moviegoers (Postrel, 2019). The system also made it possible to enforce the Hays Code and maintain the G (general audience) rating for all movies.

In 1948, the Supreme Court's landmark antitrust[2] decision required the studios to abandon theater ownership, which severed their control over the content. However, this decision (in U.S. *v.* Paramount Pictures, Inc.) improved the prospects for independent theaters and international films. Because of the decision, filmmakers independent of the studios, and those who worked internationally, gained the chance to compete and tell stories that appealed to diverse audiences.

The history of antitrust goes back to 1890 when Congress

> passed the Sherman Antitrust Act, which made it illegal to monopolize or engage in practices that restrain trade. The Clayton Antitrust Act, adopted by Congress in 1914, made it illegal to engage in price-fixing or discrimination, to bring about mergers of businesses or corporations that reduce competition, or to allow directors of one corporation to sit on the board of another. (Schultz, 2009)

In U.S. *v.* Paramount Pictures, sometimes called the "Paramount Consent Decrees," the Court ruled that the movie studios had violated the law. The major studios had established an efficient production, distribution, and exhibition system. Yet, this system prevented competition in exhibiting movies in theaters.

---

[2] Antitrust laws are designed to protect and promote competition in a free market, preventing abuse by monopolies or trusts. A trust is formed by companies joining together to eliminate competitors.

U.S. Supreme Court Reverses Rulings

The Paramount Decrees regulated movie theater distribution for over 70 years until 2019, when the U.S. Supreme Court reversed the ruling.

> The Division has concluded that these decrees have served their purpose, and their continued existence may actually harm American consumers by standing in the way of innovative business models for the exhibition of America's great creative films. (U.S. Department of Justice)

We noted a similar reversal in 1952 when the Supreme Court rejected its former decision that denied movies First Amendment protection. This change came with the Court's decision in Burstyn, Inc. *v.* Wilson, which overturned the 1915 ruling in Mutual Film Corporation *v.* Industrial Commission of Ohio and ended movie censorship. Alongside, it struck down a New York state law that required government permission to show films.

> Film censorship statutes that came and went between 1907 and 1981 in seven states, and dozens of municipalities, were based on prior restraint—that is, they required that movies be examined before they could be shown. Licenses were denied to movies found obscene, sacrilegious, indecent, inhuman, immoral, or likely to incite criminal activity. (Wittern-Keller, 2009)

In the 1952 Burstyn case, a New York distributor had lost his license to show *The Ways of Love* (Rossellini, 1950). The film was judged sacrilegious and banned even after the New York Film Critics Circle had voted it the best foreign-language film of 1950. The Supreme Court ruled that motion pictures "were a significant medium for communicating ideas," therefore, censorship defied the First

Amendment (Green, 2009).

Then in 1965, with the Supreme Court's decision in the Freedman *v.* Maryland case, the MPAA[3] lost its ability to censor any film. The MPAA abolished the Hays Code and replaced it in 1968 with a voluntary rating system much like today's guidelines.

In the mid-1960s, the 16–24 age group accounted for a sizeable percentage of box office tickets. Because of this and the competition from TV, the industry began producing movies with greater freedom in subject matter to appeal to a younger market. By 1993, two-thirds of Hollywood films were R-rated (Greenberg, Siemicki, Dorfman, Heeter, Lin, & Stanley, 1993).

Unfortunately, freedom of expression means pornography still represents a portion of the movie industry. Its victims include those addicted to it and may become more violent because of it. Still, more importantly, victims include children, those who are trafficked, who are predominantly women and children. First Amendment protection for movies is problematic for those who want to limit pornography to protect these victims. Like many public issues, dealing with uncensored movie content is complicated, much more so than described briefly here. One complication is that, given both the artistic and scientific value of some depictions of human bodies, pornography is difficult to define.

A more precise definition of pornographic materials was sought in the case of Miller *v.* California in 1973, one that could stop its transmission. The decision in the case generally restated earlier laws

---

[3] The MPPDA had become the MPAA in 1945. In 2019, to recognize its global presence, the MPAA officially changed its name to the Motion Picture Association (MPA).

on obscene material, but its added description can help in local situations. In its ruling, the Court stated that "if the work, taken as a whole, lacks serious literary, artistic, political, or scientific value," it has no free speech protection.

However, in the Internet context especially, it is still challenging to apply obscenity laws and enforce them. Luzwick (2017) argues that "prosecutors should use the sex trafficking provision of the TVPA [Trafficking Victims Protection Act of 2000], 18 U.S.C. § 1591, to prosecute sex trafficking within the pornography industry."

On the other hand, because of the policy changes in the latter half of the 20th century, sexuality is no longer hidden from view in legitimate movie productions. Now we can learn about and acknowledge the spectrum of characteristics that accompanies this vital aspect of human existence, which was once limited to understanding conventional heterosexual reproduction.

Psychiatrists Define Human and Civil Rights

Because of limited knowledge and other more pressing concerns, no classification standard for sexuality and gender existed before the Civil War (Eskridge, 1999). Thus, no U.S. laws restricted the human or civil rights of gay people. Then from post-Civil War to the 1980s, U.S. states enacted laws to punish people considered "sexually deviant." The medical community led the way in establishing public policies by identifying certain human features and activities and judging them as undesirable.

In 1952, the American Psychiatric Association's classification of mental disorders (DSM-I) placed homosexuality under the heading of "sexual deviations," calling the same-sex sexual orientation a "sociopathic personality disturbance."

In 1954, a psychiatrist's book, Seduction of the Innocent (Wertham), claimed comic books' depiction of violence potentially influences juvenile delinquency. After its publication, the Comics Code Authority (CCA) came into being.

In *DSM-II*, in 1968, homosexuality remained classified as "sexual deviation." Same-sex attraction would stay a mental illness for another 20 years after that.

> In *DSM-I*, homosexuality was classified with the sexual deviation disorders in the section on sociopathic personality disturbance, with retention of this diagnosis in *DSM-II*. In subsequent printings of the *DSM-II* beginning in 1973, the diagnosis of homosexuality was replaced with "sexual orientation disturbance." The only reference to homosexuality in the *DSM-III* diagnostic criteria in 1980 was "ego-dystonic homosexuality," and by 1987, homosexuality was completely removed from the *DSM-III-R* diagnostic criteria. (Suris, Holliday, & North, 2015)

"APA's [American Psychiatric Association's] 1973 diagnostic revision was the beginning of the end of organized medicine's official participation in the social stigmatization of homosexuality" (Drescher, 2015). As of the *DSM-III* (1980), same-sex attraction is no longer viewed as a mental disturbance; this revision also introduces the diagnosis of "transsexualism" for diagnosing transgender individuals. In *DSM–IV* (1994), attempting to reduce stigma, "gender identity disorder" (GID) replaced "transsexualism."

Maybe the positive gender-related changes in medical practice were reasons for the Central Conference of American Rabbis to allow religious ceremonies for same-sex couples beginning in 2000. Also in 2000, Vermont became the first state to pass a law to grant full benefits of marriage to same-sex couples.

Amazing that those changes came right after the 1996 Defense of Marriage Act (DOMA), which was passed by the 104th Congress and signed into law by President Clinton. This law had defined marriage as the union of one man and one woman. It allowed states to refuse to recognize same-sex marriages granted under the laws of other states. In 2003, Massachusetts became the first state to legalize gay marriage; then Connecticut followed in 2005.

The *DSM-5* (2012) removed "gender identity disorder" and introduced "gender dysphoria" to disassociate from the concept of a disorder and feature the emotional distress from a gender identity difference. "The *DSM-5* defines gender dysphoria in adolescents and adults as a marked incongruence between one's experienced/expressed gender and their assigned gender."

In 2014, the Presbyterian Church (USA) voted to allow same-sex marriages, making it one of the largest Christian denominations in the world to accept same-sex unions openly.

In Obergefell *v.* Hodges (2015), 576 U.S. 644, the Supreme Court ruled that the right to marry is guaranteed to same-sex couples.

U.S. Supreme Court Reaffirms Civil Rights for All

Amid the celebrations of progress in civil and human rights, challenges to certain business practices emerged around three LGBTQ discrimination cases. In Bostock *v.* Clayton County (2020), the Supreme Court upheld Title VII of the Civil Rights Act of 1964. The 1964 law had banned discrimination based on race, color, religion, sex, or national origin. The Court ruling in 2020 stated that discrimination based on sexual orientation or gender identity is also discrimination "because of sex," as prohibited by Title VII.

In each of the three cases, an employer fired a long-time employee solely because of being a gay or transgender person. The ruling is hailed as one of the most important legal decisions regarding LGBTQ rights in U.S. history, a significant victory for human beings and civil liberties (Foreman, 2020).

Consequently, under the law, the daily decisions of Georgia employers must honor all individuals' rights to life, liberty, and the pursuit of happiness, the "unalienable rights" given to human beings by their Creator. Our Declaration of Independence says that we created our government to protect those rights.

I am confident that the writers of the Civil Rights Act of 1964 thought they had considered all possible ways in which employers unjustly discriminate on the basis of sex. Still, maybe now they must spell out all possible connotations and permutations of the other categories too. With cynicism, one might wonder if they considered the case of a capable and honorable employee who has skin that is colored green.

YEAR	CODE
1871	Germany's Paragraph 175 outlaws sexual relations between men.
1885	Britain's Criminal Law Amendment Act—The 11th Amendment created the offense of gross indecency between men. This law covered same-sex acts not involving intercourse.
1914	Hirschfeld's research shows that same-sex attraction occurs in every culture. He advocates the repeal of Germany's anti-gay laws.
1915	Mutual Film Corporation v. Industrial Commission of Ohio, 236 U.S. 230—No free speech protection for movies.
1919	The Weimar Constitution establishes free speech and prohibits censorship in Germany.
1920	The 19th Amendment grants U.S. women the right to vote.
1922	The Motion Picture Producers and Distributors of America (MPPDA) is founded to support the American film industry.
1930	The Motion Picture Production Code (aka Hays Code) restricts images, language, and stories in Hollywood movies.

1934	Communications Act of 1934, 47 USC 151 abolishes the Federal Radio Commission (FRC) and transfers authority to the FCC. The FCC restricts obscene, indecent, or profane language on radio broadcasts. American radio's Golden Age roughly corresponds with Hollywood's studio system—1920s to 1950s.
1948	FCC rules for broadcast, Title 47 CFR, Part 1—18 U.S. C. 1464 restricts obscene, indecent, or profane language on radio and TV.
1948	United States vs. Paramount Pictures, Inc., 334 U.S. 131—Ruled an anti-trust violation, movie studios can't own movie theaters.
1952	The American Psychiatric Association's classification of mental disorders (DSM-I) defines homosexuality as a "sociopathic personality disturbance."
1952	Burstyn, Inc. v. Wilson, 343 U.S. 495—Movies gained protection under the First Amendment's free speech and free press provisions.
1954	Comics Code Authority (CCA): The Comics Magazine Association of America formed CCA to avoid government regulation. Senate hearings and Dr. Wertham's book Seduction of the Innocent (1954) sought to ban images of violence and gore in crime and horror comics.
1961	The Production Code adds an amendment allowing a conservative portrayal of same-sex attraction.
1964	Title VII of the Civil Rights Act, 42 USC. 2000e: Prohibits discrimination by employers based on race, color, religion, sex, or national origin.
1965	Freedman v. Maryland, 380 U.S. 51: Ended the state of Maryland's 1916 motion picture censorship, taking away government rating boards' power to ban a film.
1968	After years of lax enforcement, MPAA's rating system replaces the Hays Code. Then, movies are rated X for extreme violence, strongly implied sex, and graphic language.
1969	Riots erupt at the Stonewall Inn in New York City as police raid the bar to arrest gay couples.
1972	Title IX of the Education Amendments Act, 20 U.S.C. §1681 et seq: Bans discrimination in educational programs based on sex.
1973	In DSM-III, the diagnosis of homosexuality as a sexual deviation disorder is replaced with "sexual orientation disturbance."
1973	Miller v. California, 413 U.S. 15, 24—upholds Supreme Court's decisions that obscenity has no 1st Amendment protection in movies unless merited by literary, artistic, political, or scientific value.

1981	The AIDS epidemic begins. The CDC publishes the current designation, "acquired immune deficiency syndrome." The AIDS illness first spread among the gay community.
1987	DSM-III-R no longer includes the term homosexuality. "Gender identity disorder" (GID) replaces "transsexualism" for transgender individuals.
1994	Campbell v. Acuff-Rose Music, Inc., 510 U.S. 569: A commercial parody can qualify as fair use.
1996	The Defense of Marriage Act (DOMA) defines marriage as between a man and a woman.
2000	The Central Conference of American Rabbis allows religious ceremonies for same-sex couples.
2003	Massachusetts is the first state to legalize gay marriage.
2012	In DSM-5, the American Psychiatric Association replaces "gender identity disorder" with "gender dysphoria" to describe the "emotional distress over 'a marked incongruence between one's experienced/expressed gender and assigned gender.'"
2013	U.S. v. Windsor, 570 U.S. 744: Supreme Court finds Sec 3 of DOMA unconstitutional in denying federal recognition of same-sex marriages.
2014	The Presbyterian Church (USA) votes to allow same-sex marriages during its 221st General Assembly, making it one of the largest Christian denominations in the world to accept same-sex unions openly.
2015	Obergefell v. Hodges, 576 U.S. 644 guarantees same-sex couples the right to marry.
2016	North Carolina House Bill 2 bans transgender people from using public bathrooms if the gender on the bathroom door does not match the gender on their birth certificates.
2019	U.S. Justice Department files a motion to terminate the so-called "Paramount decrees" that regulated the movie industry for over 70 years. Once again, movie studios can own movie theaters.
2020	Bostock v. Clayton County, No. 17–1618 590 U.S. ___ prohibits workplace discrimination based on sexual orientation or gender identity.

ABOUT THE
MOVIES ON CHATHAM GROUP

Mary Reed

U NDERSTANDING THAT IT IS PRIMARILY an inactive and silent activity, still, movie-watching has a fulfilling way of drawing families and friends together. It seems that the most memorable films in life remain there because of who you were with when you watched them. Possibly at a time when you could laugh, cry, scream, or roll your eyes simultaneously.

Or, maybe it was when you felt an arm extend around the back of your theater seat, that arm belonging to a new exciting love interest. Can you picture the theater, the weather outside, what you were wearing, and of course, the name of the movie?

Sometimes, we can enter those rarefied spaces in our fantasy lives because a movie provides a vicarious emotional experience. This emotionality is why we believe movies are so wonder-filled.

Our Movies on Chatham investigation began in 2010 when Pam Hassebroek invited some friends over to watch a movie with her.[1] Long before then, she had pondered the media's influence on young people, noting the increasing realism of violence and crime in film and TV. An exploration seemed like a worthwhile effort with its growing presence online, in real-life news stories, and on TV during primetime. In addition, she knew she could learn more from a

---

[1] *The International* (Tykwer, 2009) was the first movie the group watched. Who could resist Clive Owen and Naomi Watts on a global chase to pursue corporate criminals?

focused study that involved discussion with others. Yet, she had no idea whether anyone else would be interested in attending regular sessions to do this.

Since then, the gathering has developed into a faithful and vibrant group. Sadly, a few valued members have moved away or turned their attention to their own or a family member's health problems. Despite their departures, the group has remained stable at 12–14 women. We always have food and drink, and Jerry Hassebroek's guacamole is a favorite item.[2] A set of informal guidelines has kept it functioning for an entire decade.

To manage our movie choices, we first identify a topic or theme. We then turn to the arduous task of selecting only four or five movies that embody that theme. In that process, we search for relevant films, particularly those considered significant in film history; we look for quality, identifying films with positive critical and popular reception. As the last and most essential filter, we choose movies we believe our group will enjoy.

By design, the group represents women from various backgrounds, which sometimes brings very different perspectives to after-screening discussions. Moreover, not one group member can be considered a "token" of any particular demographic. We include only women in the group to eliminate potential restraint during discourse in men's presence.[3]

---

[2] We include his recipe on page 221 to add to the enjoyment of your group's experience.

[3] Including only women allows control for sex, one of many potential demographic variables in an audience reception study. However, many other factors can affect an audience member's reading of a film, e.g., age, beliefs, culture, life experience, state of mind.

We also try to inhibit preconceived bias that could, consciously or otherwise, either enhance or discredit opinions expressed by other women in the group. For this reason, we don't formally introduce anyone, nor do we provide opportunities for individuals to present their histories to the group as a whole. Instead, new people introduce themselves informally. And this is not to say that members haven't learned more about each other during evenings together. Still, we don't emphasize identities or pedigrees.

To support and reinforce the idea of open discussion, we established our own *Chatham House rule* a few years ago to eliminate or reduce potential privacy concerns. We considered that women not wishing to be quoted outside the group might hold back on details when revealing their opinions or disclosures.

The British Chatham House aims to foster mutual understanding through debate, dialogue, and independent analysis ("Chatham House," 2021). Our group's design attempts to cultivate these same methods toward our shared knowledge of film. Movies on Chatham's rule is identical to that posted on the official Chatham House website.

OUR CHATHAM HOUSE RULE

When a meeting, or part thereof, is held under the Chatham House Rule, participants are free to use the information received, but neither the identity nor the affiliation of the speaker(s), nor that of any other participant, may be revealed.

—CHATHAM HOUSE, The Royal Institute of International Affairs

To explore the film world further, Movies on Chatham has now ventured beyond its movie room. Members have traveled near and far: to attend meetings and workshops, e.g., those presented by WIFTA (Women in Film and Television Atlanta); to SCAD

(Savannah College of Art and Design) Atlanta for a look at amazing costumes from memorable films; to attend film festivals in Atlanta and Crested Butte, CO; and to the Society for Cinema and Media Studies (SCMS) conferences.

With a flourishing film industry in Georgia, field trips to filming locations are excellent opportunities for a getaway. The group particularly enjoyed visiting the set of *The Walking Dead* in Senoia. We look forward to watching the growth of the Trilith Studios south of Atlanta in Fayetteville. Originally Pinewood Atlanta, the studios have been used for numerous films and television programs, notably by Marvel Entertainment.

We invite you to join us on this enriching journey to discover how movies reflect and affect our cultures and each one of us.

Finally, we sincerely hope you have as much fun delving into *Movies on Chatham Presents* as we did in preparing it.

FOOD AND DRINK

Jerry Hassebroek's Guacamole

Adapted from On Cooking (2010)[1]

INGREDIENTS:

1 small plum tomato, finely chopped

3 green onions, finely chopped

2 tablespoons cilantro, chopped

1 tablespoon freshly-squeezed lemon juice

1 garlic clove, minced and mashed

½ teaspoon dried oregano

½ teaspoon kosher salt

½ Jalapeno, chopped or diced

4 ripe Haas avocados (slightly soft when squeezed)

PREPARATION:

★ The first six ingredients (through oregano) can be prepared, mixed, and refrigerated in advance.

★ At serving time, half each avocado, remove the seed, spoon into a bowl. Mash the avocado with a fork until creamy.

★ Using a fork, blend the other ingredients with the avocado and serve with chips or crackers.

Note: The amount of each ingredient can be varied to taste.

---

1 Early editions of *On Cooking* (Labensky, Hause, & Martel) are available online for free download.

Gluten-Free Chocolate Brownies

While Jerry's guacamole is a hands-down favorite (in addition to popcorn), many of our group members also like to indulge in a dessert item. Since most prefer chocolate, brownies are always a welcome addition to an evening of movies. However, some have found they are healthier when eating a gluten-free diet.

We know that baking from scratch is enjoyable when time is available, but all in the group have agreed that simple is best when preparing for Movie Night.

In 2019, Emily from *One Lovely Life* did our work for us in comparing gluten-free brownie mixes. Her top choice was King Arthur Flour Gluten-free Brownie Mix, to which you add eggs, butter/oil, chocolate chips, and nuts.[2] Missing from her list, a reader added the Betty Crocker Gluten-Free Brownie Mix as a favorite. Another suggested using dark chocolate chips.

The site also offers a "make-from-scratch" recipe for "The Perfect Gluten-Free & Paleo Brownies for those who are adventurous."[3]

Beverages

Add beverages, and you're all set. We like Pinot Noir and Meiomi in red wine, Chardonnay and Pinot Grigio in white. Ginger ale is a popular soft drink; we always have crushed ice and bottled water to drink, too—Lipsey and sometimes Dasani.

---

[2] Find the brownie mix taste test at https://www.onelovelylife.com/the-best-gluten-free-brownie-mix/

[3] Find the "make-from-scratch" recipe at https://www.onelovelylife.com/the-perfect-gluten-free-brownies/

ACKNOWLEDGMENTS

We are so grateful for a project that allows us to share our passion for movies. Toward that end, we express our heartfelt appreciation to the Movies on Chatham group, having met faithfully in monthly meetings since 2010. Your dedication has helped to pursue our mission by building a spirit of camaraderie and mutual trust. Thanks to your eye-opening comments, our movie room has livened up and filled up with stimulating and enlightening conversation. As hospitality director extraordinaire, Jayne Hasson made sure that we always had food and just the proper libations. We love you all.

More than we ever imagined, researching and compiling project entries was a considerable task. Without the researchers and writers regularly working together, it would not yet be complete.

We are indebted to those who proofread the manuscript, Judy Gray and Dell Reardon, and from whose counsel we benefited. Very thankful also for those who made significant helpful and productive comments on various elements: Jerry Hassebroek, Carter Hassebroek of Solotech Nashville, and Professor Nadine Kaslow of the Emory University School of Medicine.

Professors Anne Balsamo at UT Dallas and Jay David Bolter at Georgia Tech introduced the media and communication concepts that inspired this work. Thank you extends to them especially.

The patience and support of our husbands and families have enabled us to persevere—most notably, Jerry Hassebroek. He has offered unfailing encouragement in all research (and hospitality) efforts over these years. This book is certainly no exception.

CONTRIBUTORS

DR. PAM HASSEBROEK is Editor of the *Movies on Chatham Presents* series and Director of the Movies on Chatham study. A STEM guru turned social scientist, she earned degrees at TCU, UT Austin, and Georgia Tech and studied at Oxford University in England. A researcher in engineering, media communication, and information security, Pam's work has been published in journals and conferences in the Americas, Europe, Asia, and the Middle East. Her most recent contributions to cybersecurity and cyber terrorism research are at Georgia Tech and the National Academies' Computer Science and Telecommunication Board (CSTB). She lives in Atlanta with her husband, Jerry. Two children and precious grandchildren are in both near and far-flung places.

LUCY COTA is Research Director for *Movies on Chatham online.* An Atlanta native, UGA graduate, and former Atlanta Public Schools teacher, Lucy finds unique angles for examining film contexts, informing and enhancing lively discussions among enthusiasts. While devoted to the study, Lucy finds time for bridge, multiple book clubs, and three adored grandchildren (not necessarily in that order).

MARY REED is Staff Writer, a regular contributor to *Movies on Chatham online* and her personal blog. An Emory University graduate and former analyst at Accenture, she serves as medical billing assistant for Reed Imaging Services in Atlanta, even as she manages a family of five. Mary longs for spare time.

GLOSSARY OF TERMS

These are terms we use in discussing and writing about films. Some are from other sources, which we list in the Bibliography under the "Back Matter" heading.

A FILM

A film is a photographic recording of images from either the natural world or a recording of images created artificially using animation techniques or special effects. Its visual elements give movies universal power in communication.

★ In the broad context of cinema (apart from a physical medium), a film is a text—a cultural artifact—created by a specific social group. The group, e.g., a society, has specific cultural symbols that reflect that group and, in turn, affect it and others outside. As a film study group, we are interested in film as an object of study—as a cultural artifact. Thus, we consider the film a vital art form, a popular entertainment source, and a forceful teaching—or indoctrinating—method.

A TEXT

A text is a work of communication, a body of language—a collection of symbols. A text is a narrative. It has a sequence, i.e., a beginning, middle, and end. It can be a recording: a document or movie, live communication, such as the content of a speech, or a musical concert.

Examples include a painting, a book's contents, or an anthology of books like *The Encyclopedia Britannica* or the *Bible*. However, a text may be a single symbol, such as a cave painting or an image at a street crossing.

It is a cultural product regarded as an object of critical analysis (who produced it; who created it; what message it communicates, etc.).

Note that while a typical connotation of a text regards a written form, we have extended that definition to include other types. Communication occurs between a sender and receiver through five perception methods—hearing, seeing, feeling, smelling, and tasting. In our critical analysis of a text, we consider all of these senses as objects of study.

AGITPROP

Agitprop is political propaganda spread chiefly in the arts. Short for "agitatsiya propaganda" (agitation and propaganda), its techniques help influence public opinion. "Despite its Russian roots, American writers and tweeters have adapted it to the 21st century, usually to accuse someone of promoting ideology" (Rossman, 2017).

AUDIO MOTIF

Audio or sound motifs emotionally condition the audience for a character's setting or particular actions.

AUDIENCE RECEPTION

In audience reception models, a movie has little inherent meaning. Instead, individual audience members interpret meaning from what they see on screen.

AUTEUR THEORY

The 1950s-era auteur theory holds that a director's film reflects the director's personal creative vision as the primary "auteur" (French for "author"). Even when the film's production is part of an industrial process, the author's creative voice may be distinct enough to shine through studio complexities. In some cases, film producers exert a similar "auteur" influence on films.

BLACK HUMOR

In black humor, dismal topics and events are treated in a humorous or satirical manner.

BACKSTAGE

The backstage areas of a theater are not part of the house or stage. These areas include dressing rooms, green rooms, and other offstage places (e.g., wings and storage spaces).

CELLULOID

Celluloid is another name for the film used in cinematography. The original photographic film began as cellulose nitrate, a highly flammable compound used for making explosives, plastic, and varnish. The transparent material was then coated with a light-sensitive emulsion. Because of its use in making films, the term came to stand for movies in general.

CINEMA

For most viewers and critics, cinema (movies, films) is storytelling and entertainment. In early cinema, a camera recorded performances exclusively through celluloid film and lens-based methods. Today, various techniques (lighting, film arts, film stocks, lenses, editing, etc.) modify the original record obtained by filming equipment.

CINEMATOGRAPHY

Cinematography is an art form, photography that is unique to motion pictures. The creative and interpretive process results in original authorship rather than a simple recording.

COMIC CLIMATE

In contrast to verisimilitude, the comic climate often requires the audience to suspend belief.

DEUS EX MACHINA

Deus ex machina denotes a situation in a storyline where a character or event enters unexpectedly or questionably to resolve a complex dilemma or plot.

DIRECTOR

The director is the person responsible for overseeing all aspects of filmmaking.

DISSOLVE

Used in the post-production process of film and video editing, a dissolve is a gradual transition from one image to the next.

DOCUDRAMA

A docudrama (or documentary drama) is a re-enactment of actual events performed by actors.

DUTCH ANGLE

A Dutch angle is a camera position where the cinematographer rotates the camera relative to the shot's horizon or vertical lines. (See: *Wikipedia*, Dutch angle.) The camera angle often depicts madness, unrest, and disorientation in German Expressionism. The word Dutch was often a substitute for the similar word Deutsch, which means German.

EMOTIONAL ENGAGEMENT

Philosophical discussions of emotional engagement with films begin with a question that applies to other art forms: Why care about film characters? What happens shouldn't matter like the circumstances of real people do. Even so, we do get emotionally involved with them.

The following are some ideas about this.

IDENTIFICATION THEORY

Identification theory proposes that we identify with characters.

As we identify with a particular character, we perceive a connection to that persona; we see ourselves in her stories. Naturally, then, her fate matters to us.

Film philosophers argue that identification theory can't entirely explain our emotional engagement with characters because we have a variety of attitudes and feelings toward them. Even if we identify with some of the characters, this theory doesn't explain why we have emotional reactions to other characters we don't identify with.

IMAGINATION THEORY

Imagination theory proposes that a movie helps us imagine a character's situation. Further, that emotional engagement begins with curiosity about something we may never have experienced. What would it feel like to have this happen? Because we can imagine the outcome we want, which affects us emotionally, fictional films have an emotional impact.

IMAGINATION THEORY SUB-CATEGORIES

SIMULATION THEORY

Imagining situations and people in a film brings about typical emotional responses, e.g., fear, anger, or sadness; except that the emotions are virtual. When responding emotionally to an imagined situation, one feels the same way as in a similar real case. Most people would feel frightened if they experienced a monster running amok in person. Simulation theory suggests that one might enjoy the frightening feeling in a safe context.

However, responding as in the actual situation is not usually the outcome. For example, when we see a villain tying little Nell to the railroad tracks, we are concerned about her and outraged by the villain's actions. Yet, we are always aware that this is not an actual situation, so we don't try to save her.

THOUGHT THEORY

We know that thinking can bring about real feelings. For example, when I hear that a colleague received an unfair review, the thought of the injustice makes me angry. Our thoughts also influence our emotions as we watch a film. Therefore, thought theory rejects the notion of virtual emotion.

This theory has promise, but … should just a thought (not a belief) bring an emotional response? If I believe a character is abusing someone, isn't that a moral issue? The situation may not produce emotion without a belief system. Could we describe this better as moral outrage?

ENSEMBLE CAST

Actors and performers in an ensemble cast have roughly equal amounts of importance and screentime, unlike those casts where some are more developed than others. Examples: *Peyton Place* (Robson, 1957); *Book Club* (Holderman, 2018).

FICTIONAL (NARRATIVE) FILM

A fictional film tells a fictional or fictionalized story, where believable narratives and characters help convince the audience that the unfolding fiction is real. If verisimilitude (the simulation of reality) is the goal, actors must convincingly deliver dialogue and action to engage the audience.

FILM CRITICISM

Film criticism is the comparison, analysis, interpretation, and evaluation of movies, individually and collectively. A critic aims to reveal the contexts and elements that provide meaning to the film, its successes, and limitations.

Film criticism applies to two types of activity:

1) Journalistic criticism, in newspapers and popular media; and

2) Academic criticism in journals publish the work of film scholars. Scholarly research adds to scientific discussion.

FILMOGRAPHY

A filmography lists films that share a similar characteristic, e.g., by one director or actor or on one subject.

GOLDEN AGE OF HOLLYWOOD

The Golden Age is set between 1930 (when movies with sound began) and the 1960s (when the Hays Code ended).

IRONY

Irony is something contrary to what one expects and is often wryly amusing as a result.

ITALIAN NEOREALISM

Neorealism is an Italian national film movement characterized by stories set among the poor and working-class, filmed on location, and frequently using non-professional actors.

MISE-EN-SCÈNE

Mise-en-scène refers to everything in the scene and its arrangement—sets, props, actors, costumes, and lighting. The mise-en-scène influences the verisimilitude of the setting.

MOTION PICTURE

Motion picture seems like a strange term but undoubtedly carries the cinema's early history with it. In any event, we all understand it—just as we know the meaning of picture shows and films.

MULTIPLE EXPOSURE

In multiple exposure, a photography and cinematography technique, the camera shutter is opened more than once to expose the same film frame.

The resulting image contains the subsequent reproduction(s) superimposed over the original. The camera technique can create ghostly images or add people and objects that weren't initially in a scene as an artistic visual effect.

NARRATIVE

A narrative describes an experience, event, or sequence of events in story form. Both fiction and non-fiction film communication is typically narrative, similar to novels and history books. It has a beginning, a middle, and an end.

NON-DIEGETIC VS. DIEGETIC SOUND

Non-diegetic sound is sound originating from outside the story world. Usually, the music soundtrack of a movie is non-diegetic, as are voice-overs by a narrator.

PARODY

A parody is a humorous imitation—a comedy film that makes fun of or re-creates an original work. Characters or settings belonging to the original are used comically or ironically in another. In the U.S. Supreme Court ruling Campbell v. Acuff-Rose Music (1994), parody "is the use of some elements of a prior author's composition to create a new one that, at least in part, comments on that author's works." The movie *Airplane!* (Abrahams, Zucker, & Zucker, 1980) parodies popular disaster films.

PERSUASION

Persuasion relates to the power, intention, or ability to influence or direct (origin: Medieval Latin 1580–90). Persuasive communication affects emotions, our subjective mental processes. A particular text persuades more or less depending on our knowledge, habits, experiences, imagination, intelligence, awareness, and belief system.

Further, we may fear the negative consequences of persuasion—

for either a viewer or society. "Religious and political leaders, film critics, studio executives, and most ominously, many consumers agree, many movies are excessively violent and mean-spirited, gratuitously sexual and profane, and mindlessly similar and formulaic" (O'Donnell, 1992).

PHILOSOPHY OF FILM

Philosophy of art is a traditional area of academic research. In a sub-field, film philosophy, researchers investigate film as an art form equivalent to drama, dance, and painting.

PRODUCER

A producer is a person who is responsible for all of the business and production aspects of making and releasing a film.

PRODUCTION COMPANY

A production company is responsible for developing and filming a specific production or media broadcast.

PRODUCTION STUDIO

A studio is an artist's workroom. A production studio serves as a center for producing a film or other artistic product. The studio may or may not have a financial interest in the film or broadcast beyond providing facilities and other required components. Filmmakers often shoot in secured studios with limited access for privacy and safety reasons.

PROP

In filmmaking, prop is a slang term for property. Properties are objects used by actors and set decorators to help the audience visualize the story setting.

PYROTECHNICS

Pyrotechnics is a term for a range of special effects props—gas flame, fireworks, explosions, etc. These materials and mechanisms create visual drama and stunning scenes in filmmaking.

RITUAL THEORY

In a ritual view, communication is a cultural practice that shapes societies (Carey, 2009). The ritual model contrasts with the concept that communication is simply the transmission or exchange of information.

SOCIAL COGNITIVE THEORY OF GENDER DEVELOPMENT

Social cognitive theory conceptualizes that part of human behavior develops by observing others in a context of social interaction, experience, and media influence. Thus, a child's development relates to perceptions set by gender typing, the expectations for roles and behavior in a particular culture based on biological reproductive organs (Bussey & Bandura, 1999).

SELECTIVE EXPOSURE THEORY

Selective exposure theory conceptualizes an individual's tendency to favor information that reinforces pre-existing views while avoiding contradictory information. According to this theory, people tend to select specific aspects of exposed information based on their perspectives, beliefs, attitudes, and prior decisions.

SOCIAL SATIRE

Social satire uses humor, irony, exaggeration, or ridicule in a text to expose and criticize social groups, often in contemporary politics and popular trends.

STUDIO SYSTEM

The studio system was a vertically integrated film production, distribution, and exhibition system in major motion picture studios in the 1930s and '40s.

SUBJECTIVE

The term "subjective" relates to what occurs inside a person's mind—i.e., emotions, prejudices, ideas, philosophies, belief systems—rather than strictly observing. We communicate facts (evidence, observations) and subjective conceptions (thoughts, beliefs) similarly through many media types.

SUBSTITUTION STOP TRICK

A stop trick is a film special effect that occurs in two steps as follows: 1) A camera shoots an object in a scene, then the camera is turned off, and the item moves out of sight. 2) The camera turns back on to recapture the scene. When a viewer watches the film, it seems that the object has disappeared.

SYMBOLIC INTERACTION THEORY

As symbolic interactions, we acquire "subjective" meanings (interpretations of symbols) as a product of social interaction. We then use these meanings to interpret the world. Our interpretive process is ongoing and changing as we continuously interact with others, in person or via various media forms.

TIME-LAPSE PHOTOGRAPHY

In time-lapse photography, the frame rate at which the image is projected and viewed is much faster than when the photographer captured it. Thus, one may consider time-lapse photography as the opposite of slow-motion photography.

VERISIMILITUDE

Verisimilitude is the appearance of being truthful or authentic, believability.

VIRTUAL REALITY

Virtual reality is an artificial, computer-generated environment displayed on hardware devices. The goal is for a user to experience the environment as actual.

VISUAL COMMUNICATION

The visual elements of cinema give motion pictures a universal power of communication. Visual communication is more powerful than words alone. It is more memorable and has higher importance, thus impacting an audience more significantly.

During the silent film era, [Hugo Münsterberg] sought to understand what it was about the film that made it conceptually distinct from the theater. He concluded that close-ups, flashbacks, and edits were unique to film and constituted its nature.

WIT

Wit is intelligent humor, saying or writing usually funny things that add a quick twist to an experience. A witty person is skilled at making smart remarks. Types of wit include the pun and repartee or play on words.

FILMS CITED

BIBLIOGRAPHY

PREFACE

About (2020). *The News Literacy Project*. https://newslit.org.

Ball-Rokeach, S. J. (2001). The politics of studying media violence: Reflections 30 years after The Violence Commission. *Mass Communication and Society* 4(1): 3–18.

Berger, J. (2016). *Invisible influence*. Simon & Schuster.

Bolter, J., & Grusin, R. (1999). *Remediation: Understanding new media*. The MIT Press.

Briscoe, S. (2021, Jan 12). U.S. laws address deepfakes. *Security Management*. https://www.asisonline.org/security-management-magazine/latest-news/today-in-security/2021/january/U-S-Laws-Address-Deepfakes/

Cantril, H. (1940). *The invasion from Mars: A study in the psychology of panic*. Princeton University Press.

Carey, J. W. (1989). Chapter 1. A cultural approach to communication. In J. W. Carey (Ed.), *Communication as culture: Essays on media and society*. Unwin Hyman.

Dewey, J. (1910). *How we think*. D.C. Heath & Co. https://www.gutenberg.org/files/37423/37423-h/37423-h.htm

Doherty, W. (2019, Jun 18). The American Catholic Church censors the movies. *Marian University*. https://mushare.marian.edu/fp_hss/19

Fake news making headlines nationwide. (2016, Dec 19). *SchoolJournalism.org*. https://www.schooljournalism.org/fake-news-making-headlines-nationwide/

Geena Davis Institute on Gender in Media. (2020). *Mount Saint Mary's University*. https://seejane.org/about-us/

Harris, N. B. (2015, Feb). How childhood trauma affects health across a lifetime. *TED*. https://www.ted.com/speakers/nadine_burke_harris_1

Kael, P. (2019, Jun 16). *Day for Night (La Nuit Américaine, 1973)*—Review. *Scraps from the Loft*. https://scrapsfromtheloft.com/2019/06/16/day-for-night-la-nuit-americaine-review-pauline-kael/

Katz, E., & Lazarsfeld, P. F. (1955). *Personal influence: The part played by people in the flow of mass communications*. Free Press.

Klapper, J. T. (1960). *The effects of mass communication*. Free Press.

Linder, D. O. (1895, Apr 3). Famous trials: Testimony of Oscar Wilde on cross

examination. *University of Missouri-Kansas City School of Law*.
https://famous-trials.com/wilde/346-literarypart

Mills, C. W. (1959). *The sociological imagination*. Oxford University Press.

Murphy, G., Loftus, E. F., Grady, R. H., Levine, L. J., & Greene, C. M. (2019).
False memories for fake news during Ireland's abortion referendum.
Psychological Science, 30(10), 1449-1459. doi:
10.1177/0956797619864887 https://cpb-us-
e2.wpmucdn.com/faculty.sites.uci.edu/dist/c/571/files/2019/11/Murph
y_IrelandAbortion_PS2019_on-line.pdf

News literacy resources. (2021). *Associated Press Institute*.
https://www.americanpressinstitute.org/youth-news-literacy/resources/

O'Neill, B. (2011). Media effects in context. In Virginia Nightingale (Ed.), *The
handbook of media audiences*. Blackwell.

Staiger, J. (2000). *Perverse spectators: The practices of film reception*. New York
University Press.

Steinmetz, K. (2017, Mar 17). Beyond 'he' or 'she': The changing meaning of
gender. *Time Magazine*. https://time.com/4703309/gender-sexuality-
changing

The center for news literacy. (2016). *Stony Brook University School of Journalism*.
https://www.centerfornewsliteracy.org/

Tucher, A. (2007, Oct). Communication, community, reality, ritual, and the
'Potato Hole' Woodson. *Journal of Communication Inquiry*, 3(4), 301–
309. doi: 10.1177/0196859907305164

Wilder, L. I. (Author), & Williams, G. (Illustrator). (1932–1943). *Little house*
[Book series]. Harper.

INTRODUCTION

Campany, D. (2010, Sep 1). Moving with the times: Eadweard Muybridge I.
Tate Etc. https://www.tate.org.uk/tate-etc/issue-20-autumn-
2010/moving-times

Dickson, W. K. L. (Director). (1894). *Carmencita* [Film]. Edison Black Maria
Studio.

Doherty, W. (2019, Jun 18). The American Catholic Church censors the
movies. *Marian University*. https://mushare.marian.edu/fp_hss/19

Eadweard Muybridge exhibition. (2010, Sep 8 –2011, Jan 16). *Tate Britain*.
https://www.tate.org.uk/whats-on/tate-britain/exhibition/eadweard-
muybridge

Geiger, J. (2011). Novelties, spectacles, and the documentary impulse. In
American documentary film: Projecting the nation. Edinburgh University

Press. *www.jstor.org/stable/10.3366/j.ctt1r28f9.7*

Le Prince, L. (Director). (1888). *Roundhay garden scene* [Film]. https://archive.org/details/Roundhay_Garden_Scene

Lumière, A., & Lumière, L. (1895). *Arrival of a train at La Ciotat* [Film]. https://www.youtube.com/watch?v=t95oMkoq24Y

Paghat the Ratgirl. (n.d.). Index of silent film reviews *Carmencita* 1894. *Weird Wild Realm Film Reviews*. http://www.weirdwildrealm.com/f-WKLDickson.html

Stopping time: The horse in motion. (2010–2011). *Tate Britain*. https://www.tate.org.uk/whats-on/tate-britain/exhibition/eadweard-muybridge/exhibition-guide/horse-motion

Sue, D. W., & Spanierman, L. (2020). *Microaggressions in everyday life*. Wiley.

PART I ★ CHANGING WOMEN

CHAPTER 1: *SUMMER AND SMOKE*

Devlin, A. J. (2014). Introduction. In Devlin, A. J. (with Devlin, M. J.) (Eds.). *The selected letters of Elia Kazan*. Knopf Doubleday.

Faria, M.A., Jr. (2013, Apr 5). Violence, mental illness, and the brain–A brief history of psychosurgery: Part 1–From trephination to lobotomy. *Surg Neurol Int*, 4(49). doi:10.4103/2152-7806.110146. https://www.ncbi.nlm.nih.gov/pmc/articles/PMC3640229/

Glenville, P. (1961). (Director). *Summer and smoke* [Film]. Paramount Pictures.

Jennings, C. R. (1986). *Playboy* interview: Tennessee Williams. In Devlin, A. J. (Ed.). *Conversations with Tennessee Williams* (pp. 224–250). University Press of Mississippi (Original published in *Playboy*, Apr 1973: 69–84).

Johnston, L. (1979, Nov 19). Theater Hall of Fame enshrines 51 artists. *The New York Times*. https://www.nytimes.com/1979/11/19/archives/theater-hall-of-fame-enshrines-51-artists-great-things-and-blank.html

Kazan, E. (2014). TO TENNESSEE WILLIAMS. In Devlin, A. J. (with Devlin, M. J.) (Eds.). *The selected letters of Elia Kazan*. Knopf Doubleday.

Lahr, J. (2006, Apr 17). Stage left: The struggles of Clifford Odets. *The New Yorker*. https://www.newyorker.com/magazine/2006/04/17/stage-left

Prize winners in drama. (2020). *The Pulitzer prizes—Columbia University*. https://www.pulitzer.org/prize-winners-by-category/218

Protest by Williams. (1947, Feb 3). *The New York Times*. https://archive.nytimes.com/www.nytimes.com/books/00/12/31/special

s/williams-protest.html

Ron. (2006, Feb 19). *Summer and smoke. TCM.*
http://www.tcm.com/tcmdb/title/4250/Summer-and-Smoke/user-reviews.html

Rose Williams; Sister of playwright Tennessee Williams. (1996, Sep 7). *The Los Angeles Times.* https://www.latimes.com/archives/la-xpm-1996-09-07-mn-41486-story.html

Singleton, D. (1983, Feb 26). The day American playwright Tennessee Williams died in 1983. *The New York Daily News.*
https://www.nydailynews.com/entertainment/theater-arts/day-american-playwright-tennessee-williams-died-1983-article-1.2541142

Sollosi, M. (2016, Sep 16). 15 classic Tennessee Williams adaptations. *Entertainment Weekly.* https://ew.com/movies/tennessee-williams-movies/

Stang, J. (1965, Mar 28). Williams: Twenty years after 'Glass Menagerie.' *The New York Times.*
https://timesmachine.nytimes.com/timesmachine/1965/03/28/97189749.pdf

Williams, T. (1947, Dec. 3). *A Streetcar Named Desire* [Play]. Live performance at Ethel Barrymore Theatre, New York, NY. *Broadway League database.*
https://www.ibdb.com/broadway-production/a-streetcar-named-desire-1804

Williams, T. (1948, Oct 9). *Summer and smoke* [Play]. Live performance at Music Box Theatre, New York, NY. *Broadway League database.*
https://www.ibdb.com/broadway-production/summer-and-smoke-2026

CHAPTER 2: MR. AND MRS. BRIDGE

Adams, J. (1780, May 12). Letter from John Adams to Abigail Adams, [Electronic edition]. *Adams Family Papers: Massachusetts Historical Society.* http://www.masshist.org/digitaladams/

Bishop J. L. (2003) Working women and dance in *progressive era* New York City, 1890–1920. [Master's thesis, Florida State University]. *FSU Digital Library.* https://diginole.lib.fsu.edu/islandora/object/fsu:181984

Blazina, C., & Desilver, D. (2021, Jan 15). A record number of women are serving in the 117th Congress. *Pew Research Center.*
https://www.pewresearch.org/fact-tank/2021/01/15/a-record-number-of-women-are-serving-in-the-117th-congress/

Blumberg, N. (2020, Feb 23). Joanne Woodward. *Encyclopædia Britannica, Inc.*
https://www.britannica.com/biography/Joanne-Woodward

Canby, V. (1990, Nov 23). A placid marriage, and undercurrents. *The New York Times*. https://www.nytimes.com/1990/11/23/movies/a-placid-marriage-and-undercurrents.html

Cassavetes, J. (1974). *A woman under the influence* [Film]. Faces International.

Connell, E. (1959) *Mrs. Bridge*, Viking Press.

Connell, E. (1969). *Mr. Bridge* (1st ed.). Random House.

Contrera, J. (2018, May 20). Stay in school or get married? In 1965, the President's daughter had to choose. *The Washington Post*. https://www.washingtonpost.com/lifestyle/style/stay-in-school-or-get-married-in-1965-the-presidents-daughter-had-to-choose/2018/05/20/760c3d86-5acf-11e8-b656-a5f8c2a9295d_story.html

Cowan, R. S. (1983). *More work for mother: The ironies of household technologies from the hearth to the microwave*. Basic Books.

Cukor, G. (Director). (1944). *Gaslight* [Film]. MGM.

Edmondson, C., & Lee, J. C. (2019, Jan 3). Meet the new freshmen in Congress. *The New York Times*. https://www.nytimes.com/interactive/2018/11/28/us/politics/congress-freshman-class.html

Freedland, J. (1993, May 1). Interview / Heat, dust and a woman with a New York view: Jonathan Freedland meets Ruth Prawer Jhabvala, novelist, Oscar winner and exile. *Independent*. https://www.independent.co.uk/arts-entertainment/books/interview-heat-dust-and-a-woman-with-a-new-york-view-jonathan-freedland-meets-ruth-prawer-jhabvala-2320223.html

Gelles, D. (2019, Jan 02). Julie Sweet of Accenture could see her future. So she quit her job. *The New York Times*. https://www.nytimes.com/2019/01/02/business/julie-sweet-accenture-corner-office.html

Gharry, S., & Molla, R. (2018, Sep 13). A new California law, if passed, could force companies like Facebook, Tesla and Alphabet to add more women to their boards. *Vox*. https://www.vox.com/2018/9/13/17841606/california-law-women-board

Gosnell, E. (2013, Feb 14). Evan S Connell: the modern-day Jane Austen who chronicled married life. *The Telegraph*. https://www.telegraph.co.uk/culture/books/9868580/Evan-S-Connell-the-American-author-who-was-a-modern-day-Jane-Austen.html

Grodstein, L. (2009, Fall/Winter). Evan S. Connell's *Mrs. Bridge*. *Post Road Magazine*. http://www.postroadmag.com/18/recommends/grodstein.phtml

Hassebroek, P. (2016, Dec). The Longhetti family: What's normal? *Movies on Chatham*. https://MoviesonChatham.com/2016/12/whats-normal

Hassebroek, P. (2017, Apr). In *Gaslight*: Wife's dependency and husband's secrecy. *Movies on Chatham*. https://MoviesonChatham.com/2017/04/dependency-and-secrecy

Hopkins. J. (1981, Nov 24). Bored housewives turn to shoplifting. *The Oklahoman*. https://newsok.com/article/1964865/bored-housewives-turn-to-shoplifting

Ivory, J. (Director). (1990). *Mr. and Mrs. Bridge.* [Film]. Miramax.

Jasanoff, M. (2018, Dec 31). Ruth Prawer Jhabvala and the art of ambivalence. *The New Yorker*. https://www.newyorker.com/magazine/2019/01/07/ruth-prawer-jhabvala-and-the-art-of-ambivalence

Johnson, N. (1957). *The three faces of Eve*. [Film]. Twentieth Century-Fox.

Lamb, C. (2021, Feb 13). Sister Natalie Becquart and the primacy of synodality. *The Tablet*. https://www.thetablet.co.uk/blogs/1/1709/sister-natalie-becquart-and-the-primacy-of-synodality

Layton, B. (Director). (2018). *American animals* [Film]. Ascot Elite Entertainment Group.

Lee, C. (2018, Jun 1). The real-life heist caper behind *American Animals*. *Vulture*. https://www.vulture.com/2018/06/the-real-life-heist-caper-behind-american-animals.html

Michals, D. (2015). Shirley Chisholm. *The National Women's History Museum*. https://www.womenshistory.org/education-resources/biographies/shirley-chisholm

Milligan, S. (2017, Jan 20). Stepping through history. *U.S. News*. https://www.usnews.com/news/the-report/articles/2017-01-20/timeline-the-womens-rights-movement-in-the-us

Pritchard, W. (2013, Feb 25). Portrait of a lady. *The Weekly Standard*. https://www.weeklystandard.com/william-h-pritchard/portrait-of-a-lady

Reed, M. (2016). Are psychiatric issues side effects of civilizing? *Movies on Chatham*. https://MoviesonChatham.com/2016/09/effects-of-civilizing

Rikleen, K. (2016. Mar 10). Older women are being forced out of the workforce. *Harvard Business Review*. https://hbr.org/2016/03/older-women-are-being-forced-out-of-the-workforce

Ritt, M. (Director). (1958). *The Long, Hot Summer*. Twentieth Century-Fox.

Róisín, F. (2018, Jun 11). The poignant rootlessness of Ruth Prawer Jhabvala. *Village Voice*. https://www.villagevoice.com/2018/06/11/the-poignant-rootlessness-of-ruth-prawer-jhabvala/

Rosenbaum, J. (1991, May 1). *Mr. & Mrs. Bridge. Chicago Reader.*
https://www.chicagoreader.com/chicago/mr-and-mrs-
bridge/Film?oid=1056898

Robinson, S. (n.d.) Joanne Woodward, IMDb Mini Biography. *IMDb.*
https://www.imdb.com/name/nm0940946/bio?ref_=nm_ov_bio_sm

Schwarz, C. (2010, Apr). Quiet desperation. *The Atlantic.*
https://www.theatlantic.com/magazine/archive/2010/04/quiet-
desperation/307978/

Sterritt, D. (1990, Dec 7). Effective `antidrama.' *The Christian Science Monitor.*
https://www.csmonitor.com/1990/1207/lbridge.html

The new housekeeping: Solving the servant problem. (2018, Mar 22). *George
Mason University History Matters Project.*
http://historymatters.gmu.edu/d/5301/

Wadler, J. (1990, Dec 10). The creator of *Mr. and Mrs. Bridge* goes home again
—with reluctance and no thanks for the memories. *People Magazine.*
https://people.com/archive/the-creator-of-mr-and-mrs-bridge-goes-
home-again-with-reluctance-and-no-thanks-for-the-memories-vol-34-
no-23

Wikipedia contributors. (2021, Jan 5). Carol Moseley Braun. In *Wikipedia, The
Free Encyclopedia.* https://en.Wikipedia.org/wiki/Carol_Moseley_Braun

Wikipedia contributors. (2021, Jun 19). Merchant Ivory Productions. In
Wikipedia, The Free Encyclopedia.
https://en.wikipedia.org/wiki/Merchant_Ivory_Productions

Women in the Senate. (2020). *United States Senate.*
https://www.senate.gov/artandhistory/history/common/briefing/wome
n_senators.htm

CHAPTER 3: *PEYTON PLACE*

Bailey, M. (2004, Jul 11). *Peyton Place. NotComing.*
http://www.notcoming.com/reviews/peytonplace/

Baker, C. (1956, Sep 23). Small town peep show. *The New York Times.*
https://nyti.ms/2WxmnA6

Brier, E. (2005). The accidental blockbuster: *Peyton Place* in literary and
institutional context. *Women's Studies Quarterly*, 33(3/4), 48–65.
www.jstor.org/stable/40004418

Callahan, M. (2016). Grace Metalious: *Peyton Place*'s real victim. In G. Carter
(Ed.), *Vanity Fair's writers on writers* (pp. 277–291). Penguin Books.

Clark, H. (2019, Dec 16). *Gone with the Wind* premiere: 80 years later. *Historic
Oakland Foundation.* https://oaklandcemetery.com/gone-with-the-

wind-premiere-80-years-later/

Crowther, B. (1957, Dec 13). The screen drama in *Peyton Place:* American town star of film at Roxy. *The New York Times.* https://www.nytimes.com/1957/12/13/archives/the-screen-drama-in-peyton-place-american-town-star-of-film-at-roxy.html

Dembart, L. (1976, Sep 23). Carter's comments on sex cause concern. *The New York Times.* https://www.nytimes.com/1976/09/23/archives/carters-comments-on-sex-cause-concern.html

Dick, K., & Ziering, A. (2017, Mar 12). How Florida State covered up two rape reports against Jameis Winston. *Huffington Post.* https://www.huffpost.com/entry/how-florida-state-covered_b_9421824

Doherty, W. (2019, Jun 18). The American Catholic Church censors the movies. *Marian University.* https://mushare.marian.edu/fp_hss/19

Filipovic, J. (2018, Sep). How far have we really come since Anita Hill? *Vanity Fair.* https://www.vanityfair.com/style/2018/09/christine-blasey-ford-anita-hill

Friedan, B. (1963). *The feminine mystique.* W.W. Norton and Co.

Godin, S. (2019, May 21). Steven Godin's reviews > *Bonjour tristesse. Goodreads.* https://www.goodreads.com/review/show/2828892000

Hirsh-Dickinson, S. (2007, Winter). Dirty whites and dark secrets: Sex and race in *Peyton Place* (Doctoral Dissertation). *University of New Hampshire: Durham.* https://scholars.unh.edu/dissertation/409.

'I Love Lucy,' 'Lucy is enceinte' more than 60 years later. (2013, Jul 26). *HuffPost.* https://www.huffpost.com/entry/i-love-lucy-lucy-is-enceinte_n_3652507

Kalra, G., & Bhugra, D. (2013). Sexual violence against women: Understanding cross-cultural intersections. *Indian Journal of Psychiatry, 55*(3), 244–249. https://doi.org/10.4103/0019-5545.117139

Karlos, S. (2019, May 8). Opinion: A lesson on why victims of sexual assault stay silent. *The Daily Aztec, San Diego State University.* https://thedailyaztec.com/94723/el-alma/opinion-a-lesson-on-why-victims-of-sexual-assault-stay-silent/

Keller, J. (2006, Jul). Scandal! Outrage! *Chicago Tribune.* https://www.chicagotribune.com/news/ct-xpm-2006-07-23-0607230009-story.html

Kelly, G. (2013, Mar). 50 shades of Grace: The impact of *Peyton Place* on New Hampshire 60 years later. *New Hampshire Magazine.* https://www.nhmagazine.com/March-2013/50-Shades-of-Grace/

Krauss, R. M., & Chiu, C.-Y. (1998). Language and social behavior. In D. Gilbert, S. Fiske, & G. Lindzey (Eds.), *The handbook of social psychology* (pp. 41–88). McGraw-Hill.

Mallon, T., & Holmes, A. (2014, Mar 4). What's it like reading *Peyton Place* today? *The New York Times.* https://www.nytimes.com/2014/03/09/books/review/whats-it-like-reading-peyton-place-today.html

Metalious, G. (1956). *Peyton place.* Julian Messner, Inc.

New England Historical Society contributors. (2019.) *Peyton Place*—A town, its scandals and the woman who told the world. https://www.newenglandhistoricalsociety.com/peyton-place-town-its-scandals-and-the-woman-who-told-the-world/

Novkov, J. (2016, Feb) Equality, process, and campus sexual assault. *Maryland Law Review, 75*(2), 590–620.

Payne, M. (2015, Feb 19). Erica Kinsman, who accused Jameis Winston of rape, tells her story in new documentary *The Hunting Ground. The Washington Post.* https://www.washingtonpost.com/news/early-lead/wp/2015/02/19/erica-kinsman-who-accused-jameis-winston-of-rape-tells-her-story-in-new-documentary-the-hunting-ground/

Peyton Place (1957). (2019). *AFI catalog of feature films.* https://catalog.afi.com/Catalog/moviedetails/52325

Plummer, W. (1984, May 14). Ethel Kennedy, Behind a brave front, fought to maintain a dynasty and a home. *People Magazine.* https://people.com/archive/ethel-kennedy-behind-a-brave-front-fought-to-maintain-a-dynasty-and-a-home-vol-21-no-19/

Richardson, R. (2004, May 23). 'Peyton Place' shockingly revealed life. *SentinelSource.* https://www.sentinelsource.com/news/special_reports/peyton-place-shockingly-revealed-life-by-rachel-richardson/article_451da3d9-1bc3-58b1-b8fa-7aec02cec5e6.html

Rivera, J. (2021, Jan 17). What happened to Jameis Winston? *SportingNews.* https://www.sportingnews.com/us/nfl/news/jameis-winston-buccaneers-saints/1vyiiqx2ly0lu13aeo787txkwg

Robson, M. (Director). (1957). *Peyton place* [Film]. Twentieth Century-Fox.

Romm, C. (2015, Jun 17). Before there were home pregnancy tests. *The Atlantic.* https://www.theatlantic.com/health/archive/2015/06/history-home-pregnancy-test/396077/

Sexual risk behaviors can lead to HIV, STDs, & teen pregnancy. (2020, Mar 25). *CDC.* https://www.cdc.gov/healthyyouth/sexualbehaviors/index.htm

Smith, N. (2016, Sep 26). How *Peyton Place* comforted me as a closeted teenager. *Literary Hub.* https://lithub.com/how-peyton-place-comforted-me-as-a-closeted-teenager/

Stahl, J. (2015, Apr 30). Talent trumps principle. *Slate magazine*. https://slate.com/culture/2015/05/jameis-winston-drafted-the-quarterbacks-disturbing-history-will-soon-be-a-distant-memory-for-the-nfl.html

Stroud, R. (2020, Apr 29). Jameis Winston will make about $19 million less with Saints than Bucs. *Tampa Bay Times*. https://www.tampabay.com/sports/bucs/2020/04/29/jameis-winston-will-make-about-19-million-less-with-saints-than-bucs

Sypher, F. (1993). Return to Grace Metalious. *Columbia Library Columns*, 93(1), 3–11. http://www.columbia.edu/cu/lweb/digital/collections/cul/texts/ldpd_6309312_043/ldpd_6309312_043.pdf

Toth, E. (1981). *Inside Peyton Place: The life of Grace Metalious*. University Press of Mississippi.

Toth, E. (2006, Sep 22). How to teach a dirty book. *Inside Higher Ed*. https://www.insidehighered.com/views/2006/09/22/how-teach-dirty-book

U.S. Department of State. (2016). Section 6. Discrimination, societal abuses, and trafficking in persons. *Country Reports on Human Rights Practices for 2016*. https://www.state.gov/reports/2016-country-reports-on-human-rights-practices/afghanistan/

Wiegand, S. (2014). *U.S. history for dummies* (3rd ed.). Wiley.

Williams, R. (2014, Feb 28). Françoise Sagan: 'She did what she wanted.' *The Guardian*. https://www.theguardian.com/books/2014/feb/28/francois-sagan-bonjour-tristesse

CHAPTER 4: *CHARADE*

Barson, M. (2020, Apr 09). Stanley Donen. *Encyclopædia Britannica*. https://www.britannica.com/biography/Stanley-Donen

Colette, S. (1944). *Gigi*. La Guilde du Livre.

Collar, C. (2017, Jun 29). Stop. Worshiping. Audrey Hepburn. *Outtake*. https://medium.com/outtake/stop-worshiping-audrey-hepburn-3d4f0506f06

Crowther, B. (1963, Dec 6). Audrey Hepburn and Grant in *Charade*: Comedy melodrama is at the Music Hall: Production abounds in ghoulish humor. *The New York Times*. https://www.nytimes.com/1963/12/06/archives/screen-audrey-hepburn-and-grant-in-charadecomedymelodrama-is-at-the.html

Donen, S. (Director). (1963). *Charade* [Film]. Stanley Donen Productions.

Dotti, L. (2015). *Audrey at home: Memories of my mother's kitchen* (1st ed.). Harper Design.

Eder, B. (2010, Sep 21). *Charade*: The spy in Givenchy. *The Criterion Collection.* https://www.criterion.com/current/posts/64-Charade-the-spy-in-givenchy

Fleming, I. (1959). *Goldfinger.* Jonathan Cape.

Gonzales, C. (2017, Jun 27). Iconic movies with LGBT leads and themes. *The Houston Chronicle.* https://www.chron.com/entertainment/movies/article/Iconic-movies-with-LGBT-leads-and-themes-11247078.php

Higgins, B. (2015, Jun 4). Throwback Thursday: Shirley MacLaine recalls filming lesbian drama *Children's Hour* in 1961. *Hollywood Reporter.* https://www.hollywoodreporter.com/news/throwback-thursday-shirley-maclaine-recalls-799165

James, C. (1993, Jan 21). Audrey Hepburn actress, is dead at 63. *The New York Times.* https://www.nytimes.com/1993/01/21/movies/audrey-hepburn-actress-is-dead-at-63.html

Kismaric, C., & Heiferman, M. (2007). *The mysterious case of Nancy Drew and the Hardy Boys.* Fireside. ISBN 1-4165-4945-5.

Le, M. (2016). I ate like Audrey Hepburn for 5 days and learned her secret. *Spoon.* https://spoonuniversity.com/lifestyle/audrey-hepburn-for-5-days-ate-like

Loos, A. (1952). *Gigi: A comedy in two acts.* Random House.

McDonough, M. (2018, Mar 12). Hubert de Givenchy, French clothing designer who transformed Audrey Hepburn into a style legend, dies at 91. *The Washington Post.* https://www.washingtonpost.com/local/obituaries/hubert-de-givenchy-french-clothing-designer-who-transformed-audrey-hepburn-into-a-style-legend-dies-at-91/2018/03/12/f64f83f0-25fe-11e8-b79d-f3d931db7f68_story.html

McNeil, L. (2015, Jun 23). Audrey Hepburn weighed 88 lbs. after World War II, son reveals. *People Magazine.* https://people.com/bodies/audrey-hepburn-weighed-88-lbs-after-world-war-ii-son-luca-dotti-says

McNeil, L. (2017, Aug 24). Why Audrey Hepburn refused to have her wrinkles photoshopped. *People Magazine.* https://people.com/movies/why-audrey-hepburn-refused-to-have-her-wrinkles-photoshopped/

Miller, F. (2007, Mar 27). *Staircase. TCM.* https://www.tcm.com/tcmdb/title/91239/staircase#articles-reviews?articleId=159647

Newton, M. (2013, Dec 13). *Charade*: The last sparkle of Hollywood. *The Guardian*. https://www.theguardian.com/film/2013/dec/13/Charade-audrey-hepburn-cary-grant

Nordquist, R. (2020, Mar 6). Intertextuality. *ThoughtCo*. https://www.thoughtco.com/what-is-intertextuality-1691077

Stein, R. (2018, Nov 7). When Michael Tilson Thomas and Audrey Hepburn teamed on Anne Frank piece. *San Francisco Chronicle*. https://datebook.sfchronicle.com/music/when-michael-tilson-thomas-and-audrey-hepburn-teamed-on-anne-frank-piece

V, M. (2014, Feb 3). *Charade*: Audrey Hepburn as Reggie Lampert. *Girls do film*. https://girlsdofilm.wordpress.com/2014/02/03/*Charade*-audrey-hepburn-as-reggie-lampert/

Westbrook, B. E. (2000, July 1). Second chances: The remake of Lillian Hellman's *The Children's Hour*. *Bright Lights Film Journal*. https://brightlightsfilm.com/second-chances-remake-lillian-hellmans-childrens-hour/

Wikipedia contributors. (2020, Apr 27). *Charade* (1963 film). In *Wikipedia, The Free Encyclopedia*. https://en.Wikipedia.org/w/index.php?title=Charade_(1963_film)&oldid=953456753

Wikipedia contributors. (2021, Jan 10). Nancy Drew. In *Wikipedia, The Free Encyclopedia*. https://en.Wikipedia.org/w/index.php?title=Nancy_Drew&oldid=999410507

Wyler, W. (Director). (1966). *How to steal a million* [Film]. Universal.

CHAPTER 5: *BOOK CLUB*

Bennett, J. (2019, Jan 8). I am (an older) woman. Hear me roar. *The New York Times*. https://www.nytimes.com/2019/01/08/style/women-age-glenn-close.html

Chen, S. (2019, Dec 13). *Book club*: Movie review. *Common Sense Media*. https://www.commonsensemedia.org/movie-reviews/book-club

Chu, C. (2017, Jan 29). In the time you spend on social media each year, you could read 200 books. *Quartz*. https://qz.com/895101/in-the-time-you-spend-on-social-media-each-year-you-could-read-200-books/

Danusha_Goska1. (2018, Jun 1). Like eating plastic fruit. *IMDb*. https://www.imdb.com/review/rw4186339/

Driscoll, M. (2012, Dec 3). E L James as 'Publishing Person of the Year' draws outcry from literary world. *The Christian Science Monitor*.

https://www.csmonitor.com/Books/chapter-and-verse/2012/1203/E-L-James-as-Publishing-Person-of-the-Year-draws-outcry-from-literary-world

Epstein, M., & Bell, S. (2016). *Rocks and clouds*. Steidl.

Haneke, M. (Director). (2001). *The piano teacher* [Film]. Kino.

Holderman, B. (Director). (2018). *Book club* [Film]. Paramount.

Hunt, K. (2016, Sep 22). A history of radical thinking: How women created book clubs. *Broadly: Vice Magazine*. https://broadly.vice.com/en_us/article/nejbvk/a-history-of-radical-thinking-how-women-created-book-clubs

James E.L. (2012). *Fifty Shades of Grey*. Vintage Books.

Jelinek, E. (1988). *The Piano Teacher*. Weidenfeld and Nicolson.

Luscombe, B. (2012, Apr 18). The world's 100 most influential people: 2012: E. L. James. *Time Magazine*. https://web.archive.org/web/20130814025500/http://www.time.com/time/specials/packages/article/0,28804,2111975_2111976_2112140,00.html

Nelson, I. (2012, Jan 7). Once upon a time in Quincy: Sarah Atwater Denman was a passionate philanthropist, humanitarian. *The Herald-Whig*. https://www.whig.com/story/16468648/once-upon-a-time-in-quincy-sarah-atwater-denman-was-a-passionate-philanthropist-humanitarian

Ott, E. (Curator). (2012). Turning the page: Technology & innovation in 19th-century books, *Rare Book School, University of Virginia*. https://rarebookschool.org/all-programs/exhibitions/turning-the-page/1/

Otto, A. (2009, Sep 15). The evolution of American book clubs: A timeline. *MinnPost*. https://www.minnpost.com/books/2009/09/evolution-american-book-clubs-timeline/

Rosin, H. (2012). *The end of men: And the rise of women*. Riverhead Books.

Smith, S., Choueiti, M., & Pieper, K. (2017, Feb). Over sixty, underestimated: A look at aging on the "silver" screen in best picture nominated films. *USC Annenberg School of Communication and Journalism*. https://annenberg.usc.edu/sites/default/files/2017/05/30/MDSCI_Over%20Sixty%20Underestimated%20Report%20Final.pdf

Wikipedia contributors. (2020, May 19). *Fifty shades of grey* [Film]. In *Wikipedia, The Free Encyclopedia*. https://en.Wikipedia.org/w/index.php?title=Fifty_Shades_of_Grey_(film)&oldid=957516053

PART II ★ CELEBRATING LGBTQ

CHAPTER 6: *THE CELLULOID CLOSET*

Aalai, A. (2018, Jul 28). Facts about human behavior that defy our assumptions. *Psychology Today*.
https://www.psychologytoday.com/us/blog/the-first-impression/201807/facts-about-human-behavior-defy-our-assumptions

Altman, L. (1981, Jul 3). Rare cancer seen in 41 homosexuals. *The New York Times*. https://www.nytimes.com/1981/07/03/us/rare-cancer-seen-in-41-homosexuals.html

American Psychological Association. (2008). Sexual orientation and homosexuality. *APA*. https://www.apa.org/topics/lgbt/orientation

Borders, M. (2012, Jun 11). Badass hall of fame: Vito Russo. *Birth.Movies.Death*. https://birthmoviesdeath.com/2012/06/11/badass-hall-of-fame-vito-russo

Dyer, R. (1977). *Gays in film*. British Film Institute.

Dyer, R. (1983). Review essay: Vito Russo, *The celluloid closet: Homosexuality in the movies*. 9 (2), 52–56. https://repository.upenn.edu/svc/vol9/iss2/4

Eckert, P., & McConnell-Ginet, S. (2013). An introduction to gender. In *Language and Gender* (2nd ed.). (pp. 1–36). Cambridge University Press. doi:10.1017/CBO9781139245883.002

Friedman, J., & Epstein, R. (Directors). (1996). *The celluloid closet* [Film]. HBO.

Gelbert, B. (2011, Sep). Vito Russo, pioneering gay film historian & gay & AIDS activist, is remembered in comprehensive new bio, *Celluloid Activist*, by Michael Schiavi. *New York Q News*. http://newyorkqnews.com/2011/09/cell/index.html

Gender pronouns. (2020). In *Lesbian, Gay, Bisexual, Transgender, Queer Plus (LGBTQ Resource Center, University of Wisconsin-Milwaukee*. https://uwm.edu/lgbtrc/support/gender-pronouns/

Guo, J. (2016, Jan 8). Sorry, grammar nerds. The singular 'they' has been declared Word of the Year. *The Washington Post*. https://www.washingtonpost.com/news/wonk/wp/2016/01/08/donald-trump-may-win-this-years-word-of-the-year/

Herek, G. (1991). Stigma, prejudice, and violence against lesbians and gay men. In John C. Gonsiorek & James D. Weinrich (Eds.) (1991), *Homosexuality: Research implications for public policy*. Sage.

Kennedy, M. (2011, Jul 10). 'Celluloid activist,' by Michael Schiavi: biography. *SFGate*. https://www.sfgate.com/books/article/Celluloid-Activist-by-

Michael-Schiavi-2355090.php

LPC designates six individual landmarks with LGBT associations during pride month. (2019, Jun 18). *Landmarks Preservation Commission*. https://www1.nyc.gov/site/lpc/about/pr2019/lpc-designates-six-individual-landmarks-with-lgbt-associations-during-pride-month.page

Lugowski, D. M. (1999). Queering the (new) deal: Lesbian and gay representation and the depression-era cultural politics of Hollywood's production code. *Cinema Journal*, 38 (2), 3–35.

Mann, W. J. (2001). *Behind the screen: How gays and lesbians shaped Hollywood*. Viking.

Osmond, D. (2003, Mar). Epidemiology of HIV/AIDS in the United States. *University of California San Francisco*. http://hivinsite.ucsf.edu/InSite?page=kb-01-03

Parker, K., Horowitz, M., & Stepler, R. (2017, Dec 5). Americans are divided on whether differences between men and women are rooted in biology or societal expectations. *Pew Research Center*. https://www.pewsocialtrends.org/2017/12/05/americans-are-divided-on-whether-differences-between-men-and-women-are-rooted-in-biology-or-societal-expectations/

Parker, T. (1972). *Screening the sexes*. Holt, Rinehart and Winston.

Russo, V. (1987). *The celluloid closet: Homosexuality in the movies* (Revised ed.). Harper & Row. (Original work published 1981)

Russo, V. (1988, May 9). Why we fight [Transcript of speech]. *ACT UP Demonstration*. https://actupny.org/documents/whfight.html

Schiavi, M. (2009). Looking for Vito. *Cinema Journal*, 49 (1), 41–64.

Schiavi, M. (2011). *Celluloid activist: The life and times of Vito Russo*. University of Wisconsin Press.

Shepard, B. (2011, Apr 13). 'Celluloid Activist' by Michael Schiavi. *Lambda Literary*. https://www.lambdaliterary.org/2011/04/celluloid-activist-michael-schiavi/

The celluloid closet. (2016). *Top Documentary Films*. https://topdocumentaryfilms.com/the-celluloid-closet-special-edition/

Tomlin, L. (2011). Editorial review. In M. R. Schiavi (Ed.), *Celluloid activist: The life and times of Vito Russo*. University of Wisconsin Press.

CHAPTER 7: *WILDE*

Adut, A. (2005, Jul). A theory of scandal: Victorians, homosexuality, and the fall of Oscar Wilde. *American Journal of Sociology*, 111(1), 213–48. https://doi.org/10.1086/428816

Associated Press. (2019, Apr 3). Brunei will stone adulterers to death, same penalty for gay sex. *Courthouse News.* https://www.courthousenews.com/brunei-will-stone-adulterers-to-death-same-penalty-for-gay-sex/

Bostock v. Clayton County, No. 17–1618 590 U.S. ___. (2020, Jun 15). *Supreme Court of the United States.* https://www.supremecourt.gov/opinions/19pdf/17-1618_hfci.pdf

Bristow, J. & Mitchell, R. N. (2016, Jan 13). On Oscar Wilde and plagiarism. *The Public Domain Review.* https://publicdomainreview.org/2016/01/13/on-oscar-wilde-and-plagiarism/

Cahill, N. (2020, Feb 5). Civil rights icon convicted of gay sex in 1950s, pardoned in California. *Courthouse News.* https://www.courthousenews.com/civil-rights-icon-convicted-of-gay-sex-in-1950s-pardoned-in-california/

Carlin, G. (1973). Class clown: Seven words you can never say on television [Audio recording]. *The Orchard Music.*

Castleman, M. (2018, Oct 1). "Unconventional" sex is actually pretty common. *Psychology Today.* https://www.psychologytoday.com/us/blog/all-about-sex/201810/unconventional-sex-is-actually-pretty-common

Dorland, W. A. N. (1900). *The American illustrated medical dictionary.* W.B. Saunders Company. https://books.google.com/books?id=dO_HhmD10AIC

Downey, M. (1994, Jul 10). It's time to shuck the corn in Cobb. *Los Angeles Times.* https://www.latimes.com/archives/la-xpm-1994-07-10-sp-13996-story.html

FCC admin. (2017, Feb 15). TV: Obscene, indecent and profane broadcasts. *FCC.* https://fccid.io/blog/2017/02/15/tv-obscene-indecent-profane-broadcasts/

Federal Communications Commission. (n.d.). Obscenity, indecency and profanity. *FCC.* https://www.fcc.gov/general/obscenity-indecency-and-profanity

Flood, A. (2011, Apr 27). Uncensored *Picture of Dorian Gray* published. *The Guardian.* https://www.theguardian.com/books/2011/apr/27/dorian-gray-oscar-wilde-uncensored

Friedman, D. M. (2014). *Wilde in America: Oscar Wilde and the invention of celebrity.* W.W. Norton & Company.

Ganesan, G. K. (2018, Sep 24). Should homosexuality be a crime? *Paradox.* https://www.gkg.legal/should-homosexuality-be-a-crime/

Gates, G. (2011, Apr) How many people are lesbian, gay, bisexual, and

transgender? *UCLA Williams Institute.*
https://williamsinstitute.law.ucla.edu/publications/how-many-people-
lgbt/

Georgia Voice editors. (2012, Mar 30). Marietta's Theatre on the Square was
ground zero for anti-gay resolution. *Georgia Voice.*
https://thegavoice.com/culture/mariettas-theatre-on-the-square-was-
ground-zero-for-anti-gay-resolution/

Ghoshal, N. (2016, Jul 12). Dignity debased: Forced anal examinations in
homosexuality prosecutions. *Human Rights Watch.*
https://www.hrw.org/report/2016/07/12/dignity-debased/forced-anal-
examinations-homosexuality-prosecutions

Gilbert, B. (Director). (1997). *Wilde* [Film]. BBC.

Harris, F. (1916). Oscar Wilde, His life and confessions/chapter 7. In
Wikisource.
https://en.wikisource.org/w/index.php?title=Oscar_Wilde,_His_Life_a
nd_Confessions/Chapter_7&oldid=3955281

Hoerr, N. L., & Osol, A. (Eds). (1956). *Blakiston's new Gould medical dictionary,*
(2nd ed.). McGraw-Hill.

Hughes-Johnson, A. (2020, Oct 14). Women at Oxford 1878–1920. *Education
and Activism.* https://www.firstwomenatoxford.ox.ac.uk/

Iborel (2020, Oct 20). Mostly true: there would be « LGBT free zones » in
Poland. *Eucheck France.* https://www.eucheck.fr/2020/10/20/are-there-
lgbt-free-zones-in-poland/

Kaufman, M. (Director). (1997). *Gross indecency: The three trials of Oscar Wilde*
[Play]. New York, NY.

Kaufman, M. (Director). (2002). *The Laramie project* [Film]. HBO.

Klein, M. (2013, Apr 4). The end of normal sex. *Psychology Today.*
https://www.psychologytoday.com/us/blog/sexual-
intelligence/201304/the-end-normal-sex

Lewin, A. (Director). (1945). *The picture of Dorian Gray* [Film]. MGM.

Map of countries that criminalise LGBT people. (2020). *Human Dignity Trust.*
https://www.humandignitytrust.org/lgbt-the-law/map-of-
criminalisation/

McNally, T. (1992). *Lips Together Teeth Apart* [Play]. Penguin Books.

Meyer, I. H. (2019, Jun 27). How do you measure the LGBT population in the
U.S.? *Gallup.*
https://news.gallup.com/opinion/methodology/259457/measure-lgbt-
population.aspx

Moulson, G. (2017, Mar 22). German cabinet oks plan to annul homosexuality
convictions. *Courthouse News.*

https://www.courthousenews.com/german-cabinet-oks-plan-annul-homosexuality-convictions/

Paulson, M. & Kishkosky, S. (2015, Jun 22). Gay-themed play about Oscar Wilde hits a Kremlin roadblock. *The New York Times*. https://www.nytimes.com/2015/06/22/theater/gay-themed-play-about-oscar-wilde-hits-a-kremlin-roadblock.html

Peach-2. (1999, Jun 7). Interesting portrait. *IMDb*. https://www.imdb.com/title/tt0120514/reviews

Schwirtz, M. (2012, Feb 29). Anti-gay law stirs fears in Russia. *The New York Times*. https://www.nytimes.com/2012/03/01/world/asia/anti-gay-law-stirs-fears-in-russia.html

Soloway, J., & Sperling, A. (Executive producers). (2014–2019). *Transparent* [TV series]. Amazon Studios.

Steakley, J. (1999). Cinema and censorship in the Weimar Republic: The case of *Anders als Die Andern*. *Film History*, 11(2), 181–203. ISSN 0149-7952. http://www.jstor.org/stable/3815322

Walshe, E. (2014). *The diary of Mary Travers*. Somerville Press. (See: https://www.independent.ie/entertainment/books/book-reviews/books-oscar-wildes-father-was-also-a-scandal-30460310.html).

Wikipedia contributors. (2020, Sep 3). Magnus Hirschfeld. In *Wikipedia, The Free Encyclopedia*. https://en.Wikipedia.org/w/index.php?title=Magnus_Hirschfeld&oldid=976544753

Wilde, O. (1890, Jul). The picture of Dorian Gray. *Lippincott's Monthly Magazine* (46), 25.

Wilde, O. (1907). *The writings of Oscar Wilde: Epigrams, phrases and philosophies for the use of the young*. A. R. Keller & Co.

Wilde, O. (1909). *Lady Windermere's fan and the importance of being Earnest*. Musson.

Wilde, O. (1913). De profundis. *Project Gutenberg*. https://www.gutenberg.org/files/921/921-h/921-h.htm

Wojczuk, T. (2020, Jun 30). Charlotte Cushman broke barriers on her way to becoming the A-list actress of the 1800s. *Smithsonian Magazine*. https://www.smithsonianmag.com/arts-culture/charlotte-cushman-broke-barriers-her-way-becoming-list-actress-1800s-180975221/

CHAPTER 8: *THE DANISH GIRL*

About Klinefelter Syndrome. (2019, May 19). *Human Genome Research Institute*. https://www.genome.gov/Genetic-Disorders/Klinefelter-Syndrome

American Psychiatric Association. (2020). What Is gender dysphoria? *American Psychiatric Association.* https://www.psychiatry.org/patients-families/gender-dysphoria/what-is-gender-dysphoria

American Psychological Association. (2015). Guidelines for psychological practice with transgender and gender-nonconforming people. *American Psychologist*, 70 (9), 832–864. doi: 10.1037/a0039906 https://www.apa.org/practice/guidelines/transgender.pdf

Barber, K. E. (2008). Johann Blumenbach and the classification of human races. In *The Columbia Encyclopedia*, (6th ed.). Columbia University Press. https://www.encyclopedia.com/science/encyclopedias-almanacs-transcripts-and-maps/johann-blumenbach-and-classification-human-races

Bauer, H. (2017). *The Hirschfeld archives: Violence, death, and modern queer culture.* Temple University Press. ISBN 9781439914335.

Bissinger, B. (2015, Jun 25). Caitlyn Jenner: The full story. *Vanity Fair.* https://www.vanityfair.com/hollywood/2015/06/caitlyn-jenner-bruce-cover-annie-leibovitz

Boorstein, M. (2014, Dec 13). Gay Christians choosing celibacy emerge from the shadows. *The Washington Post.* https://www.washingtonpost.com/local/gay-christians-choosing-celibacy-emerge-from-the-shadows/2014/12/13/51c73aea-6ab2-11e4-9fb4-a622dae742a2_story.html

Bradford, B. (2007). *The fallacy of assignable gender*: About the book. Xlibris publishing. https://www.xlibris.com/bookstore/bookdetail.aspx?bookid=SKU-0035627049

Burnside, A. (2021, Feb 18). The Biden administration should increase LGBTQ public benefit access and data collection. https://www.clasp.org/blog/biden-administration-should-increase-lgbtq-public-benefit-access-and-data-collection

Burton, N. (2015, Sep 18). When homosexuality stopped being a mental disorder. *Psychology Today.* https://www.psychologytoday.com/us/blog/hide-and-seek/201509/when-homosexuality-stopped-being-mental-disorder

Chappell, N., & Schutt, A. (2018). Hyperandrogenemia. In *Encyclopedia of reproduction* (2nd ed.) 4, 70–76. doi:10.1016/B978-0-12-801238-3.64518-X

Ebershoff, D. (2000). *The Danish girl*. Phoenix.

Eugenides, J. (2013). *Middlesex*. Fourth Estate.

From GI Joe to GI Jane: Christine Jorgensen's story. (2020, Jun 30). *National*

WWII Museum.
https://www.nationalww2museum.org/war/articles/christine-jorgensen

Ganz, J. (2020, Jun 10). Caitlyn Jenner reflects on 'emotional' transition 5 years later. *New York Daily News*. https://www.nydailynews.com/snyde/ny-caitlyn-jenner-speaks-transition-anniversary-20200610-ortw4ciymjbjpdd5qyeajn2iyq-story.html

Gerda Wegener (Danish, 1885–1940). (2021). *Artnet Worldwide Corporation*. http://www.artnet.com/artists/gerda-wegener/

GLAAD media reference guide: *AP & New York Times* style. (2013). *GLAAD*. https://www.glaad.org/reference/style

GLAAD media reference guide: In focus: Covering the transgender community. (2020). *GLAAD*. https://www.glaad.org/reference/covering-trans-community

Hadjimatheou, C. (2012, Nov 30). Christine Jorgensen: 60 years of sex change ops. *BBC*. https://www.bbc.com/news/magazine-20544095

Herman, R. (1976, Aug 27). 'No exceptions,' and no Renée Richards. *The New York Times*. https://www.nytimes.com/packages/html/sports/year_in_sports/08.27.html

Hirschfeld, M. (2000). *The homosexuality of men & women*. Prometheus Books. (Original work published 1914)

Hooper, T. (Director, Producer). (2015). *The Danish girl* [Film]. Focus Features.

Horvath, H. (2020, Jul). Activist-driven transgender research methods are reckless and will lead to harms. *University of California, San Francisco*. https://www.researchgate.net/publication/343039750_Activist-driven_transgender_research_methods_are_reckless_and_will_lead_to_harms

Hoyer, N. (pseudonym)/ Harthern-Jacobsen, E. L. (Ed.). (2004). *Man into woman: An authentic record of a change of sex*. Blue Boat Books Ltd. (Original work published 1933)

Johnson, R. (May 2, 2019). What no one is telling you about Caster Semenya: She has xy chromosomes. *LetsRun*. https://www.letsrun.com/news/2019/05/what-no-one-is-telling-you-about-caster-semenya-she-has-xy-chromosomes/

Jorgensen. C. (1972, Apr 26). Christine Jorgensen speaking at UCLA 4/26/1972. *UCLA Communications Studies Archive*. https://youtu.be/HeY3_zs1u08

Krafft-Ebing, R. von (1906). *Psychopathia sexualis, with especial reference to the antipathic sexual instinct, a medico-forensic study* (12th ed.). Rebman. *Internet Archive*. https://archive.org/details/bub_gb_hg8A35JWBXQC

(Original work published 1886)

Lane, C. (2012, May 1). American sex and American psychiatry. *Psychology Today*. https://www.psychologytoday.com/intl/blog/side-effects/201205/american-sex-and-american-psychiatry

Liptak, A. (2015, Jun 27). Supreme Court ruling makes same-sex marriage a right nationwide. *The New York Times*. https://www.nytimes.com/2015/06/27/us/supreme-court-same-sex-marriage.html

Longman, J. (2016, Aug 18). Understanding the controversy over Caster Semenya. *The New York Times*. https://www.nytimes.com/2016/08/20/sports/caster-semenya-800-meters.html

Longman, J. (2020, Sep 8). Track's Caster Semenya loses appeal to defend 800-meter title. *The New York Times*. https://www.nytimes.com/2020/09/08/sports/olympics/caster-semenya-court-ruling.html

Medical model of disability. (2008). In W. Kirch (Ed.), *Encyclopedia of public health*. Springer.

Mêlé, C. (2016, Apr 13). In North Carolina and Mississippi, backlash grows over rights law. *The New York Times*. https://www.nytimes.com/2016/04/13/us/north-carolina-mississippi-gay-rights-boycott.html

Meyer-Bahlburg, H. F. (2010). From mental disorder to iatrogenic hypogonadism: Dilemmas in conceptualizing gender identity variants as psychiatric conditions. *Archives of sexual behavior*, 39(2), 461–476. https://doi.org/10.1007/s10508-009-9532-4 https://www.ncbi.nlm.nih.gov/pmc/articles/PMC2844928/

Mikalson, P., Pardo, S., & Green, J. (2012, Dec). First, do no harm: Reducing disparities for lesbian, gay, bisexual, transgender, queer, and questioning populations in California. *California Department of Public Health*. https://cpehn.org/sites/default/files/lgbtq_population_report.pdf

Nagoski, E. (2021). *Come as you are: The surprising new science that will transform your sex life*. Simon & Schuster.

Oswald, R. (1919). *Different from the Others (Anders als die Andern)* [Film]. Richard-Oswald-Produktion.

Rapper, I. (Director). (1970). *The Christine Jorgensen story* [Film]. United Artists.

Sasson, E. (2015, Apr 27). America has not reached a transgender tipping point. *The New Republic*. https://newrepublic.com/article/121653/bruce-jenner-interview-cox-photos-not-transgender-tipping-point

Schillace, B. (2021, May 10). The forgotten history of the world's first trans clinic. *Scientific American.* https://www.scientificamerican.com/article/the-forgotten-history-of-the-worlds-first-trans-clinic/

Sex, gender and genetics. (2019). *Personal Genetics Education Project.* http://pged.org/wp-content/uploads/2019/05/InfoBrief-SexGenderGenetics.pdf

Spitzer, R. L. (2003, Oct 1). Can some gay men and lesbians change their sexual orientation? 200 participants reporting a change from homosexual to heterosexual orientation. *Arch Sex Behav*, 32(5), 403–17; discussion 419–72. doi: 10.1023/a:1025647527010.

Spitzer, R. L. (2012, May 24). Spitzer reassesses his 2003 study of reparative therapy of homosexuality. *Arch Sex Behav*, 41(5), 757. https://doi.org/10.1007/s10508-012-9966-y

Steakley, J. (1999). Cinema and censorship in the Weimar Republic: The case of *Anders als Die Andern*. *Film History*, 11(2), 181–203. ISSN 0149-7952. http://www.jstor.org/stable/3815322

What is intersex? (2008). *Intersex Society of North America.* http://www.isna.org/faq/what_is_intersex

Wikipedia contributors. (2020, April 23). Sexual identity. In *Wikipedia, The Free Encyclopedia.* https://en.Wikipedia.org/w/index.php?title=Sexual_identity&oldid=952615572

Witkin, R. (2014, May 1). Hopkins hospital: A history of sex reassignment. *The Johns Hopkins News-Letter.* https://www.jhunewsletter.com/article/2014/05/hopkins-hospital-a-history-of-sex-reassignment-76004/

CHAPTER 9: *BEHIND THE CANDELABRA*

Associated Press. (2014, Jan 23). Behind the bars: Liberace's former lover jailed for up to 20 years after failing drug test while on probation. *Daily Mail.* Retrieved from https://www.dailymail.co.uk/news/article-2545059/Liberaces-former-lover-Scott-Thorson-jailed-20-YEARS-failing-drug-test-probation.html

Curto, J. (2020, Apr 17). Steven Soderbergh, *Contagion* director, to lead industry coronavirus committee. *New York Magazine.* https://www.vulture.com/2020/04/steven-soderbergh-contagion-coronavirus-committee.html

HBO. (2013). *Behind the candelabra:* Interview: Jerry Weintraub. *HBO.*

https://www.hbo.com/movies/behind-the-candelabra/interview-with-jerry-weintraub.html

Kastrenakes, J. (2013, May 3). Steven Soderbergh tweets a thrilling crime novella. *The Verge*. https://www.theverge.com/2013/5/3/4296620/steven-soderbergh-twitter-novella-bitchuation

Lastliberal (2013, May 26). They have no idea he's gay. *IMDb*. https://www.imdb.com/review/rw2804071/

Segal, D. (2013, May 10). The boy toy's story. *The New York Times*. https://www.nytimes.com/2013/05/12/fashion/scott-thorson-the-boy-toys-story.html

Soderbergh, S. (Director). (2013). *Behind the candelabra* [Film]. HBO.

Soderbergh, S. (Director). (2018). *Unsane* [Film]. Bleecker Street Media.

Soderbergh, S. (Director). (2019). *High Flying Bird* [Film]. HBO.

Spielberg, S. (Director). (1975). *Jaws* [Film]. Universal Pictures.

Steven Spielberg (2021). *IMDb*. https://www.imdb.com/name/nm0000229/

Thorson, S., & Thorleifson, A. (1990). *Behind the candelabra: My life with Liberace*. Knightsbridge Pub Co Mass.

CHAPTER 10: *THE BIRDCAGE*

Als, H. (2019, Sep 6). *Giovanni's Room* revisited. *The New York Times*. https://www.nytimes.com/2019/09/05/t-magazine/james-baldwin-giovannis-room.html

Baldwin, J. (1956). *Giovanni's Room*. The Dial Press.

Bellott, G. (2019, Apr 25). James Baldwin in Paris: On the virtuosic shame of *Giovanni's Room*. *Literary Hub*. https://lithub.com/james-baldwin-in-paris-on-the-virtuosic-shame-of-giovannis-room/

Fleming, J. (2021). *How to be human, An autistic man's guide to life*. Simon & Schuster.

Williams, P., & Asher, K. (Writers). (1979). *Rainbow connection* [Music].

Holden, S. (1996, Mar 15). Film review: Literally and figuratively, unclothing a dreamboat. *The New York Times*. https://www.nytimes.com/1996/03/15/movies/film-review-literally-and-figuratively-unclothing-a-dreamboat.html

Khazan, O. (2014, Feb 27). The dark psychology of being a good comedian. *The Atlantic*. https://www.theatlantic.com/health/archive/2014/02/the-dark-psychology-of-being-a-good-comedian/284104/

Koplinski, C. (2015, Mar 19). Film capsules, March 19, 2015. *Champagne, IL The News-Gazette*. https://www.news-gazette.com/arts-entertainment/local/2015-03-19/film-capsules-march-19-2015.html

La Cage aux Folles. (2020). *The Internet Broadway Database*.
https://www.ibdb.com/broadway-production/la-cage-aux-folles-4231

Lorber, J. (1994). *Paradoxes of gender*. Yale University Press.

Molinaro, É. (Director). (1978). *La cage aux folles* [Film]. United Artists.

Nichols, M. (Director). (1996). *The birdcage* [Film]. United Artists.

Petersen, A. H. (2014, Sep 23). Scandals of classic Hollywood: The long suicide of Montgomery Clift. *Vanity Fair*.
https://www.vanityfair.com/hollywood/2014/09/scandals-of-classic-hollywood-montgomery-clift

Peterson, M. (2017. Oct 13). Nathan Lane on enduring impact of *The Birdcage:* 'People still talk to me about it.' *The Morning Call*.
https://www.mcall.com/entertainment/arts-theater/mc-ent-nathan-lane-birdcage-state-theatre-easton-20171006-story.html

Poiret, J. (1973). *La Cage aux Folles* [Play].

Roisman, G., Clausell, E., Holland, A., Fortuna, K., & Elieff, C. (2008, Jan). Adult romantic relationships as contexts of human development: A multimethod comparison of same-sex couples with opposite-sex dating, engaged, and married dyads. *Developmental Psychology*, 44(1), 91–101. doi: 10.1037/0012-1649.44.1.91

Scott, A. O. (2014, Aug 12). Robin Williams, an improvisational genius, forever present in the moment. *The New York Times*.
https://www.nytimes.com/2014/08/12/movies/robin-williams-an-improvisational-genius-forever-present-in-the-moment.html

Shafer, D. (Director). (1995). *Man of the year* [Film]. Seventh Art Releasing.

Stack, L. (2015, Mar 8). Dirk Shafer, *Playgirl* centerfold who revealed he was gay, dies at 52. *The New York Times*.
https://www.nytimes.com/2015/03/08/arts/dirk-shafer-playgirl-centerfold-who-revealed-he-was-gay-dies-at-52.html

Tóibín, C. (2016, Feb 26). The unsparing confessions of *Giovanni's Room*. *The New Yorker*. https://www.newyorker.com/books/page-turner/the-unsparing-confessions-of-giovannis-room

BACK MATTER

American Psychiatric Association, Committee on Nomenclature and Statistics. (1952). *Diagnostic and statistical manual of mental disorders*. American Psychiatric Press.

American Psychiatric Association, Committee on Nomenclature and Statistics. (1968). *Diagnostic and statistical manual of mental disorders* (2nd ed.).

American Psychiatric Press.

Berkvist, R. (2011, Apr 9). A director of classics, focused on conscience. *The New York Times*. http://www.nytimes.com/2011/04/10/movies/sidney-lumet-director-of-american-classics-dies-at-86.html

Bordwell, D., & Thompson, K. (2003). *Film art: An introduction* (7th ed.). McGraw-Hill.

Bussey, K., & Bandura, A. (1999). Social cognitive theory of gender development and differentiation. *Psychological Review*, 206(1), 676–713.

Carey, J. W. (1989). Chapter 1. A cultural approach to communication. In J. W. Carey (Ed.), *Communication as culture: Essays on media and society*. Unwin Hyman.

Chatham House rule. (2021). *Chatham House*. https://www.chathamhouse.org/about-us/chatham-house-rule

Dentith, S. (2000). *Parody* (The new critical idiom). Routledge.

Drescher, J. (2015). Out of DSM: Depathologizing homosexuality. *Behavioral Sciences*, 5(4), 565–575. https://www.ncbi.nlm.nih.gov/pmc/articles/PMC4695779/#sec8-behavsci-05-00565title

Eskridge, W. (1999). *Gaylaw: Challenging the apartheid of the closet*. Harvard University Press.

Fleming, V. (1939). *Gone with the wind* [Film]. MGM.

Foreman, M. (2020, Jun 16). Historic win. *Haas Jr.* https://www.haasjr.org/perspectives/historic-win

Green, W. C. (2009). Burstyn v. Wilson (1952). *The First Amendment Encyclopedia*. https://www.mtsu.edu/first-amendment/article/92/burstyn-v-wilson

Greenberg, B. S., Siemicki, M., Dorfman, S., Heeter, G., Lin, G., & Stanley, G. (1993). Sex content in r-rated films viewed by adolescents. In B. S. Greenberg, J. D. Brown, & N. Buerkel-Rothfuss (Eds.), *Media, sex and the adolescent*. Hampton Press, Inc.

Kuhn, A., & Westwell, G. (2012). *A dictionary of film studies*. Oxford University Press.

Labensky, S. R., Hause, A. M., & Martel, P. (2010). *On cooking: A textbook of culinary fundamentals*. (5th ed.). Prentice-Hall.

Luzwick, A. J. (2017). Human trafficking and pornography: Using the Trafficking Victims Protection Act to prosecute trafficking for the production of Internet pornography, *Northwestern University Law Review*, 112(2), 355-375. https://scholarlycommons.law.northwestern.edu/nulr/vol112/iss2/5

Münsterberg, H. (1916). *The photoplay: A psychological study*. D. Appleton & Company.

O'Donnell, P. (1992, summer). Killing the golden goose: Hollywood's death wish. *Beverly Hills Bar Journal*.

Postrel, V. (2019, Dec 6). Hollywood shows how antitrust laws can flop. *Bloomberg*. https://www.bloomberg.com/opinion/articles/2019-12-05/hollywood-shows-how-antitrust-laws-can-flop

Rossman, S. (2017, May 11). What is 'agitprop'? *USA Today*. https://www.usatoday.com/story/news/nation-now/2017/05/11/agitprop-what-agitprop/317957001/

Suris, A., Holliday, R., & North, C. (2016, Jan 18). The evolution of the classification of psychiatric disorders. *Behav. Sci*, 6(5). doi:10.3390/bs6010005

Schultz, D. (2009). Media exemption to antitrust laws. *The First Amendment Encyclopedia*. https://mtsu.edu/first-amendment/article/1128/media-exemption-to-antitrust-laws

Sternberg, J. (Director). (1930). *Morocco* [Film]. Paramount.

TV Tropes contributors. (2020, Jun 18). Useful notes / The Hays code. In *TV Tropes*. https://tvtropes.org/pmwiki/pmwiki.php/UsefulNotes/TheHaysCode

U.S. Department of Justice. (2019, Nov 22). Department of Justice files motion to terminate Paramount consent decrees. *Justice News*. https://www.justice.gov/opa/pr/department-justice-files-motion-terminate-paramount-consent-decrees

Vaughn, S. (1990, Jun). Morality and entertainment: The origins of the motion picture production code. *The Journal of American History*, 77(1), 39-65. doi:10.2307/2078638

Wikipedia contributors. (2020, Aug 12). Weimar Constitution. In *Wikipedia, The Free Encyclopedia*. https://en.Wikipedia.org/w/index.php?title=Weimar_Constitution&oldid=972571879

Wertham, F. (1954). *Seduction of the innocent*. Farrar & Rinehart.

Wittern-Keller, L. (2009). Freedman *v*. Maryland (1965). *The First Amendment Encyclopedia*. https://mtsu.edu/first-amendment/article/349/freedman-v-maryland

INDEX

structure, 124
societal, society
  capitalism, 26.43
  democracy, 27
  discrimination, 1
  elites, 148
  industrialization, 26
  male dominance, male-
    dominated, 50, 64
  misfit, 196
  paternalism, 44
  upper-middle-class, 51
Soderbergh, Steven, 184, 187, 189
Some Like it Hot (film), 169
Sotomayor, Sonia, 40
Staircase (film), 88
Stanford, Leland, 3
stereotypes, stereotypical, 68, 126, 196
Stone, Peter, 81, 85
Stonewall Inn, 129
  riots, 129
Stonewall National Monument (SNM), 128–129
suburban housewife, 29–30
  boredom, 33–35
suffragists, 38

T

TGNC (transgender and gender non–conforming), 166
Thomas, Clarence, 71
Thorson, Scott (aka Jess Marlow), 187–188
Tootsie (film), 169
transvestism, 145
Turing, Alan, 136n2
Turner, Lana, 60, 63

Turpin, Luci Baines Johnson, 34
Tyler, Parker, 128

U

U.S. National LGBTQ Wall of Honor, 128
U.S. Supreme Court, 40, 111
  rulings, 118, 144, 154, 169

V

Valenti, Jack, 131
Victim (film), 87
Victorian–era
  elites, 137
  ideology, 14
  intolerance, 147
  repression, 17
  restrictive rules, 50
  social class distinctions, unequal privileges, 12
violence
  acts of, 125
  Afghanistan, 27, 68
  anal examinations, 140
  assault, 38, 145
  Florida State University (FSU), sexual assaults, 69–70
    Jameis Winston, football player, 69–71
  microaggression, 8
  rape, 59, 66–70, 107, 145, 187
  sexual, 69, 108, 140, 145
  victim of
    negative social reactions, 69
    psychological effects, 140
    role, 108
    women, 65–70

We invite our readers to . . .

*Find a group of people who challenge and inspire you, spend a
lot of time with them, and it will change your life.*
—AMY POEHLER

www.ingramcontent.com/pod-product-compliance
Lightning Source LLC
Chambersburg PA
CBHW070717280326
41926CB00087B/2396